THE DARKNESS AND THE DAWN

THE DARKNESS AND THE DAWN

Empowered by the Tragedy and Triumph of the Cross

CHARLES R. SWINDOLL

WORD PUBLISHING

NASHVILLE

www.wordpublishing.com

A Thomas Nelson Company

The Darkness and The Dawn
By Charles R. Swindoll

Copyright ©2001 by Charles R. Swindoll, Inc.
Published by Word Publishing, a Thomas Nelson Company,
P. O. Box 141000, Nashville, Tennessee 37214.

Unless otherwise indicated, Scripture quotations used in this book are from the
New American Standard Bible (NASB)
© 1960, 1962, 1963, 1971, 1972, 1973, 1975, 1977,
by the Lockman Foundation. Used by permission.

ISBN 0-8499-1347-0

Printed in the United States of America

01 02 03 04 05 06 07 08 BVG 9 8 7 6 5 4 3 2 1

Dedication

*Ever since the inception of
Stonebriar Community Church
of Frisco, Texas, in the fall of 1998,
we have felt that the Lord's hand
has been on our ministry.*

*We have experienced a love that is deep,
a worship that is authentic and meaningful,
a joy that is rare, and a harmony
that pastors often dream about but
seldom have the pleasure of witnessing.*

*A major reason these ingredients are so evident in our church
is the excellent leadership that is present
among our Board of Elders.
It is my distinct privilege to serve
alongside these fine men
as we pray together
and
grow in the Word together
and
lead our church together for God's greater glory.*

*Because of their unselfish dedication
and commitment to the work of ministry,
I gratefully dedicate this book
to these six faithful servant-leaders:*

STAN BAXTER   JIM GUNN
DAVID CHAVANNE   JOHNNY KOONS
DICK CREWS   BILL SOUSA

Contents

Introduction

Heart attack. Those two words sent a chill up my spine. I could hardly believe the physician was talking about me. I found myself crawling into my own inner cave of emotional darkness, facing for the first time in my entire life the reality of my own mortality. I shall never forget the feeling.

It was 5:50 A.M. on October 14, 2000, only four days before my sixty-sixth birthday. I was experiencing only minimal pain, but because of its location, and because it wouldn't go away, my wife and I decided to check it out. Because we did, I'm alive today. And pain free. According to the latest report of my cardiologist, Dr. Jack Spitzberg, as well as the studied opinion of my personal physician, Dr. Kenneth Cooper, my heart has suffered "no permanent damage."

A small stainless steel stent was inserted into the circumflex artery in my heart, which enables the blood to flow freely as it once did. Over a short period of time, I am told, my body will accept this tiny hollow tube of steel, and life for me will return pretty close to normal.

What a contrast between the frightening words I heard that dark morning in mid-October, "heart attack," and the latest report I remember each dawn as I enjoy a hot cup of coffee with my faithful wife, Cynthia: "no permanent damage." The darkness brought on by the fear of uncertainty is gone. The dawn of renewed hope and revived dreams has made me into a new man with a greater determination than ever to serve my Lord and to fulfill His plan for the balance of my life—whatever that may include.

To say that I am full of gratitude would qualify as the understatement of the year.

Interestingly, I had embarked on a new publishing project when all of that occurred back in October 2000. I had begun writing the book you are holding in your hands. For well over forty years I have been intrigued by the two extremes our Lord experienced at the end of His ministry on earth: the agony of His torturous suffering and death, followed by the ecstasy of His glorious resurrection and triumph over the grave. Time spent meditating on both extremes of His final days on earth always left me hungry for more information, more insights, more understanding.

It seemed to me that these contrasting extremes deserved the kind of time and attention only a book could provide. Sermons on these themes are certainly helpful, as are songs and hymns. But if we hope to go into any depth of understanding and personal application, we need the opportunity to revisit these scenes much more carefully and slowly. Once we have invested the meditation they deserve, they will empower us to worship Him who died for us, as we should, and to exalt Him who was raised that we might live transformed lives, as we so desire.

And so I set out to focus my thoughts on both the tragedy and the triumph of our Savior, with not even the slightest idea that, during the process, God would take me through my own darkness and dawn. Perhaps it was the Father's plan to take me through all that to enable me to write at a level I could not otherwise have achieved. If that occurs, I am, again, full of gratitude.

My thanks to several good and capable servants with whom I have had the joy of working on this project. My editors, Judith Markham and Mary Hollingsworth, deserve special recognition for their tireless efforts and insightful comments. My longtime friend and coworker in our Pastoral Ministries Department at *Insight for Living*, Bryce Klabunde, provided needed and helpful counsel on historical details, biblical background, and linguistic research. I am grateful for his keen eye, which kept me from making embarrassing errors. And again I am indebted to Julie Meredith, who assisted me in gaining permissions for the quotations used in this volume. I thank my many dear friends at Word Publishing, especially Joey Paul and David Moberg, for their belief in this project and their compassionate understanding, as well as their prayer-filled encouragement during those days when my rehabilitation required an extension of the deadlines (Ugh, those deadlines—an author's dread!).

I must also mention the loving support of those men with whom I serve: my fellow elders at Stonebriar Community Church. In more ways than they realize, they minister to me consistently, deeply, and affirmingly. Mine is an enviable role to fill. As I have often said to them, there isn't a pastor in the country who wouldn't love to be in leadership alongside a team like those fine and gracious servant-leaders. If you knew them, you would understand better why I chose to dedicate this book to them.

Finally, to my wife and family, whom I love in stronger and more meaningful ways than I ever did before October 14, 2000, I want to express my profound affections and devotion. Each has been with me through the depths of my darkness, and each was there in the glorious light of my new dawn. I give my God great praise for allowing me an extension of time on this earth to demonstrate to them how I treasure their presence and delight in their companionship.

And with that, I ask you to join me as we leave this present, familiar world and walk into the imaginary time tunnel. Return with me to those few, yet epochal, days twenty centuries ago when our precious Lord walked into the awful darkness, which He did not deserve, only to arise into the sunlit dawn of triumph, providing us a victory from which we shall never know defeat.

As we journey together into one sacred scene after another, may we, together, to borrow from Charles Wesley's grand words, be "lost in wonder, love, and praise."

—CHUCK SWINDOLL
Dallas, Texas

The Darkness

It is curious that people who are filled with horrified indignation whenever a cat kills a sparrow can hear the story of the killing of God told Sunday after Sunday and not experience any shock at all.

—DOROTHY SAYERS[1]

He was despised and forsaken of men, a man of sorrows, and acquainted with grief.

—ISAIAH 53:3A

And so after receiving the morsel he went out immediately; and it was night.

—JOHN 13:30

1
The Suffering Savior

No wound? no scar?
Yet, as the Master shall the servant be,
And, pierced are the feet that follow Me;
But thine are whole: can he have followed far
Who has no wound, no scar?"[2]

— AMY CARMICHAEL

1
The Suffering Savior

The Scottish essayist and historian, Thomas Carlyle, used to say that the easy, somewhat superficial optimism of Ralph Waldo Emerson maddened him. Carlyle believed it stemmed from Emerson's rather sheltered life, for no dark shadow had ever fallen across the man's path. To Carlyle, his contemporary over in America seemed like a man who, standing far back from even the spray of the sea, threw chatty observations on the beauty of nature to those dear souls battling for life with the huge waves beating against them, threatening to sweep them away.

Who knows? Perhaps Carlyle was right in his evaluation of Emerson; we cannot say for sure. But if my personal experience as an adult in the real world is at all reliable, I'm compelled to believe differently. Since he was merely a man and a part of our fallen race of humanity, even the brilliant and gifted Emerson must have had his share of sorrows and felt the sting of rough wind across his face.

The shadow of suffering falls across every path. Even the One who left heaven when He came to live among us was inseparably linked to that shadow. As one of His own followers later wrote, "He came to that which belonged to Him . . . and they who were His own did not receive Him and did not welcome Him" (John 1:11, *The Amplified Bible*).

No one knows what Christ looked like. But this has not deterred countless painters—among them some of the greatest artists of all time—from applying brush and paint to canvas to give their own creative version of His likeness. Two of the more memorable paintings I have seen bear the same title: "The Shadow of the Cross." Though originally painted by different artists, highlighting different scenes, both convey the same theme.

The first pictures a scene inside Joseph's carpenter shop, where Joseph is working alongside Jesus. Jesus, portrayed as a young teenager, has paused from His work to look out the shop window. He stands at full height, stretching His arms wide. In doing so, He is casting an ominous shadow across the wall behind Him. A shadow in the form of a cross.

The second painting depicts Jesus as a little lad, running with outstretched arms to His mother, the sun on His back. Cast upon the path before Him is the dark shadow of the cross.

Both paintings leave the indelible impression on the viewer that the cross was with Christ from the very beginning . . . from His earliest days. We may not know what He looked like, but it is clear to all who examine the inspired record that He was intimately acquainted with suffering.

Certainly the cross was a looming reality throughout His life. Although Scripture does not tell us how, His young mind understood that the cross was ahead. His own words testify to this, even before He began His ministry, He sensed a compelling call to be about the things of His Father (Luke 2:49). Furthermore, while training His disciples, He was not hesitant to tell them about the suffering that lay ahead (Mark 8:31–33; Luke 9:44–45). Though such comments confused and even irritated His disciples, Jesus made it clear that each day brought Him closer to His hour of agony.

The Old Testament also gives us a stunning pen portrait of the shadow of the cross. Although writing about seven centuries before Jesus was born, Isaiah vividly foretells the Savior's suffering and death. As we examine this portrait, we see Christ from three perspectives: as men saw Him; as God saw Him; and as Christ saw Himself.

It's All in How You Look at It

Who has believed our message?
And to whom has the arm of the LORD been revealed?
For He grew up before Him like a tender shoot,
And like a root out of parched ground;
He has no stately form or majesty
That we should look upon Him,
Nor appearance that we should be attracted to Him.
He was despised and forsaken of men,
A man of sorrows, and acquainted with grief;
And like one from whom men hide their face,
He was despised, and we did not esteem Him.

—Isaiah 53:1–3

What did Christ look like to the men, women, and children who met Him? To be completely honest about it, probably not much like the images we see in art museums, stained-glass windows, carvings and murals.

From the clues that Scripture gives us, it would seem that His physical appearance was not impressive. He wasn't tall, dark, and handsome. As the prophet foretold, the coming Anointed One had no "appearance that we should be attracted to Him." He didn't have pomp or flair—no stately form or majesty.

Instead, "He grew up . . . like a tender shoot." Not a tall, stately reed; just a little, tender shoot. Fully human, a man with very real emotions, skin with delicate nerve endings, and tear ducts that were activated by sadness and grief. No untouchable giant of a man, He found Himself moved with compassion and stung by sharp words. Though undiminished Deity, He lived among us in true humanity . . . like a tender shoot.

Isaiah also says that He appeared "like a root out of parched ground." This "parched ground" may refer to the land of Israel, which was nothing more than dust under a Roman boot when Christ came to earth. The world hated the Jews then as much of the world does now. Rome ruled over what they called Palestine with a rod of iron. And in the midst of that, Jesus must have seemed like a tender, fragile, vulnerable shoot making its way out of hard parched ground.

He had "no stately form or majesty that we should look upon Him." Or, as *The Living Bible* puts it, there was "nothing to make us want Him." Men looked upon Him and they didn't want Him. John, who did see Christ in the flesh, says the same thing: "He came to His own, and those who were His own did not receive Him" (John 1:11). They didn't want Him. There was no apparent reason "that we should be attracted to Him."

"Aha!" you say. "What about the message we occasionally hear today that Jesus Christ swept into the Middle East and the first-century world was amazed at His presence and followed Him by the droves? That's not true, at least not for long. The majority of the people ultimately hated Him! They didn't want Him around. He wasn't the most sought-after celebrity of the day. He would never have made *Time's* cover, at least not the first-century edition, as "Man of the Year." Israel didn't want Him as their Savior. Oh, they wanted *a* savior—a man on a white horse to deliver them from their oppressors. But they did not want *the* Savior, because Jesus was not what they expected, not what they desired; so they despised Him.

"He was despised and forsaken." The Hebrew word that is translated "despised" is a term that means "to regard as negligible or worthless." In other words, Isaiah tells us that when people viewed Jesus, they would say, "He's worthless." This Hebrew term also means "to deplore and to give scorn to someone." They scorned Him. They deplored Him. He wasn't what they expected. Clearly, they despised Him.

The shadow darkens. He was not only despised; he was also *"forsaken* of men." Here the original language literally means "wanting in men." He didn't have a band of followers that would impress the public. No groupies. No hangers-on. No fans who would be a draw for others to associate with Him. He was "wanting in men."

In the eyes of men, He was "a man of sorrows, and acquainted with grief." He was a person "from whom men hide their face." Being despised, Jesus was seen as One the people "did not esteem." He was not considered valuable, and so they turned away or ignored Him.

Psychologists sometimes use the word "discount" to describe this kind of treatment. To discount someone is to nullify any of his or her significance—to ignore him . . . to treat her as nothing. Criticism is not the greatest insult; neither is gossip or an outburst of anger. The greatest insult is to ignore a person—to act as if that person doesn't count, doesn't matter, doesn't even exist. That's what Isaiah describes here. The people personified the ultimate discount: They just didn't care if He was around.

Early in His ministry, Jesus knew what it meant to be wounded by the behavior of others. Such treatment was severely demonstrated, which surely scarred His tender spirit. Such scars within are not visible, but they are real wounds and are terribly painful.

Amy Carmichael describes the importance of our recognition of Christ's wounds in her poem, *No Scar?*

> Hast thou no scar?
> No hidden scar on foot or side or hand?
> I hear thee sung as mighty in the land,
> I hear them hail thy bright ascendant star,
> Hast thou no scar?
> Hast thou no wound?
>
> Yet I was wounded by the archers, spent.
> Leaned Me against a tree to die; and rent
> By ravening beasts, they compassed Me, I swooned;
> Hast thou no wound?
> No wound? No scar?
>
> Yet, as the Master shall the servant be,
> And, pierced are the feet that follow Me;
> But thine are whole: can he have followed far
> Who has no wound, no scar?"[3]

This is where some believers go astray. They become disturbed when followers of Christ are dismissed as extremist or oddball by the media and other critics—when they are unpopular in Hollywood, in sophisticated circles in New York, and within the beltway of Washington D.C. They forget that being a follower of Christ has never been a popular thing to be—that it has never been easy. Though written long ago, Amy Carmichael's question remains relevant: "Hast thou no wound, no scar?"

Now, we've seen how men and women perceived Jesus, and how even His own people, the Jews, viewed Him. But what was God's perspective of His own Son? Isaiah describes it this way:

> Surely our griefs He Himself bore,
>   And our sorrows He carried;
>   Yet we ourselves esteemed Him stricken,
>   Smitten of God, and afflicted.
> But He was pierced through for our transgressions,
>   He was crushed for our iniquities;
>   The chastening for our well-being fell upon Him,
>   And by His scourging we are healed.
> All of us like sheep have gone astray,
>   Each of us has turned to his own way;
>   But the LORD has caused the iniquity of us all
>   To fall on Him.
>
> —ISAIAH 53:4–6

And then, later in the same narrative, this bold, categorical statement appears: "But the Lord was pleased to crush Him, putting Him to grief" (53:10a).

God saw Jesus as our substitute. God also saw His Son's suffering as a part of His sovereign will. The Savior's suffering, therefore, pleased Him. Yet the Father was not unconcerned about His Son when He went to Calvary. The people of Jesus' day may have dismissed Him as insignificant, but certainly not the Father! He describes the sufferings of His Son in vivid terms: "Griefs." "Sorrows." "Stricken." "Smitten." "Afflicted." "Pierced through." "Crushed." "Chastening." "Scourging." God had placed on His Son all of our iniquity, and He gives us a clear picture of what that meant to Him, God the Father.

Isaiah 53 is a portrait of a crushed, chastened, scourged individual. I cannot overemphasize this. We need to revisit the scene in order to have a realistic image of the Savior of the Scriptures. Despite all of His power and His unquestioned majesty, we must not picture Him as some kind of Super-hero. He was, truly, the Suffering Savior. Crushed and broken and bleeding, He pursued His God-ordained mission when He went to the cross for us.

Recently we have seen renewed interest in World War II, in everything from Tom Brokaw's bestselling book, *The Greatest Generation,* to Tom Hanks' hit movie, *Saving Private Ryan.* But those of us who are old enough to remember that war and that era need no reminders. Although I was just a boy in elementary school during that turbulent time, I will never forget the news photographs that were released and printed when the war had ended and the gates of those chambers of horror at places like Dachau and Auschwitz were opened. Or the photos of torture from Corregidor. Concentration camp victims . . . prisoners of war . . . reduced to gaunt, bleeding human skeletons. Crushed and broken survivors. Brave men and women stumbling out into a new existence of freedom and the sunlight of new hope.

Such tragic images give us a glimpse of what the Savior must have looked like, what He must have experienced when He endured the agony of the cross.

The people dismissed His appearance and His significance. The Father saw Him as the Suffering Substitute. But how did Christ see Himself?

Perhaps the most vivid portrait of all is the one Christ paints of Himself through Isaiah's pen:

> He was oppressed and He was afflicted,
> Yet He did not open His mouth;

Like a lamb that is led to slaughter,
And like a sheep that is silent before its shearers,
So He did not open His mouth.
 By oppression and judgment He was taken away;
And as for His generation, who considered
That He was cut off out of the land of the living,
For the transgression of my people to whom the stroke was due?
His grave was assigned with wicked men,
 Yet He was with a rich man in His death,
 Because He had done no violence,
 Nor was there any deceit in His mouth.

—ISAIAH 53:7–9

As He carefully draws the picture, as He guides the strokes of Isaiah's stylus from one word to the next, Christ describes Himself as "oppressed" and "afflicted." *Oppressed* means "to be pressed hard, to be driven." It could even be taken to mean "to be plagued" or "hard-pressed." *Afflicted* means "to be bowed down, to be made low, to be forced into submission." Yet, in spite of and through all this, "like a sheep that is silent before its shearers, so He did not open His mouth."

In a former pastorate I knew a man who had lived in the West, up in the high plains. He was familiar with sheep raising, and I've never forgotten one of his descriptions.

"When he shears the wool from the sheep, the shearer wants to take a full pelt, without cutting into it," he said. "But when you shear, you have a fight on your hands. You have to set the sheep on its haunches and then start with the belly and work around the sides. What you have on your hands is just one long wrestling match. It takes several people to get the job done.

"But you know something?" he added (and this was the amazing part to me), "When you lead a sheep to slaughter, he's just as silent and as passive as can be."

I think of that when I read Isaiah 53:7–8: "He was oppressed and He was afflicted, yet He did not open His mouth; like a lamb that is led to slaughter, and like a sheep that is silent before its shearers, so He did not open His mouth."

Peter, who saw the Savior tried and crucified, records Jesus' silence in similar terms:

> For you have been called for this purpose, since Christ also suffered for you, leaving you an example for you to follow in His steps, WHO COMMITTED NO SIN, NOR WAS ANY DECEIT FOUND IN HIS MOUTH; and while being reviled, He did not revile in return; while suffering, He uttered no threats, but kept entrusting Himself to Him who judges righteously; and He Himself bore our sins in His body on the cross, that we might die to sin and live to righteousness; for by His wounds you were healed.
>
> —I PETER 2:21–24

And here, once again, we find a reference to the wounds of the Suffering Savior. In the original, the word is "wound" (literally, "bruise"–singular), not "wounds" (plural). One writer has described Jesus' appearance after the awful torture and the brutal blows of scourging as "one massive bruise."

Isaiah refers to this in these terms: "His appearance was marred more than any man, and His form more than the sons of men." Some commentators and translators have described it this way: "His appearance was marred more than that of a man," meaning that when you looked at Him, you didn't even see Him as a man because His face and body were so bruised, swollen, and bleeding.

As a climax to this important section of Isaiah 53, we come upon what has been called "a holy paradox."

> But the LORD was pleased
>> To crush Him, putting Him to grief;
>> If He would render Himself as a guilt offering,
>> He will see His offspring,
>> He will prolong His days,
>> And the good pleasure of the LORD will prosper in His hand.
>
> —ISAIAH 53:10

Jesus was not murdered. He gave up His life willingly. Furthermore, as we have already noted, the Father found satisfaction in the death of His Son. The crushing of His Son was planned by the Father. That massive wounding, those crushing blows, were all designed by a loving Father. A holy paradox indeed! The crucial question is "Why?" Why would it please the Father to allow His Son to be bruised?

Author John Piper does a splendid job of answering that question:

> Why did God bruise His Son and bring Him to grief? He did it to resolve the dissonance between His love for His glory and His love for sinners." . . .
>
> It was not for His own sin that the Father bruised the Son. It was because He wanted to show us mercy. He wanted to forgive and heal and save and rejoice over us with loud singing. But He is righteous. That means His heart was filled with a love for the infinite worth of His own glory. But we were sinners. And that means that our hearts were filled with God-belittling affections. So to save sinners, and at the same time magnify the worth of His glory, God lays our sin on Jesus and abandons Him to the shame and slaughter of the cross.[4]

The Father has prepared the same canvas for you that He did for His Son. Based on A. W. Tozer's words, it's doubtful that God can use anyone greatly until He has hurt him deeply. If we're to be shaped and molded into the image of Christ, then we should be prepared for the reality of that image. We must be prepared to suffer and, in fact, to die (to self) before we can live the life our Savior has designed for us to live.

Dimitri Vail was one of the foremost portrait painters in America. Many famous individuals had their portraits painted by this gifted artist, who was known for one thing: realism. In fact, his work is so realistic that you might think you are looking at an enlargement of a photograph. On several occasions I have visited Vail's gallery in Dallas. One day, as I was walking through the exhibits, I noticed a picture I had never seen before hanging in a dark corner without a light focused in its direction. Most of Vail's pictures were beautifully displayed, with lovely frames and exquisite lighting. This one sat on an easel and seemed almost crudely presented. It had no frame, no light, no name.

Who is that? I wondered. All the other portraits were readily identifiable, even without the famous names listed beneath them. But this one, painted in shades of gray and brown, dark blue and streaks of black, was unidentified. I was intrigued.

"Who is this?" I finally asked the woman who was working in the gallery.

"Oh, that's a self-portrait" she said. "That's Mr. Vail himself."

As I stood and studied the somber, sad-looking face, she added, "And you know what? He looks just like that."

That's the way it is with our Lord. He may allow many individuals to have portraits of prominence—to look attractive, upbeat, and impressive to the public. But when it comes to His own portrait, He paints it under the shadow of the cross, with the browns and grays and blacks of realism. No frame. No fame. No spotlight. It's the truth on display. It's the Man of Sorrows, who was acquainted with grief—the One who was pierced through for our transgressions and crushed for our iniquities. And because the Lord allowed our sins to fall on Him, we give Him our highest praise as we sing, "Worthy is the Lamb that was slain. . . ."

And you? What about *your* portrait? Are you still working on polishing your image? Still trying to impress? Still attempting to escape the pain or deny the struggles of being reshaped into the image of Christ?

The shadow of suffering falls across *every* path, including yours. But the beauty of those dark shades and dismal colors is in the result, for in the process we become more like Christ.

2
The Cup of Sacrifice

When I survey the wondrous cross
On which the Prince of glory died,
My richest gain I count but loss,
And pour contempt on all my pride.[1]

— ISAAC WATTS

2
The Cup of Sacrifice

I've had some pretty amazing meals in my lifetime. They span the extremes, from the sublime to the sensational, from the most primitive to the most formal, fashionable, and elegant. I've been invited to banquets in governors' mansions and have sat at the captain's table on ocean cruises. I've also eaten in rugged hunting lodges and around campfires with my family, enjoying delicious fresh-caught fish, and I've tried to choke down hospital meals that tasted like a mixture of wet plaster and soggy cardboard.

Having done more than my share of eating (!) in my more than six decades, I can tell you that, if given a choice, I much prefer a small, intimate setting to a large, impersonal gathering. As a matter of fact, the more I study the New Testament and examine how the people of that era ate their meals, the more I think I would have felt right at home with them, especially among Jesus and His disciples. Almost without exception, they kept their meals simple, and they kept the group small. No five- or six-course meals. No elegant banquets or flashy decorations. And no formal, sophisticated protocol. Nowhere was this more evident than when they ate the Passover meal together.

Centuries have passed since the evening our Lord sat in the upper room and shared that last simple meal with His disciples. Simple, yet extremely significant. During those centuries, that meal has taken on enormous significance. Unfortunately, it has also taken on the trappings of religion—the "extras" of complicated rituals and denominational distinctives. In doing so, it has lost, I believe, some of the profound simplicity that surrounded the table when Jesus and His men met together that final night.

First of all, let's consider why they were together.

> Now the Feast of Unleavened Bread, which is called the Passover, was approaching. And the chief priests and the scribes were seeking how they might put Him [Jesus] to death; for they were afraid of the people. . . . Then came the first day of Unleavened Bread on which the Passover lamb had to be sacrificed. And He sent Peter and John, saying, "Go and prepare the Passover for us, that we may eat it."
>
> —LUKE 22:1–2, 7–8

Every year, on the fourth Thursday of November, many Americans prepare a lavish meal. We invite our nearest and dearest—family and friends—and celebrate the Thanksgiving meal. This is the holiday that remains my all-time favorite of the year. It is a time when we gather for two simple reasons: to have a meal and to remember.

Passover might be considered the Thanksgiving celebration of the Jews. It's not a Thanksgiving with turkey and trimmings, pilgrims and Plymouth Rock, but a time of remembrance of something far more significant.

When the Hebrews were in Egypt, God called Moses to lead them out of slavery and into the Promised Land. On the night of that great Exodus, God told His servant, in effect, "Moses, give these instructions to the Hebrews. Tell each household to choose a perfect lamb—one that is unblemished, without scars or imperfections. They are to take that spotless lamb, kill it in the way I have specified, and drain the blood into a pan. Take that blood and smear it on the doorway of their homes. For tonight, Moses, the Angel of the Lord will visit Egypt. Any home with blood on the door, he will 'pass over' that home and leave it untouched. But if he finds no blood on the door, death will enter that home, and the oldest son will die. There will be no exception, Moses. The Destroyer will 'pass over' only when he sees the blood." (See Exodus 12:12–13, 29)

That began the single most important of all the Jewish observances. Appropriately, it is called "Passover." God made it clear that they were to remember that epochal night from then on; and when they did, they were to explain its significance to their children. The meal became, from that day on, the Jews' most important celebration.

WHERE THEY WERE

On His last night with His disciples, Jesus celebrated the Passover, as devout Jews had been doing for centuries. Appropriately, He used that feast of remembrance to turn their attention to His own approaching death.

> And He sent Peter and John, saying, "Go and prepare the Passover for us, that we may eat it." And they said to Him, "Where do You want us to prepare it?" And He said to them, "Behold, when you have entered the city, a man will meet you carrying a pitcher of water; follow him into the house that he enters. And you shall say to the owner of the house, 'The Teacher says to you, "Where is the guest room in which I may eat the Passover with My disciples?"' And he will show you a large, furnished, upper room; prepare it there." And they departed and found everything just as He had told them; and they prepared the Passover.
>
> —LUKE 22:8–13

Notice that Jesus does not send Peter and John to a specific address. He gives them no house number, no street name, not even a section in the city of Jerusalem. He simply tells them to look for a man carrying water.

A *man* carrying water? In those days, the women went to the wells to fetch the water. So a man carrying water would be very noticeable, even in the crowded streets of Jerusalem, busy with all the traffic that surrounded a great religious festival like the Feast of Passover. One wonders if, in fact, he was the only man carrying water in the entire city of Jerusalem.

Once Peter and John spotted a man carrying water, they were to follow him. He would lead them to a house, where they were to enter and say to the owner: "The Teacher says to you, 'Where is the guest room in which I may eat the Passover with My disciples?'" The owner would then lead them to a large, furnished, upper room. In other words, he would lead them to a room on the second floor of the house.

The instructions were clear. Jesus had made the arrangements, and they were to follow through just as He had explained.

WHAT THEY DID

> And they departed and found everything just as He had told them; and they prepared the Passover.
>
> —LUKE 22:13

As time passed and the Jews, each year, celebrated the Passover Feast of remembrance and thanksgiving, the required ingredients of that feast were passed down from generation to generation in the traditional teachings of the six hundred thirteen Laws of the Torah. This included the slaughtering and preparing of "the Paschal lamb" (Exodus 12:6); the obligation to eat the Paschal lamb (that is, to participate in the Passover Seder) (Exodus 12:8); the proper preparation of the lamb (it must be roasted—Exodus 12:9); the prohibition against leaving any remains of the Lamb (Exodus 12:10); the requirement to eat matzah (unleavened bread) during Passover (Exodus 12:18); the obligation to tell one's child the story of the liberation from Egypt (Exodus 13:8). These are just a few of the specific instructions from the Torah regarding Passover. Nothing all that complicated, but what was stated was to be followed to the letter.

The Feast of Passover was centered around three items: roasted lamb, bitter herbs, and unleavened bread. The roasted lamb was central. It was to remind them of the sacrifice of the spotless lamb and the blood spread on the doorposts of believing Hebrew homes. The bitter herbs were a mixture of lettuce, endive, roots, peppermint, and dandelion. As the sting and bite of those bitter herbs touched the tongue, they offered a vivid taste of the stinging years that the Hebrew fathers had spent in slavery. The unleavened bread was to remind them of the haste with which the Hebrews had to prepare to leave with Moses, their deliverer.

The disciples did precisely as Jesus had directed them. They found the proper place and prepared the necessary ingredients for the Passover.

THE FINAL MEAL

And when the hour had come He reclined at the table, and the apostles with Him.

—LUKE 22:14

At the risk of losing favor with those who are lovers of great works of art, I need to say something that some may not enjoy reading, and that is this: Leonardo da Vinci did Christianity a great disservice with his painting "The Last Supper." Not to the world of art, you understand; artistically his painting is a masterpiece. But historically and biblically the masterpiece is not anywhere near authentic.

In da Vinci's painting, Jesus and His disciples are sitting on one side of the table, in chairs, "facing the camera," as it were. But Jesus and the Twelve would not have sat in chairs with high backs at a table some thirty inches from the floor. In the First Century, when people ate a meal, they sat on the floor on small pallets or rugs. In fact, they reclined around a table built low to the floor, leaning on one elbow, in a prone position.

Also, they did not eat with utensils, as we do. Bread served as a utensil to sop up or scoop up the other ingredients. Nor was their bread like our common loaf of bread; it would have been a flat loaf, perhaps somewhat like our pita bread—and at Passover, made deliberately without the leaven, it would have been flat and brittle. They would break the bread and dip it into the bitter herbs and pile on pieces of roasted lamb.

Picture Jesus and His disciples, reclining in a casual circle around a low table, facing each other and eating the Passover meal, as faithful Jews had done for centuries. Those men had eaten that meal, much as Americans have eaten our Thanksgiving meal, all their lives. No surprises. No unexpected moments . . . until . . . until Jesus began to speak to them as a group.

> And He said to them, "I have earnestly desired to eat this Passover with you before I suffer; for I say to you, I shall never again eat it until it is fulfilled in the kingdom of God."
>
> —LUKE 22:15–16

Put yourself in the place of these men. Remember, they had not had nineteen centuries of celebrations of the Last Supper behind them. They had not heard these words of the Lord read to them during countless "communion services." They had been walking with Jesus for three years, so at most they had celebrated three Passovers with Him. But they had never observed what we now call the Lord's Table; they had never heard the message that Jesus was going to give them now. This was a first . . . an absolutely startling, life-changing significant first. A total surprise.

The disciples, of course, did not have any idea how significant this gathering would be. They were barely paying attention, eating the Passover and talking among themselves. Sometimes these men could be downright contentious, and this was one of those times. They even argued over who would be the greatest in the kingdom.

Many folks today view the Twelve as immortal saints of the faith—our spiritual forefathers—but at this point in their training, they were very human, sometimes carnal, and downright ignorant men. They had no concept of what lay ahead in the coming hours: Jesus would leave them that night and go to the cross, and their faith would be tested as never before in the fires of persecution.

We'll leave all this for now and touch on it again in a later chapter. At the moment, I don't want us to drift from where we're headed in this scene as Jesus is with His men around the table.

> And while they were eating, Jesus took some bread, and after a blessing, He broke it and gave it to the disciples, and said, "Take, eat; this is My body." And when He had taken a cup and given thanks, He gave it to them, saying, "Drink from it, all of you; for this is My blood of the covenant, which is poured out for many for forgiveness of sins. "But I say to you, I will not drink of this fruit of the vine from now on until that day when I drink it new with you in My Father's kingdom."
>
> —Matthew 26:26–29

They ate together, celebrating the Passover Feast. Traditionally, as devout Jews, they would have been quoting from the ancient Scriptures, remembering the days when their forefathers were enslaved in Egypt and delivered by God through His servant Moses. Suddenly, they noticed that Jesus was no longer participating in the conversation. He looked somber—perhaps more somber than He had looked during all their years together.

As they watched with curiosity, Jesus took a piece of unleavened bread and broke it. Then He bowed His head and prayed. The passage says, "He blessed the bread." We don't know what He prayed. Perhaps He asked the Father that the disciples might begin to sense the significance of that night, the last one He would be spending with them. They didn't know it was the last, but He knew, and He wanted to help them understand what He was about to do . . . and what it would mean to them. Perhaps He prayed for strength in light of what lay ahead. Whatever the untold details might be, we know that having broken the bread and given thanks, He said, "Take this bread and eat it. This is My body."

What? What was He talking about? They must have looked back and forth at each other questioningly. The Master had never said this before. He was suddenly breaking with tradition, and they were completely confused.

Theologians, too, have been confused for centuries over that statement. Some have taught that the bread served at the Eucharist, the Lord's Table, actually becomes the body of Christ when it enters the mouth of the believer. Others believe that when the priest stands before the people and breaks the bread it becomes the body of Christ. Others say that it is *representative*—a spiritual symbol of the body of Christ. I believe that the best answer is the most simple and direct: The bread is a picture of His body, a representation of His body that was given for us on the cross.

In my wallet I carry a small picture of my family. Occasionally, someone will say to me, "We'd love to see your family, Chuck." And I'll reach into my pocket and pull out my family to show them. Not literally, of course; it's just a picture of my family. But I say, "This is my family."

That's what Jesus meant when He said to them that night, "This is My body."

If we could only gain a sense of what that moment must have been like for those twelve, suddenly disoriented disciples. Today, we have centuries of teaching and writings at our fingertips as resources; we have the four Gospels and the other books of the Bible. Furthermore, we have the entire life of Christ to put this into perspective. But there are occasions when we need to relax in the simplicity of faith, and in our time of quiet meditation we need to travel back to that upper room where Jesus broke the brittle, flat loaf of bread and told His disciples to eat it, reminding them that it was a symbol—a tangible picture—of His body that would soon be given on their behalf.

Imagine the sudden silence. Imagine the questions that swarmed through the minds of the disciples: Is He really going to die? What will happen to us? What about the kingdom He promised? Have all these years with Him been in vain? Their stomachs must have been in knots. The Gospels give no indication that a word was spoken in response. For a change, these twelve men sat in absolute, stunned silence. Words failed to describe their feelings.

While the taste of the bread was still in their mouths, Jesus picked up a cup of wine. Down through the years people have imagined Jesus using all sorts of cups, from simple clay vessels to elaborate silver chalices. Many myths have grown up around the cup Jesus used at the Last Supper, which some see as a sacred vessel. Those who promote such thinking believe the cup has somehow, somewhere been preserved and venerated through the centuries. Yet God has never wanted His people to worship or venerate any object or person other than Himself. Please remember that! For that reason alone, I'm certain there was nothing elaborate or significant about the cup that our Lord chose on that last night. It was an ordinary, everyday drinking vessel—an earthen vessel, one of several on the table, filled with wine, from which He and His disciples had been drinking.

Jesus took a cup, offered a prayer of thanks, and said to His disciples, "Drink from it, all of you."

I have often asked myself as I read this passage, for what did Jesus give thanks? He had already asked the blessing on the meal. He had already asked the blessing on the bread. Why pray again? Why give thanks? For what?

It helps to understand that the same word that is used here for "cup" is used later when Jesus prays in the Garden of Gethsemane: "Father, if it be Your will, let this *cup* pass from me; nevertheless, not My will but Yours be done." This is also a word that could be used to represent suffering. So as Jesus gave thanks for the cup, He may very well have been giving thanks for the suffering He was facing. And let's not forget that the cup of suffering would include His death on a cruel cross.

Out of obedience to the Father, Jesus took the cup of death, willing to pay the price for the sins of the world. And out of love for His followers He gave thanks for what that cup would provide—the gift of eternal life.

> And when He had taken a cup and given thanks, He said, "Take this and share it among yourselves; for I say to you, I will not drink of the fruit of the vine from now on until the kingdom of God comes."
>
> —LUKE 22:17–18

This was the end of their time together. "You will never celebrate another Passover with Me," Jesus was saying. "But there will come a day when we will celebrate together in My Father's kingdom in the Father's presence." Won't that be a glorious day? With the Father and the Son in the kingdom.

And so today, on each occasion when we observe the Lord's Table, let us give thanks that our Savior gave thanks for us and that He was compelled by love to take up that cross. As we hold that cup close to our lips, in remembrance, may we taste and see that the Lord is good. Think of the significance of that. We are not simply to feel or to read or to hear or to see, but to take into our very bodies the taste of our Savior's sacrifice.

HIS PURSUIT OF OBEDIENCE . . . AND OURS

> And He came out and proceeded as was His custom to the Mount of Olives; and the disciples also followed Him.
>
> —LUKE 22:39

After they had shared that final Passover meal in the upper room, that Last Supper, Jesus and His disciples made their way out of the city and across the Kidron Valley to a garden on the Mount of Olives. From what we read in Luke's account, we know our Savior had frequently found quiet refuge on the Mount of Olives . . . quite probably at

Gethsemane itself. It's noteworthy that He did not choose to run and hide, knowing that danger was near, as we would be tempted to do. Instead, He led His men back to that familiar place, unafraid of the capture and arrest that lay ahead. Jesus led His disciples out into a dark night to face the brutal, hostile world that was waiting to condemn Him to death.

Jesus could not pay the price for our sin by hiding in the safety of the upper room, and we cannot remain in the safety of the sanctuary. Daily we must go out into the world, where the presence of Jesus Christ in our lives will create in us a love, a tolerance, an ability to be unique even in a hostile, desperate, hateful, ugly world.

To add more to a scene this searching and intimate could dilute its impact. Perhaps a simple prayer of devotion would be our best conclusion here.

Dear Father,

Please forgive us for the many times we have observed the Lord's Table and failed to grasp the significance and symbolism of the bread and the cup. What a powerful message awaits us each time we pause in remembrance of our Lord! In the simplicity of the supper we remember His eternal love, infinite compassion, resolute obedience, boundless grace . . . the agony He endured and the ransom He paid.

Thank You, Father, for Christ our Savior . . . for the accomplishments of the cross and for the model of obedience He portrayed. Deepen our devotion as we focus our hearts on Him as never before in our lives.

Through His strong Name, I pray.

Amen.

Midnight in the Garden

King of my life, I crown Thee now.
Thine shall the glory be;
Lest I forget Thy thorn-crowned brow,
Lead me to Calvary.
    Lest I forget Gethsemane;
    Lest I forget Thine agony,
    Lest I forget Thy love for me,
    Lead me to Calvary.[1]

—JENNIE EVELYN HUSSEY, 1921

3
Midnight in the Garden

*M*y Aunt Ernestine was an accomplished, though self-taught, artist. Of all of her works, the one I liked best—and the one that intrigued me as a little boy—was a painting of the Lord Jesus in the Garden of Gethsemane. It was a large oil painting that hung above the fireplace in my maternal grandparents' home. It was, in fact, the first thing that caught your eye when you walked in the front door.

In the painting, Jesus knelt beside several large boulders, with His hands folded and His arms resting on the rugged rocks, His face looking up into heaven in an attitude of prayer. Above and behind Him rolled a cloudy, troubled sky, moonlit but moody.

One day I pulled up a chair and climbed up so that I was at the level of the painting. I pressed my nose right up against the part of the picture that fascinated me: the small droplets of blood coming out of Jesus' forehead. I was bothered by those droplets. I didn't know the story of Gethsemane then, so I imagined all manner of things. Maybe this Man was lost in the woods and was praying for God to help Him find His way out. But why was His forehead bleeding? Had He hit it on the limbs of the trees as He stumbled through the forest? Or maybe some enemy had struck Him in the face.

One afternoon I asked my granddaddy Lundy, "What does that picture mean?"

He reached down and picked me up, holding me in his arms as we stood and looked together at Aunt Ernestine's painting.

"This is a painting of our Savior when He was in the garden praying before He went to the cross," he said.

"Why is the blood there?" I asked.

"Well, let me show you," said my granddaddy. And he got his well-worn Bible and read me the part where it says that Jesus' sweat "was as it were great drops of blood falling down to the ground" during his agonizing prayer in the Garden of Gethsemane (Luke 22:44 KJV).

I never have been able to fully comprehend that kind of agony in prayer, but I believe it happened. Men of medicine tell us that the body can, at times of great stress, so break down that blood can actually ooze through the skin. A careful reading reveals that Dr. Luke does not say that the Savior actually bled. He says that His sweat "became as great drops of blood." But whatever it was, no one can overestimate the depth of agony that our Lord experienced in Gethsemane.

THE HUMANITY OF CHRIST

As we lift the veil on that night, we see just a small portion of a larger picture of the passion of Jesus. ("Passion" is a term commonly used when referring to Christ's suffering between the time of the Last Supper and His death on the cross.) What has transpired up to this point? As we saw in the previous chapter, Jesus has been in the upper room observing the Passover meal, their last supper together. Judas, the betrayer, has left to accomplish his evil scheme. Now, Jesus and His faithful eleven followers wind their way through the streets of Jerusalem, out through one of the gates of the city, across the southern steps of Herod's temple, then down into and beyond the Kidron Valley and on up the Mount of Olives to the dark and silent grove of olive trees called Gethsemane.

Gethsemane is a Hebrew word that means "oil press." Apparently there was a press in the vicinity where olives were pressed for their oil

It was here—alone and in agony—the Savior would experience the most crushing of experiences.

> And after singing a hymn, they went out to the Mount of Olives.
> . . . And they came to a place named Gethsemane; and He said to
> His disciples, "Sit here until I have prayed."
>
> —MARK 14:26, 32

Judging from the ancient olive grove that can be seen today on the Mount of Olives, this must have been a quiet, fragrant, and lovely place. Scholars of the New Testament believe Jesus and His disciples must have arrived there somewhere between midnight and one o'clock in the morning. Jesus asked His men to sit and wait while He prayed. Apparently they were to be some kind of human shield, guarding the site, lest someone interrupt His time of solitude. He did, however, take three of the group deeper into the garden with Him.

> And He took with Him Peter and James and John, and began to
> be very distressed and troubled. And He said to them, "My soul
> is deeply grieved to the point of death; remain here and keep
> watch." And He went a little beyond them, and fell to the ground,
> and began to pray that if it were possible, the hour might pass
> Him by.
>
> —MARK 14:33–35

No artist could possibly portray the anguish that began to sweep across Jesus' inner man. Words also fail in trying to describe His anguish. Here, the Greek words that are translated *very distressed* literally mean "to be struck with terror."

I cannot fully explain the why and how of Jesus' experience. I can only describe what Mark tells us. (Mark was the earliest of the four gospels written, probably written after much time spent with Peter.) Scholars verify that Mark got his information about this night directly from Peter . . . and Peter, of course, was an eyewitness. So from Peter's eyes, through Peter's lips, into Mark's pen come the words "very distressed." An anguishing sense of awe came over the Lord Jesus as He faced what lay ahead.

The verse also tells us that He became troubled, "very distressed and troubled." The word *troubled* includes the idea of being "ill at ease, filled with unrest, uncomfortable within." At that moment, just before He fell before the Father in prayer, those feelings began to close in upon Him. He did not hide His feelings from His three close friends—Peter, James, and John. He confessed He was "deeply grieved to the point of death."

About seven centuries earlier, as we saw in chapter one, Isaiah had prophesied that the Savior would be "a man of sorrows and acquainted with grief" (Isaiah 53:3). No better description of that is found in Scripture than the moment when He says, "I am deeply grieved."

What does it mean, in our human terms, to be deeply grieved? Think back a moment to a time in your own life that might be described in those terms. Maybe it happened when you lost your closest friend. Maybe it came after a long struggle with some addiction that tormented you—the humiliation of being found out and the grief that resulted. Or perhaps it was the untimely death of your mother or father.

I remember the afternoon my father called and said, "Son, I think mother is gone." I immediately drove across the city to my parents' home and there on the sofa was my mother's body. Earlier that afternoon she had decided to take a nap . . . she never awoke. There she lay, lifeless, at the relatively young age of sixty-three. And at that moment the deepest feelings of grief enveloped me.

One writer describes this moment for the Son of God in Gethsemane: "Grief enveloped Him, surrounded Him, saturated His conscious mind. It was so deep it was as if death had wrapped its fingers around His shoulders." Nowhere else in the Gospel narrative can we enter as fully into the humanity of Christ as in Gethsemane.

Troubled, distressed, and grieved beyond words, Jesus said to His disciples, "Remain here and keep watch."

Why? Why would He want them to be near Him when He was enduring such anguish? Often the human inclination is to retreat from others when overwhelmed—to hide such feelings. But Jesus didn't hide His anguish from His closest followers. He brought them face to face with His every human emotion. By doing so, He freed them from all temptation to deny such agonizing feelings in years to come. Even in His torturous struggles, He modeled a realistic, authentic example of living truthfully.

The Movement of Submission

Eight of the disciples remained near the entrance to the garden; the other three walked further into the heart of the dark, quiet Garden of Gethsemane with the Master. Then He said, "Stay right here and wait with Me." And with those words, "He went a little beyond them" and "fell to the ground, and began to pray that if it were possible, the hour might pass Him by."

In the original language in which Mark wrote, both of these verbs are in the imperfect tense, which describes continual, constant action. Thus, it could actually read like this: "He began falling to the ground and praying, and then falling to the ground and praying, and then falling and praying." In that sense, my Aunt Ernestine and other artists miss the picture when they portray Jesus kneeling quietly in the moonlight, praying with carefully folded hands in a serene fashion. That's not the way it happened. If I read this correctly, Jesus fell on the ground and prayed; He then got up, walked a little further, once again sank to the ground and prayed. He repeated this over and over as, in the anguish of His soul, He continued crying out, "Abba!"

> And He went a little beyond them, and fell to the ground, and began to pray that if it were possible, the hour might pass Him by. And He was saying, "Abba! Father! All things are possible for Thee; remove this cup from Me; yet not what I will, but what Thou wilt."
> —Mark 14:35–36

Abba is a word from Aramaic, the language Jesus spoke. *Abba* was an intimate word, a familial term for the close relationship between child and parent. The best equivalent in our language is the word "daddy." In using that term Mark preserves the sense of intimacy, immediacy, and agony the Holy Spirit wanted preserved.

"Oh, Daddy!" Jesus is saying. "If it is at all possible, Father, oh, my Father, let this agony that I am facing go by. Let there be another way. All things are possible for You."

When some would question how the Son of God could be truly human, let them look at this scene in Gethsemane, where the oil of His anguish was pressed out like the oil from the olives. Here, in the darkness of the garden, His humanity gushes out. I'm so grateful that this dark scene has been preserved. Otherwise I fear we would look upon the Lord Jesus as some kind of divine robot, who went through the motions of redemption without the deepest of feelings involved—just another divine appointment. But it was not like that at all. Jesus was not only undiminished deity, He was also, in every way, true humanity, subject to the identical feelings we have, whether it be joy or sorrow, fear or confidence, exhilarating ecstasy or sheer agony.

At this moment, the totally innocent, sinless Son of God faces and accepts the torture and death that shortly awaits Him. And so He addresses His Father in familiar terms: "If it is possible, let this pass." If there is any other way to redeem humanity, to pay the ultimate price for their sin, may that come to pass. And then He prays the words that have become the most familiar words in our prayer life, "Yet not what I will, but what You will."

Can you count the number of times you've said that? I can't. How many times I have gone before the Lord and said, "Lord, these are my desires, and as best as I can search my heart, I honestly believe this is Your will. But it may not be, and no matter what, I want Your will, not mine. These represent my desires, and You have told me to commit myself and my desires to You, and the delight of my heart will be completely satisfied. And so not my will but Yours be done." Interestingly, these sentiments are all based on the prayer that Jesus prayed in the garden. That's where it all started: "Not my will but Yours."

Notice the movement here:

> And He came and found them sleeping, and said to Peter, "Simon, are you asleep? Could you not keep watch for one hour? "Keep watching and praying, that you may not come into temptation; the spirit is willing, but the flesh is weak." And again He went away and prayed, saying the same words. And again He came and found them sleeping, for their eyes were very heavy; and they did not know what to answer Him. And He came the third time, and said to them, "Are you still sleeping and taking your rest? It is enough; the hour has come; behold, the Son of Man is being betrayed into the hands of sinners. "Arise, let us be going; behold, the one who betrays Me is at hand!"
>
> —MARK 14:37–42

Jesus didn't just bow once for a brief prayer in the garden and then go out to face His crucifixion. He prayed, and then He went back to the disciples. He then returned to prayer, and then once again came back to the disciples. Three times He went back to pray. This is the movement of submission: "Not My will, but Yours be done."

What an incredible experience that should have been for the disciples. Yet they did not hear Him. Instead, "He found them sleeping."

The verse says He found "them" sleeping, but He talked to Peter. Do you know why He addressed Peter? Because just a short time before, after the Passover meal, well-meaning Peter had said to the Master, "Even though all may fall away, yet I will not" (Mark 14:29). And so He singled out Peter, the very one who had promised, "I will never fall away," and said, "Simon, are you asleep?"

Notice that Jesus called him Simon, the disciple's given name, rather than Peter (meaning "rock"), the name the Lord had earlier bestowed upon him. It's almost as if the Lord is implying, "We're back where we started, Simon. You still have such a long way to go!" We can't help but wonder how Peter must have felt—the embarrassment of being asked, "Are you asleep? Could you not keep watch for one hour?" Then, graciously, Jesus urges, "Keep watching and praying."

Earlier Jesus had said "Watch." Now He says to Peter, James, and John, "Watch and pray." Why? "That you may not come into temptation." What was that temptation? Surely it was more than just the temptation to fall asleep again. I believe it was the very temptation that they would fall into during the next few hours: the temptation to defect. Right now was the time for the disciples to pray for steel in their souls. Right now was the time for them to watch and pray, while there was no enemy around, because when the enemy came, the temptation would be to fall away from the Savior. Jesus told them to watch and pray so that might not happen . . . so that they would not be tempted to leave Him.

Jeremiah gives us an interesting insight on the matter of putting steel into our souls when things are good so that when things get tough we can handle them.

> If you have run with footmen and they have tired you out,
> Then how can you compete with horses?
> If you fall down in a land of peace,
> How will you do in the thicket of the Jordan?
> —JEREMIAH 12:5

Anyone who was running with the footmen was with the infantry. But if a person could not keep up with a man on foot, what would he do when the cavalry appeared, when there was a battle with soldiers on horses? If a warrior fell down in a time of peace, what would he do in the jungle of the Jordan, in the wilderness, when the real hand-to-hand combat occurred?

An excellent principle of life is tucked away here: Capitalize on times of peace. Use moments of serenity to put steel in your soul, so you won't yield when life gets hard and heavy.

At this moment you may be experiencing tremendous prosperity in your business or your personal life. You may find yourself coasting along, and it looks like a beautiful tomorrow. If so, let me challenge you: Right now you are in the perfect place to prepare yourself. Times of peace and prosperity provide the ideal moments to equip yourself for the inevitable tests of famine and hardship.

That's what Jesus was saying in Mark 14:38: "'Keep watching and praying, that you may not come into temptation; the spirit is willing, but the flesh is weak.'" This was all too evident, as Jesus returned a third time and found them sleeping.

> And He came the third time, and said to them, "Are you still sleeping and taking your rest? It is enough; the hour has come; behold, the Son of Man is being betrayed into the hands of sinners. Arise, let us be going; behold, the one who betrays Me is at hand!"
>
> —MARK 14:41–42

Once again the disciples are sound asleep, maybe even snoring, yet this time He gently wakes them without rebuke. This is the picture for the artist to portray. Here is unvarnished realism. The disciples have virtually defected already, yet Jesus hovers over them like a mother over a sleeping baby, saying, "It is enough."

He has gone to the Father in prayer. He has requested another alternative, if that were possible. It is not. Now He sees that the only way through is the way of the cross, and He is resigned to it. And in that sweet, submissive spirit, He says, "The hour has come . . . the one who betrays Me is at hand."

There's a sense of quiet resolve recorded in all four of the gospels as they describe this scene. Jesus slips out of the garden to face His betrayer, Judas, and the hostile multitude. Then, in the flickering torchlight, He is led away as a captive.

This was God's plan, and He was ready to accept it.

THE CRUCIBLE OF DECISION

Perhaps you are in the crucible of decision—a time of deep, searching struggle in your soul. God has made it fairly clear to you that this is what He wants of you, and this is His will for your life. But it involves giving up certain rights that you enjoy, certain desires that are significant and important to you. Letting God have His way can be an uncomfortable thing.

Perhaps you are single, and you have realized that it is God's plan that, at least for the foreseeable future, you should remain single. I remember a young woman who was suddenly jilted by her fiancé. She came to me with tears streaming down her cheeks. "I have been through three difficult months," she said, "but I believe that it is God's will, at least for an extended period of time, that I make no further plans for falling in love." She said this not with bitternes or morbid resignation, but with a quiet submission to His plan.

Maybe you have found yourself suddenly face-to-face with a situation that, a year ago, you would never have dreamed could be true in your life . . . but now it is. God is "pressing" you in the midst of your own Gethsemane, saying, "I want to have My will in your life. I want you to release your rights. I want you to be willing to accept My will . . . regardless. And I want you to stop wrestling with Me. I want to have My way with you."

This is "your cup."

God might have pinpointed something that no longer has any place in your life. Perhaps it is an illicit relationship, or your unfair treatment of another person. Maybe it is an attitude of prejudice or revenge. Whatever it is, you're in the garden, facing a tough decision, wrestling with "the cup" God has called to your attention.

It is time that, in a very real sense, you walk where our Savior walked and kneel with Him at Gethsemane. Use it as a time to search your life, saying, "Lord, not my will, but Yours be done."

I have found, in my own life, that there are at least four stages the Lord takes us through in the process of bringing us to the place of full surrender.

First, *we must all journey through the darkness of our own Gethsemane.* Just as Jesus "arrived at the place," so must we (Luke 22:42).

Second, *while there, we must suffer through our own anguish.* No one can go through this process for us. Like our Lord, we pray, we sweat, and we wait it out alone . . . all alone.

Third, *in our anguish, we must release our own will.* In this crucible of decision, it is primarily a battle of two wills: ours and God's. We may plead and bargain, but, ultimately, if we are to emerge victorious, we must release the controls to Him. It is at *that* point—precisely at *that* time—the anguish subsides and a breakthrough occurs. The struggle ends and a quiet resolve emerges.

Fourth, *having accepted the Father's will over our own, we are then ready to face our own Calvary.* In other words, taking up our own cross and following Christ is bearable once we have passed through our Gethsemane.

It's just as Jesus taught: "If anyone wishes to come after Me [model the life I lived], let him deny himself [Gethsemane], take up his cross and follow Me [Calvary]" (Luke 9:23).

Here's the crucial question: Do you really wish to follow Christ that closely?

Three O' Clock in the Morning

Who was the guilty?
Who brought this upon thee?
Alas, my treason, Jesus, hath undone thee.
'Twas I, Lord Jesus,
I it was denied thee:
I crucified thee.[1]

—JOHANN HEERMANN

4

Three O' Clock in the Morning

*P*eter is the disciple with whom we most readily identify . . . and for good reason. He is so transparent, so human, so vulnerable, so honest, and at times so downright real that we can easily see ourselves in his actions and reactions as a disciple. And while I'm on that subject, can you think of anything more embarrassing than for the Lord to write down the unadulterated truth of your life for the entire world to read . . . for generations to come? And don't forget: That would also allow centuries of preachers to examine your failures and sins, your outbursts of anger and open denials and embarrassing betrayals, year after year after year.

To look at this more closely ourselves, we must return to the interlude between Jesus' last meal with His disciples in the upper room and His soul-searching struggle in the Garden of Gethsemane. As Jesus and His disciples made their way from Jerusalem to the Mount of Olives, He made some striking and startling comments.

STRONG WORDS BETWEEN TWO FRIENDS

When they had sung the hymn, they went out to the Mount of Olives.

And Jesus said to them, "You will all become deserters; for it is written,

'I will strike the shepherd,
and the sheep will be scattered.'

But after I am raised up, I will go before you to Galilee."

Peter said to him, "Even though all become deserters, I will not."

Jesus said to him, "Truly I tell you, this day, this very night, before the cock crows twice, you will deny me three times."

But he said vehemently, "Even though I must die with you, I will not deny you." And all of them said the same.

—MARK 14:26–31

"After I am raised up," Jesus said. But it is apparent Peter didn't pay attention to this prediction of the resurrection. All Peter heard was "You will all become deserters." The word *deserters*—or as the New International Version (NIV) translates it, "You will all *fall away*"—is taken from the Greek term that means "to stumble."

"Every one of you is going to turn against Me, depart from Me, leave Me . . . all of you will stumble."

And you can almost hear Peter say, with a sweeping gesture of his rugged fisherman hands toward the other disciples, in his familiar over-confident tone of voice, "All these others in the group may desert you, but I certainly will not!"

"Ah, Peter, but you will," says Jesus with a sigh. And then He adds a comment that must have stung. "Truly I tell you, this very night, before the cock crows twice, you will deny me three times."

Jesus makes three penetrating statements: Peter will deny Him; Peter will deny Him that very night; and Peter will deny Him three times.

I've often said that Peter suffered from foot-in-mouth disease. (Sound familiar?) He was given to boasting and overstatement because of his over-inflated opinion of himself. But let's give him the benefit of the doubt here. Perhaps he was genuinely self-assured. He really meant it! Confident of his own loyalty, his own devotion to the Master, he didn't mind stepping up and sounding as loyal as he felt. He was devoted enough to die with Him, so he said so.

After their Passover meal together and some of the things Jesus had said to them, all the disciples' emotions were high. Obviously Peter's ran even higher. "Lord, the world can come to an end before I'll deny You. All of these others may, but not I!"

And Jesus said, "No, this very night you're going to deny Me. Not once, but three separate times, before the cock crows twice."

William Barclay offers unexpected insight regarding Jesus' mention of the cock crowing.

> It may well be that the cock-crow was not the voice of a bird; and that from the beginning it was not meant to mean that. After all, the house of the high priest was right in the centre of Jerusalem. And there was not likely to be poultry in the centre of the city. There was, in fact, a regulation in the Jewish law that it was illegal to keep cocks and hens in the Holy City because they defiled holy things. But the hour of 3 A.M. was called *cock-crow,* and for this reason. At that hour the Roman guard was changed in the Castle of Antonia; and the sign of the changing of the guard was a trumpet call. The Latin for that trumpet call was *gallicinium,* which means *cock-crow.* It is at least possible that just as Peter made his third denial the trumpet from the castle battlements rang out over the sleeping city . . . and Peter remembered; and thereupon he went and wept his heart out.[2]

The Romans divided each day into three-hour segments called "hours"; and the three-hour segments of the night were called "watches." These watches determined the three-hour periods of guard duty, just as we have hours of guard duty in military service today. The night watches could also be used to indicate at which hour something occurred. The first night watch began at 6:00 P.M. and went until 9:00; the second watch was from 9:00 P.M. until midnight; the third watch was from midnight until 3:00 A.M.; and the fourth watch was from 3:00 until 6:00 A.M.

The Jews frequently used an abbreviated form when referring to these watches of the night. We find an example of this in Mark 13:35–37:

> Therefore, keep awake—for you do not know when the master of the house will come, in the evening, or at midnight, or at cock-crow, or at dawn, or else he may find you asleep when he comes suddenly. And what I say to you I say to all: Keep awake."

"Evening" referred to the end of the first watch, or nine o'clock. "Midnight" was the end of the second watch. Did you notice? "Cock-crow" was their term for the end of the third watch, or 3:00 in the morning. And "dawn" marked the end of the fourth watch.

When Jesus said, "before the cock crows twice," He was referring to the end of the third watch. If Barclay's suggestion is correct, a signal was given in the very early hours of the morning, marking the end of the third watch, and this signal was called "cock-crowing." Except, as we've seen, in this case it wasn't a rooster, but a trumpeter. At the changing of the guard for the next watch, there was a shrill sound of the trumpet. And during festival times, because of the vast numbers of people in the city, frequently two blasts were sounded, one in one direction and one in the other.

Since this was Passover, the trumpeter would have sounded twice. So that's what Jesus meant when He said to Peter, "This very night, before you hear those two blasts on the trumpet, you will have denied Me three times." This also assures us that Peter's denial took place before 3:00 in the morning.

> But he said vehemently, "Even though I must die with you, I will not deny you." And all of them said the same.
>
> —MARK 14:31

The others soon picked up the refrain of this loyal, yet vulnerable disciple. "Me too." "That's right, Peter, me too." "I will not deny You, Master." They were all so loyal, there in the safety of the quiet, sheltered garden . . . in the comfort of their inner circle. Little did they realize what faced them beyond that garden, at three o'clock in the eerie morning darkness of the soul.

For the moment, however, they had only to watch and wait as the Master passed through His own time of agony, His own Gethsemane. All He asked them to do was to "sit here while I pray" and "keep awake." However . . .

> He came and found them sleeping; and he said to Peter, "Simon, are you asleep? Could you not keep awake one hour?"
>
> —MARK 14:37

He came and found Peter, James, and John sleeping. But it is worth noting that He only addressed one of "them." He singled out Peter. Why? Because Peter was the one who earlier that same evening had declared so boldly, "Even though all the rest fail You, I will not!" And yet here he was, snoring away. He was too weak to keep watch or to stay awake. But let's not be too hard on Peter. Who among us hasn't made the same error? We come on strong and over-commit, only to flame out before very long.

Furthermore, Peter wasn't alone when it came to defection. Only a short time later, when Judas arrived to betray Jesus into the hands of His enemies, look what happened: "They all left Him and fled" (Mark 14:50).

Everyone who had earlier said, "I will never leave You, Master. I will never betray You. I will never deny You. I will never fail You. Though everyone else may turn away, I will not," blew it! Every last one of the remaining eleven ran away—away into the night of fear and anonymity. "They all left Him and fled." They scattered like frightened mice.

PETER'S DARKEST HOUR

And they led Jesus away to the high priest; and all the chief priests and the elders and the scribes gathered together. And Peter had followed Him at a distance, right into the courtyard of the high priest; and he was sitting with the officers, and warming himself at the fire.

—MARK 14:53–54

Peter had fled with the others when Jesus was arrested in Gethsemane. Yet he did not go far. He followed Jesus and His captors "at a distance." Standing back in the shadows in the cold morning hours, Peter watched everything unfold. He followed the crowd right into the courtyard of the high priest. The soldiers were gathered around a small fire, and carefully, with his cloak wrapped closely around him, Peter approached the embers to warm himself.

Afraid but curious, Peter's loyalty was at war with his fear. And so he followed Jesus at a distance . . . a safe distance.

Now the chief priests and the whole Council kept trying to obtain testimony against Jesus to put Him to death; and they were not finding any. . . . And some began to spit at Him, and to blindfold Him, and to beat Him with their fists, and to say to Him, "Prophesy!" And the officers received Him with slaps in the face.

—MARK 14:55, 65

Jesus was tormented, humiliated, spit upon, cursed, and falsely accused. He stood there silent and bleeding. Then they began to mock Him. They blindfolded Him and slapped His face, challenging Him to "Prophesy! Tell us who hit you!" And off in the shadows, taking it all in, stood frightened Peter, haunted by the memory of his own words. "I will never deny You, Master. Though all others fall away, I won't fail You." They pulsated in his mind. He couldn't erase the condemnation of his own words.

> And as Peter was below in the courtyard, one of the servant girls
> of the high priest came, and seeing Peter warming himself, she
> looked at him, and said, "You, too, were with Jesus the Nazarene."
> —MARK 14:66–67

Perhaps someone poked the fire, causing it to blaze up and flash light across Peter's face. At that moment a servant girl from the household of the high priest recognized him. Possibly she had seen Peter, sometime earlier, walking alongside Jesus and the disciples through the streets of Jerusalem, where they had become a familiar sight.

"You are one of the Nazarene's followers," the girl said. Whether it was said accusingly or matter-of-factly, we are not told. Regardless of her tone, however, Peter forgot his earlier words to Jesus.

> But he denied it, saying, "I neither know nor understand what
> you are talking about." And he went out onto the porch.
> —MARK 14:68

This was a bold, flat-out denial—nothing subtle about it. Peter then removed himself to an even safer distance. And with that, he withdrew further as he took another step down to calm all suspicion . . . and then he took another, for the serving maid wouldn't give up.

> And the maid saw him, and began once more to say to the
> bystanders, "This is one of them!" But again he was denying it.
> —MARK 14:69–70

This time the young woman addressed the crowd standing nearby. "Listen, this is one of them." And once again Peter openly denied any association with Jesus of Nazareth.

> And after a little while the bystanders were again saying to Peter,
> "Surely you are one of them, for you are a Galilean too."
> —MARK 14:70

How did they know Peter was from the area of Galilee? Well, as one of the Gospels says, "For the way you talk gives you away" (Matthew 26:73). Most Galileans found it difficult to pronounce some of the gutturals in the dialect spoken in Jerusalem at the time. Native Judeans picked up on that. Also, Galileans were sometimes considered ignorant and unlearned people, for while the Romans, especially the officers, usually spoke several languages, the Galileans were, at best, bilingual. Thus, when Peter barked out, "I'm not! I do not know Him! I do not understand what you're talking about," the bystanders easily spotted him as Galilean.

Our speech often betrays us. A number of years ago my wife and I were enjoying a lovely evening at one of the finest restaurants in the city of Dallas. In keeping with the décor, the servers wore Egyptian attire. Surrounded by that ambiance, we felt as if we were in old Morocco. Until the young woman assigned to our table walked over and asked, "Y'all ordered y'all's dranks yet?"

At that moment we knew we were still in Texas.

If you encounter a New Englander anywhere in the world, they will want to "pahk the cah in the yahd." And people from the state of "New Joisey" usually give themselves away. We mark ourselves by our speech. So it's not difficult to understand why the bystanders identified Peter as a Galilean.

At that point, Peter reverted to the lowest form of speech in any language: profanity.

> But he began to curse and swear, "I do not know this man you are talking about!" And immediately a cock crowed a second time.
>
> And Peter remembered how Jesus had made the remark to him, "Before a cock crows twice, you will deny Me three times." And he began to weep.
>
> —MARK 14:71–72

This could mean that he blasphemously called down curses from God: "If I am a liar, may God strike me dead." Or perhaps he used the obscene language of the street, as if to say, "Don't connect me with the Nazarene's disciples."

Whatever form this cursing and swearing took, it was effective. His finger-pointing critics were silenced.

But his curses had scarcely fallen from his lips before two things occurred that shook Peter to the core. First, the trumpet sounded the end of the third watch. And then it sounded again. The shrill blast of cock-crow . . . twice! It sent a chill up Peter's spine.

For the second, we must turn to Luke's Gospel:

> But Peter said, "Man, I do not know what you are talking about." And immediately, while he was still speaking, a cock crowed.
>
> And the Lord turned and looked at Peter. And Peter remembered the word of the Lord, how He had told him, "Before a cock crows today, you will deny Me three times."
>
> —LUKE 22:60–61

We're not told where Jesus was standing, but wherever He was, He had a clear view of Peter out on the porch. For at the loud blast of the *gallicinium,* which pierced the night air, "the Lord turned and looked at Peter." And Peter remembered what Jesus had predicted: "Truly I tell you, this day, this very night, before the cock crows twice, you will deny me three times." Talk about humiliation!

What was the look? Was it a look of surprise? No. Jesus had told Peter that he was going to betray Him. Was it a look of anger and rejection? Never. I think it must have been a look of sorrow and enormous disappointment: "What have you done, Peter? You've numbered yourself among these, my enemies and betrayers. You've done exactly as I said you would, Peter. Oh, my longtime friend, look at what you have done."

It was not a look of wrath or indifference or even surprise, but a look of mixed emotions: aching sorrow and wounded love—a love that had not ended, despite Peter's cruel and repeated denials, a love that would not let him go. Peter saw loving, unmerited grace in Jesus' eyes, and it melted his heart.

> And he [Peter] began to weep.
>
> —MARK 14:72B

Not one of us can look with judgment upon Peter. Not one. Why? Because, in our sinful nature, we have all denied Christ.

Perhaps in our workplace we have numbered ourselves with the bystanders. Maybe in some social situation we have compromised, denying the very Lord we claimed to love and worship on the previous Sunday morning. Perhaps, at an opportune moment to share our faith in Jesus Christ, we have kept silent, afraid of being branded "a religious fanatic." Silence itself can be a denial.

PETER'S OPEN CONFESSION

As I mentioned earlier, scholars tell us there is evidence that Mark got his information from Peter—certainly the details pertaining to this very personal event. That's why Mark has such insight into Peter's denial. Peter may have said, "Mark, let me tell you what actually happened." And then he openly offered his confession. Peter did not whitewash his own failure—his own denial of the Master.

Peter didn't hold back. He opened his life like a book and said, "This is true, Mark . . . these things happened, but where sin abounded, grace super-abounded!" He could even have added, "I come to you under the blood of Christ, shed on the cross, which promises me complete, constant, unending, infinite forgiveness. I have sinned, but I have fully confessed my cowardly denial before God and now, because you needed to know, before you." Surely Peter never forgot his Lord's warning that Satan wanted to sift him as wheat . . . but grace came to his rescue.

And thus we come to the question this poses for each of us:

What are the denials in *my* life?

How have I betrayed my Lord?

Am I warming myself at some fire of compromise?

Am I lurking in the shadows of silence?

The test of our testimony is not how we act before the *friends* of the cross but our conduct and actions before the *enemies* of the cross.

> Upon the cross of Jesus
> Mine eye at times can see
> The very dying form of One
> Who suffered there for me;
> And from my stricken heart with tears
> Two wonders I confess,
> The wonders of redeeming love
> And my own worthlessness.[3]

Were Peter still alive, he could sing that grand hymn with true conviction and meaning! But since he is not, we can turn to the letter he wrote and catch a glimpse of his perspective, as he extends hope and encouragement to those enduring times of severe testing. He understood. He'd been there . . . done that.

Read his words with great feeling, now that you've heard his confession:

> In this you greatly rejoice, even though now for a little while, if necessary, you have been distressed by various trials, that the proof of your faith, being more precious than gold which is perishable, even though tested by fire, may be found to result in praise and glory and honor at the revelation of Jesus Christ; and though you have not seen Him, you love Him, and though you do not see Him now, but believe in Him, you greatly rejoice with joy inexpressible and full of glory.
>
> —1 PETER 1:6–8

The Six Trials of Jesus

Man of Sorrows! what a name
For the Son of God, who came
Ruined sinners to reclaim:
Hallelujah! What a Savior![1]
—PHILIP P. BLISS

5
The Six Trials of Jesus

*M*ost Christians have never made a serious study of what transpired immediately before Jesus' crucifixion. We tend to jump from Gethsemane to Golgatha, omitting many, if not all, the events in between. In making that leap, they lose much of the history and theology, not to mention the local color of Jesus' era; as a result, they also lose important details that led to the final verdict about Jesus.

Put bluntly, the trials that resulted in Jesus of Nazareth's being nailed to a cross provide the classic example of an unfair and illegal rush to judgment. Biased and fallacious in every way, these trials represent the darkest day in the history of jurisprudence. The accused was the only perfect and completely innocent person who has ever lived. Yet He was declared guilty ... guilty of crimes He never committed. Tragically, His alleged crimes resulted in His being condemned to arguably the most painful form of capital punishment ever devised. Death for a capital offense, according to first-century Roman law, was by crucifixion.

But there is a bright side to all this darkness. Looking at Jesus' death from a theological perspective, we see that it was the fulfillment of His earthly mission. The primary purpose for His leaving heaven and becoming a member of the human race was to pay the price for sin and redeem us from its penalty—death. In other words, Jesus came to die. By dying in our place, as our sacrificial substitute, the Lamb of God was able to take away the sin of the world (John 1:29). Humanly, what seemed a cruel tragedy at the time must be seen, spiritually, as a triumph.

It would not be an exaggeration to say, therefore, that the trials, suffering, death, and subsequent resurrection of Christ are, in fact, the bedrock truth of Christianity, forming the foundation of the faith. Because this is true, I am all the more surprised at how few followers of Jesus have carefully, thoughtfully, and thoroughly studied the events surrounding our Savior's death, particularly the trials He endured. Yes, trials . . . not one, but six.

AN ISSUE OF TIME

Before we take a careful look at these events, we need to review the chronology, both in terms of time and in terms of the unfolding of events as recorded in the Gospels.

In the Roman world—the Gentile world—time was reckoned from midnight to midnight (as we measure time today). One second after midnight began the new day, and the day ended at the stroke of midnight. From midnight to midnight was one day. According to the Jewish calendar, however, the new day began at one second past six o'clock in the evening, and the day ended at the stroke of six o'clock the next evening. From six o'clock in the evening to six o'clock the next evening was one day.

In the previous chapter, we learned that the nighttime hours were measured by "watches." Between six in the evening and six in the morning, the time was divided into four watches of three hours each. The first watch was from six to nine, the second watch from nine to midnight, the third watch from midnight to three, and the fourth watch from three to six in the morning.

From six in the morning until six in the evening, the day was divided into "hours." For example, in Matthew's record of the crucifixion, he refers to two different times of the day: "Now from the sixth hour darkness fell upon all the land until the ninth hour" (Matthew 27:45).

Now if you reckon time with the Jewish day beginning at 6:00 A.M., then the sixth hour would be noon. Therefore, Matthew says that at noon darkness fell across the sky and cast its ominous shadow over the earth until the ninth hour, or three in the afternoon. That represented three full hours of darkness in the middle of the day.

THE IMPORTANT EVENTS

Now, with an understanding of this dual measurement of time (Jewish and Gentile), let's take a quick look at the events surrounding the death of Christ.

Jesus and His disciples left the upper room in the evening, following their Last Supper together, and went to the Garden of Gethsemane, where Jesus prayed and His disciples slept. We can't say exactly what time it was, but it was probably after midnight when Jesus began praying, sometime during the third watch of the night (midnight to three). How long Jesus prayed we don't know, but long enough for him to return three different times and find the disciples sleeping.

Judas and the mob must have arrived on the scene sometime after 1:00 A.M. Then began the series of trials, the first of which took place at the residence of Annas, the former high priest. That took place about 2:00 A.M. A second unofficial trial was held at the home of his son-in-law, Caiaphas, at around 3:00. Next came the third trial, a formal hearing before the Sanhedrin, the seventy men who formed the Supreme Court of the Jews. The gospel narrative states that this took place "when it was day." Thus, we can assume that this third trial must have at least been at 6:00 A.M. It was at His fourth trial, about 6:30 or 7:00, "when morning had come," that Jesus had His first interrogation by Pilate, the leading Roman official. Shortly after that came an audience before Herod Antipas, the tetrarch or governor of Galilee. That was His fifth trial. Herod then sent Jesus back to Pilate for a second and final time . . . trial number six. By 8:00 in the morning our Savior had undergone all six trials. A rush to judgment? You decide.

By 9:00, "the third hour," Jesus had traveled the *Via Dolorosa* (or Way of Sorrow), from the place of scourging to Golgotha, the public place of the skull. There He was nailed to the cross. At noon, darkness fell over the earth as He hung there, dying for the sins of all humanity. Finally, at 3:00 in the afternoon, or "about the ninth hour," the Savior of the world breathed His last and "finished" our salvation. For an overview of the trials, please see the chart in the Appendix.

Overall Illegal Maneuverings

Now, let's review those illegal maneuverings in greater detail.

Jesus' first three trials were *religious* in nature. The accusation was blasphemy, which was an offense that was admissible only in a Jewish court of law. So when Jesus stood before Annas, Caiaphas, and the Sanhedrin (trials one, two, and three), He was accused of blasphemy.

But the charge of blasphemy meant nothing in a Roman court of law. Romans had a pantheon of gods. To such a polytheistic people, blasphemy meant nothing. Therefore, when Jesus was brought before Pilate and Herod for the three *civil* trials, the charge had to be changed (an illegal act in itself). Now Jesus was accused of treason and labeled an insurrectionist by His accusers. If it could be proven that He was guilty of trying to overthrow the government of Caesar, then He would be put to death.

As I stated at the beginning of this chapter, there has never been a greater sham than the trials of Jesus Christ. Three religious trials and three civil trials . . . and all six were illegal. Let me explain.

A trial was never to be held at night, yet the first two were. The accused was allowed to have an attorney speak on his or her behalf, yet Jesus was never allowed a defense attorney. The accused could not be declared guilty without *reputable* witnesses, yet those who accused Christ were *false* witnesses.

In the greatest travesty of justice, Jesus was *declared* guilty but never *proven* guilty. As you may recall, Pilate, the same man who finally said,

"Take Him and do with Him as you wish," had earlier said, "I find no fault in Him at all." Of all the people before whom Jesus stood, the only one who gave Him even the slightest measure of justice was Pilate, who said up to the end, "I find no fault in this man."

The Jews followed the Mosaic Law, interpreted for them in the Talmud, the legal handbook of that day, while the Romans were guided by the Roman code of criminal procedure. These documents set the boundaries, and they allowed for no "gray" areas. For example, the Jewish court could not hear testimony regarding a capital crime during the hours of darkness. The language of the code read: "The members of the court may not alertly and intelligently hear the testimony against the accused during darkness."

Did the men who tried Jesus know that? Of course they did. These men formed the Sanhedrin; they were teachers of the Law. Yet they deliberately broke the Law.

Another legal detail relates to the factor of time. Members of the Jewish court, after hearing the testimony in a capital crime, were not permitted to render an immediate verdict. They were required to adjourn to their homes for two days and two nights. In the language of the code: They were to "eat light food, drink light wines, and sleep well, and once again return and hear the testimony against the accused." Then, and only then, could they vote.

One more small detail—but another illegal act. The code required that the Sanhedrin must vote one person at a time, and that the youngest members must vote first, so they would not be influenced by the older members. In Jesus' trial before the Sanhedrin, given the speed by which it all transpired, we are safe to assume that all voted quickly, emotionally, and simultaneously.

In the chart "The Trials of Jesus Christ" in the Appendix I have noted the officiating authority, the Scripture references, the accusations, the legality, the type, and the result of each of the six trials. This should help you make your own further, in-depth study of these events.

To understand why there were two phases, religious and civil, of three trials each, we need to look a little further at Jewish and Roman law. The Jews were allowed to bring the Jewish people before their own religious leaders/judges/court system, but the Jews were not allowed, under Roman law, to take a person's life. That required permission from Rome, which explains why the proud members of the Sanhedrin would appeal to Pilate—to Rome. They hoped he would find Jesus guilty and pronounce the death sentence. That's why Jesus was not stoned to death. If He had been put to death under Jewish Law, He would have been stoned. But under Roman law in the first century, the death penalty required death by crucifixion.

THE FIRST TRIAL: JESUS BEFORE ANNAS

It's time to meet the main players in this drama of injustice. In doing this, we will look at the trials of Jesus as described by the four gospel writers. Since the different writers offer unique observations and insights on what occurred, it is helpful—in fact, essential—that we take all of them into consideration as we reconstruct these events.

> So the Roman cohort and the commander, and the officers of the Jews, arrested Jesus and bound Him, and led Him to Annas first; for he was father-in-law of Caiaphas, who was high priest that year.
>
> Now Caiaphas was the one who had advised the Jews that it was expedient for one man to die on behalf of the people.
>
> —JOHN 18:12–14

The first of Jesus' six trials took place at the residence of Annas, the former high priest (perhaps he was considered as sort of a high priest emeritus). Annas was also the father-in-law of Caiaphas, the present high priest.

Annas had served as high priest from A.D. 6 to A.D. 15. So why would the mob take Jesus to this man who had been out of office for more than fifteen years?

Apparently the Jews—at least the ones in this "mob justice" crowd—

viewed Annas as the final authority. If we are correct in viewing Annas as high priest emeritus, then it would stand to reason that the Jews would respect him as an elder statesman; therefore, protocol demanded that he be consulted first. No doubt politics played a role in all this. Keep in mind that his son-in-law, Caiaphas, was now high priest.

But I don't think they had to drag Annas out of bed; I don't think he was surprised by their visit. Certainly nothing is said of his having to be awakened. I believe he was waiting for them . . . that all of this had been arranged beforehand, set up as part of the plot to condemn Jesus.

This kangaroo court, held illegally in the very early hours of the morning and in a private residence, was not a spur-of-the-moment event. It was all carefully orchestrated.

> The high priest therefore questioned Jesus about His disciples, and about His teaching.
>
> Jesus answered him, "I have spoken openly to the world; I always taught in synagogues, and in the temple, where all the Jews come together; and I spoke nothing in secret. Why do you question Me? Question those who have heard what I spoke to them; behold, these know what I said."
>
> And when He had said this, one of the officers standing by gave Jesus a blow, saying, "Is that the way You answer the high priest?"
>
> Jesus answered him, "If I have spoken wrongly, bear witness of the wrong; but if rightly, why do you strike Me?"
>
> —JOHN 18:19–23

This blow is only the beginning of a night of violence and senseless brutality. Along with the other illegalities, violence is now permitted in the courtroom. Jesus asks for truth and justice and is given physical abuse and lies. "If I am not telling the truth," He says, "provide a witness. But if I am telling the truth, why do you strike me?" The first trial ends with an unanswered, albeit excellent and relevant question.

This is the first of many questions that are never answered. The irony, of course, is that it is not Jesus on trial; it is all those around Him.

THE SECOND TRIAL: JESUS BEFORE CAIAPHAS

Annas ignored Jesus' question and "sent Him bound to Caiaphas the high priest." Trial number two is about to begin.

> And those who had seized Jesus led Him away to Caiaphas, the high priest, where the scribes and the elders were gathered together.
>
> Now the chief priests and the whole Council kept trying to obtain false testimony against Jesus, in order that they might put Him to death; and they did not find any, even though many false witnesses came forward. But later on two came forward, and said, "This man stated, 'I am able to destroy the temple of God and to rebuild it in three days.'"
>
> And the high priest stood up and said to Him, "Do You make no answer? What is it that these men are testifying against You?"
>
> But Jesus kept silent. And the high priest said to Him, "I adjure You by the living God, that You tell us whether You are the Christ, the Son of God."
>
> Jesus said to him, "You have said it yourself; nevertheless I tell you, hereafter you shall see THE SON OF MAN SITTING AT THE RIGHT HAND OF POWER, and COMING ON THE CLOUDS OF HEAVEN."
>
> Then the high priest tore his robes, saying, "He has blasphemed! What further need do we have of witnesses? Behold, you have now heard the blasphemy; what do you think?" They answered and said, "He is deserving of death!"
>
> Then they spat in His face and beat Him with their fists; and others slapped Him, and said, "Prophesy to us, You Christ; who is the one who hit You?"
>
> —MATTHEW 26:57,59–68

Isn't it interesting that everyone seems to be awake and alert this late at night? It is now about 3:00 in the morning, yet they are all wide awake, assembled, and waiting. It is nothing other than a prearranged scenario—a plot.

Caiaphas was but a puppet of Rome. Although he was the moderator and ruling member of the Sanhedrin, and his word was taken as law among the Jews, he and his cohorts were looking for people to bear false witness against Jesus. These officials, supposedly fair-minded men of reputation, called to uphold justice within the courts of the Temple, were prejudiced judges, looking for people who would lie.

The problem was, they were shy of witnesses against Jesus. Angered by the situation and by Jesus' brief but quiet responses, Caiaphas cut the trial short, judging Him "deserving of death," and allowing the accused to be physically humiliated and abused.

THE THIRD TRIAL: JESUS BEFORE THE COUNCIL OF ELDERS

Caiaphas then sent Jesus to the Sanhedrin—also called "the Council of Elders"—the seventy men who sat in ultimate authority over the Jews. That would be the third trial.

> And when it was day, the Council of elders of the people assembled, both chief priests and scribes, and they led Him away to their council chamber, saying, "If You are the Christ, tell us." But He said to them, "If I tell you, you will not believe; and if I ask a question, you will not answer. But from now on THE SON OF MAN WILL BE SEATED AT THE RIGHT HAND of the power OF GOD."
>
> And they all said, "Are You the Son of God, then?" And He said to them, "Yes, I am."
>
> And they said, "What further need do we have of testimony? For we have heard it ourselves from His own mouth."
>
> —LUKE 22:66–71

Some critics of the Scriptures have said that Jesus never claimed He was the Son of God. Yet I would like to know what Luke 22:70 means if it doesn't mean that? Perhaps He did not say the words directly: "I am the Son of God." But when Caiaphas asked Him, "Are You the Son of God?" He answered, without hesitation, "Yes, I am." He declared His identity.

That declaration was all the Sanhedrin needed. Without even attempting to examine any evidence or probe into His spotless record, they accused Jesus of blasphemy and prepared to take Him before Pilate, the Roman governor. But remember what I mentioned earlier: Blasphemy was a religious charge; it meant nothing in a Roman courtroom, which is why the Jewish leaders changed the charges against Jesus. The accusation of blasphemy would not be mentioned again, because it would carry no weight in swaying Pilate's opinion. The charge now would be insurrection and treason. Jesus, they said, was trying to overthrow the government of Rome. An interesting accusation in light of the fact that it was Jesus who publicly taught people to "'render to Caesar the things that are Caesar's; and to God the things that are God's'"(Matthew 22:21). They conveniently forgot that, however, when they went before the civil court in Jesus' fourth trial.

THE FOURTH TRIAL: JESUS BEFORE PILATE

> And early in the morning the chief priests with the elders and scribes, and the whole Council, immediately held a consultation; and binding Jesus, they led Him away, and delivered Him up to Pilate.
>
> —MARK 15:1

This brings us to the next player in our drama and probably the most fascinating character of all: Pontius Pilate.

Pilate was the Roman governor, or procurator, over Judea. He was not a Caesar. Tiberius was the Caesar, the Imperial Emperor of the Roman Empire, ruling from his headquarters in Rome. Pilate was one of his many regional representatives, the governor of Judea.

Normally Pilate resided at his comfortable and beautiful palace on the Mediterranean coast in Caesarea, but he was in Jerusalem during Passover because the crowds were so large. His presence and the entourage and soldiers that came with him were there to help maintain law and order in the streets of Jerusalem.

Now there is something we need to understand about Pilate, because there is quite a discrepancy between the way Pilate is depicted in the history books and the way he is depicted by the writers of the Gospels. In the Scriptures, Pilate vacillates. He is shifting, uneasy, seemingly eager to please the people—in particular, the Jews. The Pilate in the pages of history books looks nothing like that.

Pilate was an anti-Semitic Gentile, Roman to the core. He was an absolute wolf for Jewish blood. Because of that, he made no attempt to please the Jews. If Rome ever dealt with Jews using a velvet glove, it surely wasn't Pilate wearing it. Pilate answered not to the Roman Senate but to Tiberius himself. In the political system of that day, the governor answered to no one but the emperor. So in order for him to be removed, it took the emperor's edict.

Furthermore, Pilate was not a novice. For a man to be a governor, he had to go through the ranks. He had to be known as a brave Roman soldier. He had to be a leader. He had to be a hard administrator and a legislator. He had to be a man of decision.

And Pilate was no fool. The youngest Roman governor on record was twenty-seven years of age. Even if Pilate had been that young when he became governor, and we don't know that he was, then at this point he would have been the same age as Jesus—in his early thirties. However, it is much more likely that he was a man between forty and fifty. He was a hardened, cruel, seasoned Roman official.

This is much more in keeping with the Pilate described in a letter from Agrippa to Caligula, recorded in the writings of Philo. Caligula was the emperor after Tiberius, and this is the scathing testimony he received from Agrippa: "Pilate is unbending and recklessly hard. He is a man of notorious reputation, severe brutality, prejudice, savage violence, and murder."

As a result, Pilate was "on report," as we would say in military terms. He was under investigation by Rome. The emperor had ordered surveillance on this man, due to his suspicion after reading reports about the governor. This investigation was going on during the time when Jesus was on trial. This explains why the otherwise unbending, brutal, prejudiced Pilate appears so vacillating. This explains why he doesn't throw the Jews out of the palace when they come asking for the death of Jesus. Candidly, the man was scared. This hardened, Jew-hating Roman cared nothing about public opinion, except when his own neck was in the noose.

All of this seems confirmed by later history. Pilate was eventually banished by Caligula to Gaul, a distant region, far to the northwest of Italy, beyond the Alps. There, he suffered what sounds like an emotional or mental breakdown, and, ultimately, he committed suicide.

This was the man who would now decide the fate of the Son of God.

> And Pilate questioned Him, "Are You the King of the Jews?" And answering He said to him, "It is as you say."
> And the chief priests began to accuse Him harshly.
> And Pilate was questioning Him again, saying, "Do You make no answer? See how many charges they bring against You!"
> But Jesus made no further answer; so that Pilate was amazed.
> —MARK 15:2–5

"King" was the word that concerned Pilate. The charge of blasphemy meant nothing to him. But to a loyal Roman, Caesar was the only king— "We have no king but Casesar"—so anyone claiming to be king would be of enormous concern to Pilate, and even more so to Rome. Hence, the Jewish leaders accused Jesus of claiming to be "the King of the Jews."

And Pilate answered them, saying, "Do you want me to release for you the King of the Jews?" For he was aware that the chief priests had delivered Him up because of envy.

But the chief priests stirred up the multitude to ask him to release Barabbas for them instead.

And answering again, Pilate was saying to them, "Then what shall I do with Him whom you call the King of the Jews?"

And they shouted back, "Crucify Him!"

But Pilate was saying to them, "Why, what evil has He done?" But they shouted all the more, "Crucify Him!"

—MARK 15:9–14

Then the whole body of them arose and brought Him before Pilate. And they began to accuse Him, saying, "We found this man misleading our nation and forbidding to pay taxes to Caesar, and saying that He Himself is Christ, a King."

And Pilate asked Him, saying, "Are You the King of the Jews?" And He answered him and said, "It is as you say."

And Pilate said to the chief priests and the multitudes, "I find no guilt in this man."

—LUKE 23:1–4

Obviously Pilate did not take this charge seriously. Being full of mischief himself, he saw through the chief priests' trumped-up charge. At most, Pilate viewed Jesus of Nazareth as another strange, self-appointed Messiah.

Though I do not know the source of his remark, I distinctly recall one of my professors at seminary telling us that many people claimed to be the Messiah. According to his research, several men in Jesus' day falsely claimed to be the Messiah of Israel. Should that have been so, Pilate would have been all the more skeptical. But false prophets and phony Messiahs were not the business of the Roman government or courts.

"You take care of this Jesus yourself," Pilate told the Jews with a wave of his hand. "As far as I'm concerned, he's not guilty of anything."

But the Jewish leaders wouldn't give up:

> They kept on insisting, saying, "He stirs up the people, teaching all over Judea, starting from Galilee, even as far as this place."
>
> —LUKE 23:5

Let's take the time to observe how John records this fourth trial. Read his words slowly and carefully.

> They led Jesus therefore from Caiaphas into the Praetorium, and it was early; and they themselves did not enter into the Praetorium in order that they might not be defiled, but might eat the Passover.
>
> Pilate therefore went out to them, and said, "What accusation do you bring against this Man?"
>
> They answered and said to him, "If this Man were not an evildoer, we would not have delivered Him up to you."
>
> Pilate therefore said to them, "Take Him yourselves, and judge Him according to your law." The Jews said to him, "We are not permitted to put anyone to death," that the word of Jesus might be fulfilled, which He spoke, signifying by what kind of death He was about to die.
>
> Pilate therefore entered again into the Praetorium, and summoned Jesus, and said to Him, "Are You the King of the Jews?"
>
> —JOHN 18:28–33

Notice how legalistic the Jewish leaders were to keep themselves ceremonially pure: "They themselves did not enter into the Praetorium in order that they might not be defiled, but might eat the Passover." While guilty of false accusations, brutality, prejudice, and illegal proceedings, the scrupulous hypocrites were careful to observe the proper boundaries at the Praetorium!

This is the same trial recorded in Luke 23, but John gives us more detail, particularly the interaction between Jesus and Pilate.

"Come on in here," Pilate says, in effect. "Let's get away from the crowd. Let's you and me talk." So the two men go into the inner sanctum where Pilate presses Jesus, "Are You the King of the Jews?"

"Are you saying this on your own initiative," Jesus asks, "or did others tell you about Me?"

"I'm not a Jew, am I?" says Pilate indignantly. "Your own people turned You over to me. What have You done to offend them?"

Jesus answered, "My kingdom is not of this world. If I were truly leading an insurrection, don't you think my followers would be fighting in the streets?"

Then Pilate asks one of the most telling questions in this entire interrogation:

> Pilate therefore said to Him, "So You are a king?" Jesus answered, "You say correctly that I am a king. For this I have been born, and for this I have come into the world, to bear witness to the truth. Everyone who is of the truth hears My voice."
> Pilate said to Him, "What is truth?"
> —JOHN 18:37–38

Here is a man who holds a position of authority as significant as the governor of Judea, yet he asks this stranger he has just met, "What is truth?" Such a question forces us to wonder upon what standards Pilate made his decisions or formed his judgments? Furthermore, can you imagine the man's level of confusion? He had no clue.

To look at his question less critically, we find ourselves at a loss to interpret why he asked it. Was he being facetious or scornful? Impatient or cynical? Despairing or sincere? Hard to tell. We're left to wonder. But while we may not know *that* answer, we do know that Pilate saw Jesus as innocent of any crime. He may have considered Him a harmless philosopher or an impractical religious dreamer, but He certainly didn't qualify as a dangerous subversive. At least Pilate had the fortitude to stand against the growing ranks of Jesus' accusers and announce to them, "I find no guilt in Him" (John 18:38).

Pilate walks back out to the Jewish leaders and the mob and says, in effect, "I find no wrongdoing in this man. I've examined Him. We've talked. He's an innocent man."

But Pilate is in a tough spot himself. Every move he makes that raises their ire brings him under tighter scrutiny by Rome. Several riots have broken out in the streets of Jerusalem, and he does not want an insurrection on his hands. He now fits the description of the garden-variety politician who wants peace at any price. If he turns Jesus loose, these Jewish leaders might incite the mob to riot.

But Pilate's stubborn conscience says, "This man is not guilty." There's still enough anti-Semitism in him to keep him from giving these pompous Jews from the Temple what they want. So he searches for another out, and inadvertently he finds one. It must have made him smile deep within. Watch what happens:

> But they kept on insisting, saying, "He stirs up the people, teaching all over Judea, starting from Galilee, even as far as this place."
>
> But when Pilate heard it, he asked whether the man was a Galilean.
>
> And when he learned that He belonged to Herod's jurisdiction, he sent Him to Herod, who himself also was in Jerusalem at that time.
>
> —LUKE 23:5–7

When Pilate heard "Galilee," he must have thought, "Aha! There's my loophole." Since this Jesus was a Galilean, that would place Him under Herod's jurisdiction, "and Herod's in town!"

In predictably political fashion, Pilate passes the buck and lets someone else make the tough call.

THE FIFTH TRIAL: JESUS BEFORE HEROD

Herod Antipas, who was tetrarch over Galilee from 4 B.C. to A.D. 39, was a member of the notorious Herod family. They were a brutal bunch, bone-deep cruel, capable of murdering their own spouses and siblings. I've often referred to them as "the godfathers of the ancient world"—deceitful and dangerous, powerful and controlling.

Herod and Jesus were not unknown to each other. This was the same Herod who had had John the Baptizer beheaded, the same Herod whom Jesus called "that fox" (Luke 13:32).

> Now Herod was very glad when he saw Jesus; for he had wanted to see Him for a long time, because he had been hearing about Him and was hoping to see some sign performed by Him. And he questioned Him at some length; but He answered him nothing.
>
> And the chief priests and the scribes were standing there, accusing Him vehemently. And Herod with his soldiers, after treating Him with contempt and mocking Him, dressed Him in a gorgeous robe and sent Him back to Pilate.
>
> —Luke 23:8–11

The political ploy didn't work as Pilate had hoped. Herod Antipas, looking for an entertaining show, starts firing questions. With His innocence established in His previous examination, Jesus takes a different defense tactic. He remains absolutely silent. Though Herod anticipates a show, he finds that Jesus is not an entertainer and is not given to fulfilling curiosity. How disappointing for Herod! (And it will prove even more so for Pilate.)

Few authors do a better job of describing in a few words what transpired than Alexander Whyte:

> Herod Antipas was more of a circus-master than a serious-minded monarch; and, instead of taking up the case that had been referred to his jurisdiction, all that Herod aimed at was to get some amusement out of the accused. "He is the King of the Jews, is he? He is a candidate for my royal seat, is he? Then put the white coat of a candidate upon him and send him back to Pilate! The Governor will enjoy my jest; and it will somewhat cement our recovered friendship!"[2]

Herod, for some reason, was not in a killing mood but a playful one. He was hoping to see some kind of performance—a little miracle magic, perhaps. But nothing like that was forthcoming. Jesus refused to cooperate. Though questioned at length, the Nazarene stood absolutely silent before Herod.

So after staging his own little entertainment by dressing Jesus up in a kingly robe and mocking him, Herod shrugs the whole thing off and sends Him back to Pilate.

The Sixth Trial: Jesus Before Pilate Again

Pilate looks up from his breakfast and groans. *Oh, no.* He thought he had this nicely taken care of . . . out of his hands . . . off his plate . . . no longer his problem. Wrong. Now, what does he do?

Well, he's not yet out of ideas; so he tries another approach.

> Now at the feast the governor was accustomed to release for the multitude any one prisoner whom they wanted. And they were holding at that time a notorious prisoner, called Barabbas.
>
> When therefore they were gathered together, Pilate said to them, "Whom do you want me to release for you? Barabbas, or Jesus who is called Christ?" For he knew that because of envy they had delivered Him up.
>
> And while he was sitting on the judgment seat, his wife sent to him, saying, "Have nothing to do with that righteous Man; for last night I suffered greatly in a dream because of Him."
>
> But the chief priests and the elders persuaded the multitudes to ask for Barabbas, and to put Jesus to death.
>
> But the governor answered and said to them, "Which of the two do you want me to release for you?" And they said, "Barabbas."
>
> Pilate said to them, "Then what shall I do with Jesus who is called Christ?" They all said, "Let Him be crucified!"

And he said, "Why, what evil has He done?" But they kept shouting all the more, saying, "Let Him be crucified!"

And when Pilate saw that he was accomplishing nothing, but rather that a riot was starting, he took water and washed his hands in front of the multitude, saying, "I am innocent of this Man's blood; see to that yourselves."

And all the people answered and said, "His blood be on us and on our children!"

Then he released Barabbas for them; but after having Jesus scourged, he delivered Him to be crucified.

—MATTHEW 27:15–26

Keep in mind, up to this moment absolutely *nothing* has been proven against Jesus. He has not been found guilty of anything. Each trial has had glaring illegalities. Not one reliable witness has spoken against Him. There is not a shred of damaging evidence. Yet, strangely, He is still on trial.

At this point, Matthew informs us about a tradition of the time.

Although no other record of it can be found, there must have been the custom of releasing one prisoner at every Passover as a means of placating the Jewish population. Pilate seized on the opportunity to appeal to the masses and suggested that he would release Jesus if they demanded it. His proposal assumed that Jesus was popular with the general crowd, who did not always favor the hierarchy. . . . Pilate miscalculated the attitude of the crowd at this point.[3]

Once again Pilate thinks he may have a solution to his dilemma— another way out. He would offer them a choice between the innocent Galilean and the most notorious criminal they had imprisoned at the time, Barabbas. Barabbas was not only an insurrectionist, he was also a murderer, awaiting death by crucifixion.

I'm convinced that the center cross that day was intended for

Barabbas, whom we will discuss further in the next chapter. Pilate "knew that because of envy they had delivered Him up" (v. 18). Surely they would not carry this travesty any further. Surely they would rather have Jesus released than a man who had committed such heinous crimes, a man who was so dangerous. Brilliant idea, but again . . . wrong. "The chief priests and the elders persuaded the multitudes to ask for Barabbas, and to put Jesus to death" (v. 20).

Then Matthew introduces another character into this drama: Pilate's wife.

> And while he was sitting on the judgment seat, his wife sent to
> him, saying, "Have nothing to do with that righteous Man; for
> last night I suffered greatly in a dream because of Him."
> —MATTHEW 27:19

This is one of the most intriguing verses in the New Testament. Wouldn't you love to know what that dream was about? It must have really been something to prompt Pilate's wife to send him a note. Either Pilate had told her about his first encounter with Jesus while they were together, alone, the previous evening, or something in the dream had alerted her to what was going on. Now, along with all his other worries, he has this ominous warning to weigh into the equation.

"But the chief priests and the elders persuaded the multitudes to ask for Barabbas, and to put Jesus to death" (v.20). Look who did that! The religious people. The religious *leaders!* Why? Because Barabbas was no threat to the religious phonies. He didn't hassle the legalists. He wasn't out there preaching in the streets. He was just engaged in mob violence and, occasionally, killing people.

"Let Him be crucified!" screamed the mob.

"Why, what evil has He done?" asks Pilate. "Show me the proof."

Do you know why they didn't answer? Because they *had* no answer. Jesus had done no evil. There was no proof of a crime. And so they screamed in their murderous, hateful frenzy, "Let Him be crucified! Let Him be crucified."

Pilate had reached the peak of pressure. He knew he had a riot on his hands and that "he was accomplishing nothing." And so he washed his hands of the whole affair. He caved in to the pressure. He looked the other way. Instead of standing firm and doing what was right, he compromised.

> And when Pilate saw that he was accomplishing nothing, but rather that a riot was starting, he took water and washed his hands in front of the multitude, saying, "I am innocent of this Man's blood; see to that yourselves."
>
> And all the people answered and said, "His blood be on us and on our children!"
>
> Then he released Barabbas for them; but after having Jesus scourged, he delivered Him to be crucified.
>
> MATTHEW 29:24–26

With the ending of the sixth and final trial, rationalization goes on parade. Pilate goes through this ceremonial moment, saying verbally and symbolically, "I'm cleansing myself of all responsibility for this travesty of justice."

It says a lot that this man, known for his cruelty as a ruler, suffers pangs of conscience over Jesus' trial—so much so that he acquits himself before the Jews, whom he hated as much as he hated anything, and whom he knows are railroading this Man. No boldness or arrogance here, which is what you might expect of Pilate in this setting, before this audience. Instead he shows the weakness of conscience and a total absence of character.

In so doing, Pilate sends Jesus to the cross.

A SEARCHING SUMMATION

It is safe to say that there has never been a more unfair, illegal, or shameful set of trials conducted in the history of jurisprudence than the six trials that led to the crucifixion and death of the Lord Jesus

Christ. In this, however, there is a paradox: From those acts of injustice, the justice of God was satisfied. As men poured out their wrath upon Christ at His trials and His death, God's wrath against sin was completely released upon Christ at the cross. All of the wrath of God was poured out on Christ at that moment when He bore our sins in His body on that cruel cross. As a result, the only thing that separates lost humanity from God is rank unbelief.

The suffering and death of Christ are now history. His story. But our story goes on, for He suffered and died for you and me. His death paid the price that sin required. Therefore, God will accept us into His family, if we will simply accept His offer to believe on the Lord Jesus Christ that we might be saved.

> For God so loved the world, that He gave His only begotten Son, that whoever believes in Him should not perish, but have eternal life.
>
> For God did not send the Son into the world to judge the world, but that the world should be saved through Him.
>
> He who believes in Him is not judged; he who does not believe has been judged already, because he has not believed in the name of the only begotten Son of God.
>
> —JOHN 3:16–18

> But God demonstrates His own love toward us, in that while we were yet sinners, Christ died for us.
>
> —ROMANS 5:8

> For there is one God, and one mediator also between God and men, the man Christ Jesus, who gave Himself as a ransom for all, the testimony borne at the proper time.
>
> —1 TIMOTHY 2:5–6

Wonderful news!

The entire sweep of history hinges on this tiny window of time in the first century, and through that window we see a cross. All of history looks back to that moment—to the tragedy and triumph of that cross. First the crucifixion, then the resurrection of the Son of God. Those two epochal events secure our eternal destiny.

He suffered willingly, never once fighting back, never once really defending Himself. Before mobs and weak-willed leaders and those who would mock Him, He stood strong and He died . . . for you . . . for me. And now He lives for you and for me. What glorious news!

The Man Who Missed His Cross

There was no other good enough
To pay the price of sin;
He only could unlock the gate
Of heav'n, and let us in.[1]

—*There is a Green Hill Far Away*,
Cecil F. Alexander, 1848,
fourth stanza

6
The Man Who Missed His Cross

Although he never appears on center stage, Barabbas plays a major role in the darkness. Little would the man himself have ever guessed it, but in the sixth trial, which we discussed in the previous chapter, there he is in the sacred text of Holy Scripture. Barabbas . . . of all people!

Having been convicted and condemned to die, his cell is most likely located in the fortress of Antonia in the city of Jerusalem. From there Barabbas probably hears the crowd crying for Jesus' blood. He can't decipher every word and nuance, but he can hear the mob shouting at the top of their lungs, in their frenzy to influence Pilate.

"Barabbas! Barabbas. Give us Barabbas!" they scream.

Barabbas hears his name. Then the next thing he hears chills him to the bone: "Crucify him!" He knows he will soon be on his way to the cross.

In his mind, he goes no further than death by crucifixion. That will be the end of the trail, and a torturous end at that. No need to go beyond the driving of the nails into his flesh. Hopefully, death will come soon. All who hung on crosses hoped for quick deaths.

But for Barabbas, his life didn't end on a cross. The jailer who opened his cell didn't march him to his place of death. He set him free!

Wouldn't you love to know what happened to Barabbas after he was freed? After he learned that an innocent Man had died in his place? Wouldn't you like to know what he did with the rest of his life?

Did he continue in his evil ways, yet escape any earthly punishment? Was he arrested after another crime or, perhaps, killed in the process? Or did he come to worship the One who had died in his place? Was he, as some legends maintain, among the crowd at the foot of the cross, watching Jesus die?

If any man on this planet knew what it meant to have Jesus literally bear his cross and die in his place, it was Barabbas. And, strange as it may seem, if there is one person each one of us can identify with, it is Barabbas.

If asked to describe Barabbas, all of us could do it in one sentence: He was the man released in place of Jesus. But there is more to the story than that, much more.

To appreciate the story, we need to understand a bit about the culture and tradition of Jesus' day. According to Matthew and Mark's accounts, during Passover the governor normally released any prisoner the people wanted. Though no one seems to be able to explain how the custom began, it was clearly in place at the time of Jesus' trials.

> Now at the feast the governor was accustomed to release for the multitude any one prisoner whom they wanted.
>
> —MATTHEW 27:15

> Now at the feast he used to release for them any one prisoner whom they requested.
>
> And the man named Barabbas had been imprisoned with the insurrectionists who had committed murder in the insurrection.
>
> And the multitude went up and began asking him to do as he had been accustomed to do for them.
>
> —MARK 15:6–8

Apparently the Jewish people would approach the governor and say, "At this Passover time, we request that you release Aristobulus." And regardless of what he had done, or what he was accused of, Aristobulus would be released from prison, scot-free.

Most of the time, no doubt, that custom was a thorn in the flesh to Pilate, the anti-Semitic, brutal governor of Judea. But this time he welcomed the custom with a sigh of relief. We looked at Pilate in depth in the previous chapter, so suffice it to say that he was a man living out his career on the horns of a dilemma.

First of all, he was scared. He knew that the Jewish leaders had trumped up the charge against Jesus because they were jealous of His power over the people. But Pilate also knew that if he did not cooperate with them, they would riot. Should another bad report about his regime go back to Rome, Pilate feared, he would lose his position as governor.

His second dilemma was that he never believed that Jesus was guilty. Of all the judges that Jesus stood before in those final hours of trial, Pilate was the only one who gave Him half a chance to declare His innocence. Pilate looked for the facts, and when he found them he was not hesitant to say, "He's innocent!" When the Jews would not accept that judgment, Pilate, for some reason afraid to condemn this innocent Man, washed his hands of the matter and allowed Jesus to be crucified.

British scholar James Stalker, who has written a fine volume on Jesus' trials and death, puts it succinctly. Referring to Pilate's choice of Barabbas, he writes, "What he had considered a loophole of escape was a noose into which he had thrust his head."[2]

But the question remains: Why, of all the prisoners that were sitting in Roman cells, did Pilate select Barabbas? Why not one of the two thieves scheduled to be crucified that day—the two later crucified alongside Jesus? Why would Pilate offer to free a man with the kind of notorious criminal record that Barabbas had?

His Name

> And they were holding at that time a notorious prisoner called Barabbas.
>
> —Matthew 27:16

The word translated "notorious" comes from *episemown,* which means "to mark upon." To borrow from that meaning of the Greek term, Barabbas was a marked man. In our terms, he was "public enemy number one." He was more than simply a rabble-rouser—more than another insurrectionist fomenting unrest throughout Judea. He was no petty thief, picking pockets in the crowded streets of Jerusalem. Barabbas was a murderer, a hardened killer.

His name itself is significant. Notice that he is called "Bar-abbas." That is an Aramaic name. Aramaic was the spoken language of that day, the language spoken by Jesus and His disciples. But this was not a common Aramaic name.

As you can see, it divides easily into two parts: "Bar" and "abbas." When Jesus addressed Peter on one occasion, He called him "Simon Barjona." Simon was his given name, and Barjona was his received name. Our received name is our last name. My children have given names as their first names, but their last name is Swindoll, the same as mine. Swindoll is their received name. In biblical days, children also received their father's name. "Bar" means "son," so Simon Barjona means, "Simon, son of John."

We are not told Barabbas's given name. We are told only his received name: Bar-abbas, meaning "son of abbas." And here's the intriguing part of it: "Abbas, or "abba" means "Father." So Bar-abbas would mean "son of the father." But that doesn't make sense. Obviously the man is the son of his father. But there's more. Commentator William Barclay notes that the name "may be compounded of Bar-Rabban, which would mean 'son of the Rabbi.'"[2] Thus, this could mean that Bar-abbas was the son of a well-known rabbi, or at least a well-known man. If that were the case, his criminal activities would have been even more notorious.

This is more than mere legend or supposition. The Jewish historian Josephus agrees with Matthew, stating that Barabbas was a notorious criminal before he was caught. Possibly this was not only because of his heinous crimes but also because of the well-known family from which he came.

> When therefore they were gathered together, Pilate said to them, "Whom do you want me to release for you? Barabbas, or Jesus who is called Christ?" For he knew that because of envy they had delivered Him up.
>
> But the chief priests and the elders persuaded the multitudes to ask for Barabbas, and to put Jesus to death.
>
> But the governor answered and said to them, "Which of the two do you want me to release for you?" And they said, "Barabbas."
>
> Pilate said to them, "Then what shall I do with Jesus who is called Christ?" They all said, "Let Him be crucified!"
>
> —MATTHEW 27:17–18,20–22

In these verses Pilate refers to Jesus as "Jesus who is called Christ." It almost seems as if he is distinguishing Him from some other Jesus. Indeed, I suggest he is. According to some of the most ancient manuscripts of Matthew, two of them in particular, the gospel writer notes that Barabbas's first or given name was Yeshua (Jesus), which explains why Pilate would say, "Whom shall I release? Yeshua Barabbas or Yeshua Christ?"

Now the logical question: Why doesn't this name appear in our Bibles today?

Dr. William Riley Wilson, a keen New Testament scholar, notes this concerning the omission of Barabbas's first name. "It seems very unlikely that any Christian scribes could accidentally have included Jesus' name at this point in the text, but it is easy to see why Christian copyists would intentionally have deleted the name Jesus as a designation for the murderous Barabbas."[3]

When these texts were copied by hand, the scribes would have been careful to note when they came to the full name of Jesus, such as "Jesus, who is called the Anointed One." But when they came to the name of the murderer Barabbas, naturally they would not want to attach "Yeshua" to his name. That is Wilson's point.

"The name Jesus . . . was a common one in first-century Judea, much like James or John today. It is quite possible that Barabbas bore this name. But since the name Jesus was especially sacred to the early Church, it would have been most natural for the early Christians to dissociate it from the murderer Barabbas. This would have been accomplished by gradually omitting Barabbas's given name from the oral and written records of the trial. If this suggestion is correct, the few manuscripts which give the name Jesus Barabbas are the only surviving evidence of the insurrectionist's full name."[4]

This makes Pilate's choice of Barabbas logical. His thinking probably went something like this: "Here is a man with a given name identical to that of Jesus of Nazareth. Surely they will not want the murderer released. Surely they'd rather have the Jesus who claims to be their Messiah." Unfortunately, Pilate's plan backfired. As Stalker suggested: His hope for a loophole became his noose.

His Crime

Now at the feast he used to release for them any one prisoner whom they requested.

And the man named Barabbas had been imprisoned with the insurrectionists who had committed murder in the insurrection.

—MARK 15:6–7

Mark sheds even more light on the situation. (Often it is helpful to compare one gospel writer with another. Different narrators assist us in getting a fuller picture. We benefit from a harmony of the Gospels.) The record from Mark's gospel states, "Barabbas had been imprisoned with the insurrectionists," which verifies that the two men who were later crucified with Jesus were fellow insurrectionists with Barabbas.

Barabbas had been arrested and convicted of insurrection and murder. Insurrection is another word for rebellion against the ruling
authorities.

Barabbas was no petty pilferer or "sneak thief," writes William
Barclay in his Daily Study Bible Series. "He was a brigand or a political revolutionary." There must have been a rough audacity about him
that would appeal to the crowd. Palestine, you see, was filled with
rebellions. It was an inflammable land. In particular there was one
group of Jews called the Sicarri, which means dagger-bearers. They
were violent, fanatical zealots. They were pledged to murder and assas-
sination by any possible means. They carried daggers beneath their
cloaks, and they used them as they could. It is very likely that Barabbas
was such a man.[5]

Barabbas, the criminal whom Governor Pilate offered to the Jews in
his prisoner-release program, was a dangerous rebel, a man of violence
and murder. Our description today would be "terrorist."

His Location

All four of the gospel writers—Matthew, Mark, Luke, and John—state
or imply that Barabbas was imprisoned or bound by the Roman
authorities.

> And they were holding at that time a notorious prisoner, called
> Barabbas.
>
> —Matthew 27:16

> And the man named Barabbas had been imprisoned with the
> insurrectionists who had committed murder in the insurrection.
>
> —Mark 15:7

> But they cried out all together, saying, "Away with this man, and
> release for us Barabbas!"
>
> —Luke 23:18

> "But you have a custom, that I should release someone for you at the Passover; do you wish then that I release for you the King of the Jews?" Therefore they cried out again, saying, "Not this Man, but Barabbas." Now Barabbas was a robber.
>
> —JOHN 18:39–40

Most likely, Barabbas was imprisoned at the fortress of Antonia, the "holding tank" for all prisoners in ancient Jerusalem. During Passover the city of Jerusalem was a crowded, noisy place. The narrow streets were packed with Jews from many countries, for Jerusalem was the place to be at Passover time. The criminal element was evident as well, including various zealots rebelling against Rome, which is why Pilate had to leave his palatial headquarters in the beautiful, blue Mediterranean coastal city of Caesarea and come to Jerusalem to maintain law and order. With Pilate came a battalion of Roman soldiers, who were stationed at the barracks in the fortress of Antonia—the same stone building where Barabbas would have been held captive.

Now, where was Pilate? He could have been staying at the Hasmonian Palace. However, that was the residence of Herod Antipas when he was in Jerusalem (according to several historians), and Herod "was in Jerusalem at that time" (Luke 23:7). That suggests Pilate would have stayed at the fortress of Antonia, since this was a Roman fortress and the headquarters for the Roman soldiers in the area.

THE PAVEMENT

> As a result of this Pilate made efforts to release Him, but the Jews cried out, saying, "If you release this Man, you are no friend of Caesar; everyone who makes himself out to be a king opposes Caesar."
>
> When Pilate therefore heard these words, he brought Jesus out, and sat down on the judgment seat at a place called The Pavement, but in Hebrew, Gabbatha.
>
> —JOHN 19:12–13

This is the sixth and final trial of Jesus, and for this trial Pilate brought Jesus out to a place called "The Pavement." In Hebrew it is *Gabbatha,* which means "mosaic, or stone." This was an elevated area, paved with stone or mosaics, in a courtyard just outside the palace or the fortress, where Pilate stood or sat to pass judgments, hear cases, or dispense other rulings. Here it was that Pilate brought Jesus to interview Him and, finally, to present Him to the waiting mob. Remember, the Jewish leaders wouldn't go into Pilate's residence, because they didn't want to defile themselves at Passover time.

Now, where was this place located in relationship to where Barabbas was incarcerated? What was the distance between them?

The distance between the fortress and the palace was about two thousand feet, a little less than half a mile. From that distance, Barabbas could certainly hear the noise of the angry mob. And here is where the story gets very interesting.

Picture Barabbas, imprisoned in a cold cell in the fortress of Antonia, awaiting execution. As I said earlier, I believe the third cross was intended for Barabbas. He was awaiting execution that very day.

Barabbas paces his cell . . . angry . . . afraid . . . . Suddenly, he hears the sound of an angry mob in the distance. Did that mean his fellow zealots were rioting? Were they, perhaps, overthrowing the Roman guards and coming to his rescue? In his situation, he would be hoping for that.

Suddenly, he hears his name. "Barabbas . . . Barabbas!"

. . . "Which of the two do you want me to release for you?" And they said, "Barabbas."

—MATTHEW 27:21

But they cried out all together, saying, ". . . release for us Barabbas!"

—LUKE 23:18

Therefore they cried out again, saying, "Not this Man, but Barabbas." . . .

—JOHN 18:40

From half a mile away Barabbas could hear the mob shouting his name. And what did he hear next? Check the record, according to Matthew.

"Which of the two do you want me to release?" asked Pilate.

"Barabbas!" they shouted.

"Then what shall I do with Jesus who is called Christ?"

"Let Him be crucified!" they shouted (see Matthew 27:21–22).

Barabbas' heart begins to pound. This is no mob of zealous Jews coming to rescue him. This is a lynching party. Worse than that, a crucifixion party. He couldn't hear Pilate's lone voice asking the questions. All he could hear were the frenzied cries of the mob. "Barabbas!" . . . And then, "Let him be crucified!"

Suddenly he hears the measured tread, the deliberate slap of leather against stone pavement. Soldiers marching down the stone corridor, coming toward his cell. Closer . . . closer they come. One of them swings wide the door and growls, "Get out of here, Barabbas." His heart sinks. But then he hears, "You're free to go."

Can you imagine his shock?

Barabbas, fully expecting the soldiers to come and take him to be crucified, suddenly finds himself a free man!

A Personal Substitute

Barabbas, more than any other individual in the dark drama of Calvary, knew that he had a substitute on that center cross. A. T. Robertson writes, "There between the two robbers and on the very cross on which Barabbas, the leader of the robber band, was to have been crucified," his substitute died.[6]

Barabbas was supposed to die that very day. He was sentenced and imprisoned, awaiting death by crucifixion. Yet suddenly he was told, "You're free."

A number of legends have grown up around the character of Barabbas. They are just legends, and yet . . . a little sanctified imagination never hurts. And I have my own ideas on the subject.

I like to think that Barabbas stayed in Jerusalem that day. After all, he'd been freed. Instead of fleeing for the hills or seeking out his cronies in some back alley, he huddled in the background outside the city gate, anxious to see the Man who was dying in his place.

Barabbas missed his cross because another man literally took his place. How keenly his life models the doctrine of the substitutionary atonement. But let's not forget, Jesus was *our* substitute, too. He bore our sins and died the death that we deserve, just as He died the death that Barabbas deserved. He hung on the cross intended for Barabbas, just as He hung on the cross in our place. Like Barabbas, we were dead in our trespasses and sins until Jesus' crucified body released the blood of substitution. Like Barabbas, we were condemned to die until Jesus took our place.

Like Barabbas, we have been set free, and it is freedom for eternity.

I understand something of the feelings Barabbas must have felt, because I understand what it means to be set free from guilt and condemnation. But my question is, do you?

Are you sitting in the cold, stone dungeon of sin? Do you hear God say, "You're lost. You deserve to die. Your life condemns you."

> All of us like sheep have gone astray,
> Each of us has turned to his own way;
> But the LORD has caused the iniquity of us all
> To fall on Him.
>
> —ISAIAH 53:6

A voice calls out to you in the dungeon of your sin: "God loved you so much that He gave His Son, and, if you will believe in Him, you will never perish, but will have everlasting life."

Jesus paid the penalty for more than Barabbas. He died as a sacrifice, once and for all, for the sins of all humanity. Because He bore the cross we deserve, we're able to have an eternal peace and home in heaven we don't deserve.

The Way of the Cross

Alone thou goest forth, O Lord,
In sacrifice to die;
Is this thy sorrow naught to us
Who pass unheeding by?[1]

—PETER ABELARD, 1079–1142

7
The Way of the Cross

Sir Winston Churchill was not a man who drifted aimlessly through life. Those who knew him well and those of us who love to read his works know that he was consumed by compelling convictions of providence. His life became, to him, an unfolding sense of personal, even heroic destiny. I am not the first to suggest that leading his nation against the forces of Nazism and championing the cause of freedom, in spite of overwhelming odds, became his magnificent obsession.

When King George VI invited him, on May 10, 1940, to lead his beloved Britain against the enemy that threatened Europe, Churchill confidently accepted the challenge. As he later recounted, "I felt as if I were walking with destiny, and that all my past life had been but a preparation for this hour and for this trial."[2]

Jesus of Nazareth, too, had a magnificent obsession: the cross. Painful and anguishing though it was, He found Himself consumed by a compelling sense of Divine providence, and each day of His adult life drew Him inexorably closer to the fulfillment of His mission.

Jesus was not a helpless victim of fate; He was not a pitiful martyr. Books have been written with that very plot in mind: that Jesus had devised a plan that failed and, when the tables turned on Him, wound up on a cross, but, happily, in the process, He established a new religion. So let me set the record straight right now: Jesus' death was a necessary part—in fact, at the very core—of God's predetermined plan. His death on the cross was no afterthought on God's part but, rather, the fulfillment of the Father's predetermined plan for His Son.

Peter confirmed this in his sermon on the day of Pentecost:

> Men of Israel, listen to these words: Jesus the Nazarene, a man attested to you by God with miracles and wonders and signs which God performed through Him in your midst, just as you yourselves know—this Man, delivered up by the predetermined plan and foreknowledge of God, you nailed to a cross by the hands of godless men and put Him to death.
>
> —ACTS 2:22–23

Without removing the responsibility of guilty men—"you nailed Him to a cross"—the Apostle Peter declares the plan of God, arranged in the council of the Godhead's chamber in eternity past. Jesus' death on a cross was not only planned, but foretold—prophesied.

> But the things which God announced beforehand by the mouth of all the prophets, that His Christ should suffer, He has thus fulfilled.
>
> —ACTS 3:18

Mark the words "announced beforehand by the mouth of all the prophets." Search the Scriptures, and you will find numerous prophecies in the Old Testament, which are inescapable references to the death of the Savior. Some date as far back as nine centuries before the birth of Christ, at which time crucifixion was not even known. For example, David gives this specific description of the Savior's death:

> For dogs have surrounded me;
> A band of evildoers has encompassed me;

> They pierced my hands and my feet.
> I can count all my bones.
> They look, they stare at me;
> They divide my garments among them,
> And for my clothing they cast lots.
>
> —PSALM 22:16–18

The Psalmist says that His hands and feet would be pierced. His bones would be pulled out of joint. His clothing would be divided, and they would cast lots for His garments. He would be the object of scorn and mockery. Remarkably, He gave all of those details some nine hundred fifty years before the fact.

Seven hundred years before Christ's coming, Isaiah wrote that He would be the object of misery, torture, and pain. As we saw in previous chapters, the prophet compared Him to a sheep led to the slaughter. He would be crucified with thieves (Isaiah 53).

Planned by God so that you and I might have our sins forgiven, the death of Jesus opened the pathway to heaven—a pathway prepared and paved with His blood.

In our imagination we are going to be walking where Jesus walked on His final journey to the cross. The path is not pleasant, but it is real. We need to revisit the scene, if we hope to gain a realistic understanding of what He endured on our behalf.

DELIVERED TO BE CRUCIFIED

> When Pilate therefore heard these words, he brought Jesus out, and sat down on the judgment seat at a place called The Pavement, but in Hebrew, *Gabbatha*.
>
> Now it was the day of preparation for the Passover; it was about the sixth hour. And he said to the Jews, "Behold, your King!"
>
> They therefore cried out, "Away with Him, away with Him,

crucify Him!" Pilate said to them, "Shall I crucify your King?" The chief priests answered, "We have no king but Caesar."

So he then delivered Him to them to be crucified.

—JOHN 19:13–16

As we saw in chapter six, Pilate has washed his hands and pronounced the final sentence, turning Jesus over to the mob. Though knowing in his heart that Jesus was innocent, Pilate compromised his convictions in order to appease the people. His fear of people was greater than his fear of God.

The sixth and final trial took place around 7:30 in the morning. Jesus' final journey to the cross probably began sometime around 7:30 or 8:00. The writings of Mark tell us that Jesus' hands and feet were nailed to the cross at 9:00 in the morning; so this occurred probably an hour, or an hour and a half, before that.

PHYSICAL TORTURE: SCOURGING

Then he released Barabbas for them; but after having Jesus scourged, he delivered Him to be crucified.

—MATTHEW 27:26

In those days there were two kinds of scourging or flogging: Jewish and Roman. The Jewish method is described in Deuteronomy 25:1–3, where we are told that a person was not to be beaten more than forty times. Because the Jew was afraid of breaking that law of God, he would commonly strike the victim thirty-nine times, making sure he counted meticulously so that he didn't go beyond forty. But in Roman scourging there was no specified number of times that a victim could be beaten. Understandably, then, the Romans commonly called their torturous act of scourging "halfway death."

Before the scourging began, the victim was stripped of all his clothing and bent forward over a low, thick stump or post. At the base of the post were four metal rings. The wrists and ankles of the victim were shackled to these rings. Jesus was stripped of His garments, bent low over this post, with wrists and ankles shackled into that position.

The scourging was done by a man called a lictor—a professional in the grim art of torture. The instrument used for scourging was called a flagellum. It was a piece of wood fourteen to eighteen inches long, circular in shape, to which were attached long, leather thongs. Into these leather thongs or straps were sewn bits of glass, bone, and pieces of metal.

> The soldier who performed flagellations . . . moved to a position about six feet behind Jesus, and spread his legs. The flagellum was brought all the way back and whistled forward, making a dull drum sound as the strips of leather smashed against the back of the rib cage. The bits of bone and chain curled around the right side of the body and raised small subcutaneous hemorrhages on the chest . . .
>
> The flagellum came back again, aimed slightly lower, and again, aimed higher, and it crashed against skin and flesh. . . . The flagellum now moved in slow heavy rhythm.[3]

It was designed to reduce the naked body to strips of raw flesh and inflamed, bleeding wounds.

It was not uncommon for a man to die on the stump. As the NIV notes: "Roman floggings were so brutal that sometimes the victim died before crucifixion." [NIV note on Matthew 27:26.] Invariably, the victim passed out from pain, only to be revived by being splashed with buckets of salt water. These torturers layered pain upon pain to keep the victim conscious, wanting him to suffer as much as possible. The one in charge of this torture kept watch. It was his responsibility to stop the "discipline" if he thought the guilty one might not be revived.

Public Humiliation: Mockery and Brutality

Then the soldiers of the governor took Jesus into the Praetorium and gathered the whole Roman cohort around Him.

And they stripped Him, and put a scarlet robe on Him.

And after weaving a crown of thorns, they put it on His head, and a reed in His right hand; and they kneeled down before Him and mocked Him, saying, "Hail, King of the Jews!"

And they spat on Him, and took the reed and began to beat Him on the head.

—Matthew 27:27–30

At this point Jesus became a comic figure to the Roman soldiers. Silent, He stood before them as they began to humiliate, degrade, and mock Him in every possible way.

The first thing the soldiers did was strip Jesus of all His clothing. He stood nude before them, His face and body a mass of swollen and bruised flesh. Then, in sarcastic fashion, they jammed a crown on His head—a crown they had fashioned from thorns. They draped a scarlet robe over Him and placed a reed in His hand to represent a royal scepter. They mocked Him cruelly, bowing down before Him and hailing Him loudly as "King of the Jews!"

The Greek word referring to the scarlet robe in verse 28 is *chlamus.* It is not the word for a long flowing robe; rather, it refers to a short cloak that came only to the elbows. It was spread over the shoulders and was probably fastened with some kind of tie or button at the neck. In other words, the Son of God stood there naked from His chest down before that barracks full of base, godless men. In fact, I'm confident that is why we do not have a record of what they said to Him. Having spent time in a military barracks, I have some idea of the kind of language those who have no heart for God would have used. You can believe that as Jesus stood in that humiliating place in front of those cruel men, He heard every obscene and coarse comment aimed at Him . . . "yet He opened not His mouth."

The reference to a "crown of thorns" is intriguing (v. 29). Thorns were common in that area. The longer ones were snipped, stuffed in a basket or pot, dried, and then used as kindling to start fires. Outside public places there would be large receptacles stocked with these dried thorns and vines. Probably the soldiers went out, snatched a few thorn branches from the bucket, plaited together a crown, and, with sneers and vulgar jesting, shoved it down on His head.

Several years ago, when friends of mine were in Jerusalem, they found a fairly authentic replica of what that crown probably looked like. Some of the thorns are three and a half inches long. These sharp thorns would have torn cruelly into Jesus' scalp and forehead.

"Hail, King of the Jews!" the Romans shouted. How they hated the Jews! In their brutal mockery, they vented all of their rage on the innocent Son of God. But their hateful abuse took shape in more than costuming and words: They spit on Him and beat Him on the head with the reed scepter.

What seems remarkable to me, in my humanity, is that our Savior never retaliated in any form, never reviled in return. Peter, who was probably as close an eyewitness as any of the disciples, later remembers and writes this:

> For you have been called for this purpose, since Christ also suffered for you, leaving you an example for you to follow in His steps, WHO COMMITTED NO SIN, NOR WAS ANY DECEIT FOUND IN HIS MOUTH; and while being *reviled*, He did not revile in return; while *suffering*, He uttered no threats, but kept entrusting Himself to Him who judges righteously.
>
> —1 PETER 2:21–23 (italics mine)

It is easy to forget that Jesus was tortured, brutalized, and mistreated for an extended period of time before He was led to the place of execution. Quite likely in shock from the extensive physical trauma He had endured, He no doubt began to shake and shiver following all the blows. His face became so marked and swollen that His individual features were scarcely distinguishable. Prior to His walk to Golgotha, He was brought back before Pilate and the bloodthirsty mob. "Behold the man!" Pilate shouted to the crowd as he seized Jesus' head by the hair. "Crucify him!" they screamed in reply.

> And after they had mocked Him, they took His robe off and put His garments on Him, and led Him away to crucify Him.
> —MATTHEW 27:31

Notice that before the soldiers took Jesus to the site of execution, they redressed Him—they "put His garments on Him." In those days, the Jewish man traditionally wore five pieces of clothing: sandals on his feet, a headpiece called a turban, an inner tunic, an outer cloak, and a girdle, or what we would call a wide belt.

After the condemned criminal was executed, these garments would be divided among the soldiers, and we'll address that later.

GOING TO GOLGOTHA

Crucifixion was a common sight for those who lived under the domination of Rome. Perhaps that is why the gospel writers give us few details about Jesus' final walk to the site of execution.

Matthew simply says that the soldiers "led Him away to crucify him." Mark records that "they led him out to crucify him" (Mark 15:20). Luke tells us that "they led him away"(Luke 23:26). And John writes, "They took Jesus therefore, and He went out, bearing His own cross, to the place called the Place of a Skull, which is called in Hebrew, Golgotha" (John 19:17).

Matthew, Mark, and Luke, however, do give us one interesting detail.

> As they went out, they came upon a man from Cyrene named Simon; they compelled this man to carry his cross.
> —MATTHEW 27:32

They compelled a passer-by, who was coming in from the country, to carry his cross; it was Simon of Cyrene, the father of Alexander and Rufus.

—MARK 15:21

As they led him away, they seized a man, Simon of Cyrene, who was coming from the country, and they laid the cross on him, and made him carry it behind Jesus.

—LUKE 23:26

Once again let me remind you that crucifixion was a public event. The criminal was paraded from prison to his place of execution. The Romans wanted as many people as possible to see their "justice." Thus, following an established pattern, Jesus would have been paraded through the streets of Jerusalem to the execution site outside the city gate—a place where people were constantly coming and going. With a centurion in the lead and two soldiers on either side of Him, there was no possibility of escape, even if the victim had any physical endurance left or any friends who wanted to mount a last-minute rescue. The Romans, along with their pomp and sordid ritual for effect, were also taking no chances, especially with the Jewish zealots and insurrectionists who were capable of anything.

Many artists have painted pictures of Jesus carrying a huge cross on His back, bowed low beneath its weight. Certainly there is no way to measure the weight of the burden Jesus carried to the cross—the weight of our sin—or the degree of His suffering. However, in strictly physical terms, He would not have carried the entire cross. No man carried the two heavy timbers that formed the entire cross. The eight-foot, six-by-six piece of rugged timber, plus a crossbeam, would have been too heavy. The upright beam of the cross either remained at the execution site or was taken there by Roman soldiers ahead of time.

The victim did, however, carry the crossbeam of his own cross, which was burden enough. The beam was hoisted across his shoulders and chained to him. Then around his neck was hung a board, about twelve by twenty-four inches, on which was written a notice proclaiming his crime. That board would later be nailed above him on the cross so that everyone who passed by would know the crime for which he was being executed.

Beaten, bruised, and bleeding, our Savior staggered along the longest walk of His life. Through the narrow streets of Jerusalem crowded with the pilgrims there for Passover, who were buying and selling in the last few hours before all trading ceased at the beginning of *Shabbat* (the Sabbath), the soldiers led Jesus out to be crucified. Jesus' final walk to the cross is often called the *Via Dolorosa,* "the way of sorrow." While that is a hauntingly beautiful term (which has resulted in a beautiful musical composition), there was nothing beautiful about Jesus' stumbling, sorrowful, halting, painful journey to His place of execution.

Jesus had been tortured and beaten so badly that He stumbled under the weight of the crossbeam, unable to go on—the beam too heavy for Him to carry. Mercifully, someone was commandeered to help Him carry the beam. That "someone" was destined to play an even greater role in the future, as one New Testament scholar points out:

> This must have been a grim day for Simon of Cyrene. Palestine was an occupied country and any man might be impressed into the Roman service for any task. The sign of impressment was a tap on the shoulder with the flat of a Roman spear. Simon was from Cyrene in Africa. No doubt he had come from that far off land for the Passover. No doubt he had scraped and saved for many years in order to come. No doubt he was gratifying the ambition of a lifetime to eat one Passover in Jerusalem. Then this happened to him.
>
> At the moment Simon must have bitterly resented it. He must have hated the Romans, and hated this criminal whose cross he was being forced to carry. But we may legitimately speculate what happened to Simon. It may be that it was his intention when he got to Golgotha to fling the cross down on the ground and has-

ten as quickly as he could from the scene. But perhaps it did not turn out that way. Perhaps he lingered on because something about Jesus fascinated him.

He is described as the father of Alexander and Rufus. The people for whom the gospel was written must have been meant to recognize him by this description. It is most likely that Mark's gospel was first written for the Church at Rome. Now let us turn to Paul's letter to Rome and read 16:13. "Greet Rufus, eminent in the Lord, also his mother and mine." Rufus was so choice a Christian that he was eminent in the Lord. The mother of Rufus was so dear to Paul that he could call her his own mother. Things must have happened to Simon on Golgotha.

Now turn to Acts 13:1. There is a list of the men of Antioch who sent Paul and Barnabas out on that epoch-making first mission to the Gentiles. The name of one is Simeon that was called Niger. Simeon is another form of Simon. Niger was the regular name for a man of swarthy skin who came from Africa, and Cyrene is in Africa. Here it may well be that we are meeting Simon again. Maybe Simon's experience on the way to Golgotha bound his heart forever to Jesus. Maybe it made him a Christian. Maybe in the after days he was a leader in Antioch and instrumental in the first mission to the Gentiles. Maybe it was because Simon was compelled to carry the Cross of Jesus that the first mission to the Gentiles took place. That would mean that we are Christians because one day a Passover pilgrim from Cyrene, to his bitter resentment at the moment, was impressed by a nameless Roman officer to carry his cross for Jesus.[4]

We shall leave the first-century scene of suffering for now and return to it in the next chapter. As brutal as our Lord's experience was, it led Him toward the fulfillment of His mission—His God-given "magnificent obsession." And because of His earlier teaching regarding our taking up our cross, we need to pause right here and let the truth of His admonition make its impact in our own lives.

Taking up Your Cross

You may recall the Savior's instructions months before His trials and crucifixion transpired. Having walked with Him through this painful journey thus far, we find that those words take on much deeper meaning.

> Then Jesus said to His disciples, "If anyone wishes to come after Me, let him deny himself, and take up his cross, and follow Me"
>
> —MATTHEW 16:24

In Jesus' day "taking up one's cross" was a colloquialism that meant dying to what one wanted. In explaining the ultimate, intimate level of personal commitment to His disciples, Jesus used this common expression in a spiritual sense. "If you want to follow Me, you have to give up your own desires." They understood "take up his cross" because they were accustomed to the sight of condemned prisoners carrying the crossbeam of their cross. And when they saw a person carrying a crossbeam, they knew that person had known sorrow and suffering and had one thing ahead of him: death. So when Jesus said "you must take up your cross and follow Me," they had a clear sense of what He meant.

Do you? Can you truly say that you wish to "come after Him" that intensely, that devotedly? He will give you sufficient grace to endure, but the decision to die to what you want—to take up your own cross—is yours to make, and only yours. I challenge you to make it *now.*

> O my Lord and Savior,
> Thou hast also appointed a cross for me to take up and carry,
> a cross before thou givest me a crown.
> Thou hast appointed it to be my portion,
> but self-love hates it,
> carnal reason is unreconciled to it;
> without the grace of patience I cannot bear it,
> walk with it, profit by it.

O blessed cross, what mercies dost thou bring with thee!
Thou art only esteemed hateful by my rebel will,
heavy because I shirk thy load.
Teach me, gracious Lord and Saviour,
that with my cross thou sendest promised grace
so that I may bear it patiently,
that my cross is thy yoke which is easy,
and thy burden which is light.[5]

The Darkest of All Days

O sacred Head, now wounded,
With grief and shame weighed down,
Now scornfully surrounded
With thorns, Thine only crown:
O sacred Head, what glory,
What bliss till now was Thine!
Yet, though despised and gory,
I joy to call Thee mine.[1]

—BERNARD OF CLARIVAUX, A.D. 1091–1153

8
The Darkest of All Days

I was raised and now live in the State of Texas where, until recently, convicted murderers were executed in the electric chair. Other places use the gas chamber and, as they now do in Texas, lethal injection; and a few, I believe, still use the firing squad and the hangman's noose. None of these methods of execution is pleasant or attractive, nor are they meant to be. Execution is the ultimate punishment for the ultimate crime: giving up one's life for the deliberate act of taking the life of another person.

There is no way to make an instrument of death appealing; yet there is no doubt that some are much worse than others. Crucifixion ranks right up there on the short list of the most painful and torturous deaths ever devised.

Crucifixion differs in two major ways from the various forms of execution today.

First, today's executions are, for the most part, private events. They are private in the sense that the death itself is not viewed by the general public. At the time of execution a few are allowed to be witnesses, demonstrators may gather outside the prison, and those who demonstrate may be televised, if the execution has become notorious for some reason, but cameras are not allowed at the execution itself. In contrast, crucifixion was not only allowed to be a public event, it was designed to be memorable for those who witnessed it. The Romans wanted their subjects to have a vivid reminder that the penalty for breaking their laws was certain, brutal, and extreme.

Crucifixion actually predates the Romans by several hundred years. According to journalist Jim Bishop, the inventors of this macabre method of execution designed crucifixion as a way to inflict the maximum amount of pain on a victim before death.

> They had tried death by spear, by boiling in oil, impalement, stoning, strangulation, drowning, burning—and all had been found to be too quick. They wanted a means of punishing criminals slowly and inexorably, so man devised the cross. It was almost ideal, because in its original form it was as slow as it was painful . . . and the condemned at the same time were placed fairly before the gaze of the people.
>
> A secondary consideration was nudity. This added to the shame of the evildoer and, at the same time, made him helpless before the thousands of insects in the air . . .
>
> The Romans adopted the cross as a means of deterring crime, and they had faith in it. In time they reduced it to an exact science with a set of rules to be followed.[2]

Second, today's executions are swift and even somewhat merciful: the sudden snap of a spine, the flash of electricity through a body, the gradual sleep brought on by noxious gas, the quiet, swift death of a lethal injection. Crucifixion was designed to be an excruciatingly painful, humiliating, lingering death. Merrill F. Unger, the late biblical scholar, states that "instances are on record of persons surviving for nine days"[3] on the cross.

Today the cross is an object of veneration. Designed into exquisite jewelry and artistic statuary, the cross has become a thing of beauty. The outline of the cross is set into mosaic tiles and highlighted with indirect lighting, framed in metal and etched in lovely, mood-setting stained glass. People of the first century would be shocked to see our modern treatment of what was, to them, an object of brutality and the cruelest kind of death. It would be comparable to our wearing the image of a hangman's noose on our lapel or framing an artist's rendering of an electric chair on our living room wall. In the first century the cross meant death . . . but not just any death. It meant the most hideous, anguished death imaginable.

DEATH BY CRUCIFIXION

William Barclay calls crucifixion "the dreadful routine." Klausner, a Jewish historian, says, "Crucifixion is the most terrible and cruel death man has ever devised." Cicero, who was well acquainted with it, says, "It was the most cruel and shameful of all punishments." William Wilson, in his judicial, literary, and historical investigation of what he calls "Jesus' execution," writes, "Not only was the cross the most painful of deaths, it was also considered the most debasing. The condemned man was stripped naked and left exposed in his agony, and often the Romans even denied burial to the victim, allowing his body to hang on the cross until it disintegrated."[4]

Centuries before Christ endured the horror of crucifixion, the Persians were sending men to their deaths on crosses. The Persians worshiped Ormuzd, the god of earth; therefore, they believed that no criminal's blood should contaminate the earth by the victim's dying on it. To avoid this, they devised an ingenious plan whereby a victim could be lifted off the "pure" earth and die in that position; the body could then be removed without ever touching the earth, thus keeping the earth pure. This method of execution was passed on to the Egyptians and finally to the Romans, who embraced it and refined it further.

I am indebted to Jim Bishop for the following vivid and lengthy description of crucifixion in Jesus' day:

> The executioner laid the crossbeam behind Jesus and brought him
> to the ground quickly by grasping his arm and pulling him back-
> ward. As soon as Jesus fell, the beam was fitted under the back of

his neck and, on each side, soldiers quickly knelt on the inside of the elbows . . .

Once begun, the matter was done quickly and efficiently. The executioner wore an apron with pockets. He placed two five-inch nails between his teeth and, hammer in hand, knelt beside the right arm. The soldier whose knee rested on the inside of the elbow held the forearm flat to the board. With his right hand the executioner probed the wrist of Jesus to find the little hollow spot [where there would be no vital artery or vein]. When he found it, he took one of the square-cut iron nails from his teeth and held it against the spot, directly behind where the so-called lifeline ends. Then he raised the hammer over the nail head and brought it down with force . . .

The executioner jumps across the body to the other wrist . . .

As soon as he was satisfied that the condemned man could not, in struggling, pull himself loose and perhaps fall forward off the cross, he brought both of his arms upward rapidly. This was the signal to lift the crossbeam.

Two soldiers grabbed each side of the crossbeam and lifted. As they pulled up, they dragged Jesus by the wrists . . . When the soldiers reached the upright, the four of them began to lift the crossbeam higher until the feet of Jesus were off the ground. The body must have writhed with pain . . .

When the crossbeam was set firmly, the executioner reached up, set the board which listed the name of the prisoner and the crime. Then he knelt before the cross. Two soldiers hurried to help, and each one took hold of a leg at the calf. The ritual was to nail the right foot over the left, and this was probably the most difficult part of the work. If the feet were pulled downward, and nailed close to the foot of the cross, the prisoner always died quickly. Over the years, the Romans learned to push the feet upward on the cross, so that the condemned man could lean on the nails so as to stretch himself upward.[5]

Some historians describe a saddle-like piece of wood on the upright pole, where the victim could rest the base of his pelvis and find relief.

His arms were now in a V position, and Jesus became conscious of two unendurable circumstances: The first was that the pain in His wrists was beyond bearing, and that muscle cramps knotted His forearms and upper arms and the pads of His shoulders; the second was that His pectoral muscles at the sides of His chest were momentarily paralyzed. This induced in Him an involuntary panic; for He found that while he could draw air into his lungs, He was powerless to exhale.

To be able to keep breathing, the victim on the cross had to stay in constant motion, and so he literally dragged himself up and down, up and down, constantly, so as to make breathing possible. Eventually, he could no longer lift himself sufficiently to continue breathing.

With each second, the pain mounted. His arms, His legs, His entire torso screamed with pain; the nerves were pulled tightly, like strings of a violin across its bridge. Slowly and steadily, he was being asphyxiated, as though two thumbs were pressing against His throat.

Some suggest that victims of crucifixion died of suffocation. Others teach that they died from hunger. Still others maintain that they died from sheer exhaustion, as the body eventually wore out from the unendurable pain and the unnatural suspension of the organs and muscles.

As Harvie Branscomb summarizes: "Few more terrible means of execution could be devised. Pain, thirst, the torture of insects, exposure to brutal spectators, the horror of rigid fixation, all continuing interminably, combined to make it a supreme humiliation and torture."[6]

OUR PROFOUND GRATITUDE

Surely these terrible but necessary details have given you a better understanding of why Jesus would pray for "the cup to pass," as He agonized in the Garden. Each time I return to Golgotha and relive the horror of His final suffering, I am more deeply thankful for my Savior's willingness to suffer as He did in my place. I also realize how inadequate I am to express my profound gratitude. Few have said it better than the twelfth-century monk, Bernard of Clairvaux:

> What Thou, my Lord, hast suffered
> Was all for sinners' gain;
> Mine, mine was the transgression,
> But Thine the deadly pain.
> Lo, here I fall, my Saviour!
> 'Tis I deserve Thy place;
> Look on me with Thy favor,
> Vouchsafe to me Thy grace.
>
> What language shall I borrow
> To thank Thee, dearest friend,
> For this Thy dying sorrow,
> Thy pity without end?
> O make me Thine forever;
> And should I fainting be,
> Lord, let me never, never
> Outlive my love to Thee.[7]

❧

O Father, how exceedingly grateful we are for the Lord Jesus Christ. Although the scene we have visited occurred twenty centuries ago, it is as if we have just witnessed His death. How horrible it was! What anguish was His! The pain He bore on our behalf is more than we can even imagine. And it was my sin—our sin—that caused it all. "Mine, mine was the transgression, but Thine the deadly pain."

In this quiet moment, as tears of gratitude well, we pause to tell You how very much we love You and how grateful we are for the price our Savior paid on our behalf. All praise to You because grace abounds, forgiving our sins once for all. Because of Christ. Amen.

"Father, Forgive Them"

Seven times He spake, seven words of love;
And all three hours His silence cried
For mercy on the souls of men;
Jesus, our Lord, is crucified![1]

—*St. Cross,*
Frederick W. Faber, 1849,
third stanza

9
"Father, Forgive Them"

I confess to you, I am still in the wake of the previous chapter. It is almost impossible to visit the excruciatingly painful scene at Calvary and be able to move past it all in one sitting.

Though I realize it had to be, though I understand what it accomplished, and though I know that a brilliant dawn awaited Him who endured the darkest of all days, I am unable to shake myself free from the sound of those square nails being pounded into place. I cannot erase from my mind "the very dying form of One who suffered there for me." Perhaps I shouldn't try. And perhaps you shouldn't either.

And so, let's linger here awhile. Let's stand at the foot of His cross and watch and listen. If we pay close attention, we'll hear not one or two utterances fall from His lips, but seven, yes, seven all-important statements.

The last words a person utters are often of great importance or significance. Loved ones stand close and stay quiet, not wanting to miss those final, parting words. Never has this been truer than in the case of Jesus Christ. Before He drew His final breath on the cross, He made seven statements of incomparable significance, often called "The Seven Last Words of Christ."

In these next seven chapters I want us to listen closely to each of these statements. Timeless truths are hidden in them that we don't want to miss.

These are the Savior's final words:

"Father, forgive them; for they do not know what they are doing."

"Today you shall be with Me in Paradise."

"Mother, behold your son. Son behold your mother."

"My God, My God, why hast Thou forsaken Me?"

"I am thirsty."

"It is finished."

"Into Your hands I commit My spirit."

Christ hung on the cross for six hours before He died. He was there from nine in the morning until three in the afternoon. From nine until noon, it was daylight. At noon, you will recall, a strange and eerie darkness blanketed the skies, and this darkness lasted until after 3:00 in the afternoon. This timing is significant, because Christ's seven last statements fall into two groups: The first three were said during daylight; the last four were uttered after darkness came over the land. The first three sayings had to do with other people; the last four had to do with Jesus himself. The first three had to do with His horizontal relationships with others around Him; the last four had to do with His vertical relationship with God. The first three had to do with His compassion for others; the last four had to do with His suffering and the meaning of His death.

THE FIRST WORDS FROM THE CROSS

And when they came to the place called The Skull, there they crucified Him and the criminals, one on the right and the other on the left.

> But Jesus was saying, "Father, forgive them; for they do not know what they are doing." AND THEY CAST LOTS, DIVIDING UP HIS GARMENTS AMONG THEMSELVES.
>
> —LUKE 23:33–34

The Roman place of crucifixion was familiar to everyone in Jerusalem. This barren, rocky spot outside the city gate was so well known that it had a name. It was called *kranius* in the Greek language—a word meaning "skull," from which we get our word "cranium." In the Hebrew tongue it was called *Golgotha,* while in Latin it was *Calvary.*

I shall deliberately restrain myself from returning to the torturous details of crucifixion. But I do want to remind you that all seven of our Lord's statements were uttered while He was hanging on the cross. Amazing! While other victims cursed and screamed vitriolic words of bitterness, Jesus focused His mind first on others, then on the Father. All the more amazing, His very first words were gracious terms of forgiveness . . . after all He had been through!

We cannot begin to imagine the pathos and the pain, the suffering and the sorrow, yet we need at least to try—not out of a sadistic curiosity, but out of deep appreciation, recognition, and understanding for what our Savior suffered on our behalf. Flanked by hardened criminals, one on His right and one on His left, the sinless Son of God hung stretched out, His hands and feet impaled by iron nails, on a rough wooden cross.

As the pain increased in the bodies of those being crucified, weakness intensified. And since Jesus had been scourged and had not been given food or water since His time around the table with His men the night before (almost fourteen hours earlier), He must have been in greater pain than those two who hung beside Him. The mouths and the throats of all the condemned men on crosses cried for water. Furthermore, as He sank deeper into shock, He lost more fluids.

Two Interesting Observations

In spite of such enormous discomfort and indescribable pain, Jesus spoke words of genuine forgiveness from the cross: "Father, forgive them; for they do not know what they are doing." Pause and consider that statement. As we think about those words, a couple of significant observations come to mind.

First of all, Jesus' words are a fulfillment of Scripture—a fulfillment of what had been predicted long before those words were spoken on that dark day. "Father, forgive them" is a prayer that fulfilled a promise that had been made centuries earlier.

Writing some seven centuries before the Savior walked on earth—that's seven hundred years before Christ was born in a stable—Isaiah wrote these words:

> As a result of the anguish of His soul,
>> He will see it and be satisfied;
>> By His knowledge the Righteous One,
>> My Servant, will justify the many,
>> As He will bear their iniquities.
> Therefore, I will allot Him a portion with the great,
>> And He will divide the booty with the strong;
>> Because He poured out Himself to death,
>> And was numbered with the transgressors;
>> Yet He Himself bore the sin of many,
>> And interceded for the transgressors.
>
> —ISAIAH 53:11–12

Notice that last line: "He interceded for the transgressors." With His first words from the cross, Jesus fulfills that part of the prophecy of Isaiah. He offers a prayer to the Father on behalf of those who have tortured Him and nailed Him to a cross to die. As He "bore the sin of many," He also "interceded for the transgressors." He offers a prayer for the guilty when He prays, "Father, forgive them; they do not know what they are doing."

Second, Jesus offers this prayer of intercession more than once. Luke 23:34 introduces Jesus' words with this phrase: "But Jesus was saying." Another way of translating this from the original text, which conveys the idea of continued past action, would be to say that "Jesus was continually saying, 'Father, forgive them . . . Father, forgive them

. . . Father, again I ask You, forgive them!'" In other words, He prayed it over and over, continuing to intercede for the transgressors.

Perhaps when they drove the nails into His hands, He was praying, "Father, forgive them; they do not know what they are doing." When they nailed His feet to the beam and lifted that timber high and dropped it in the hole, with a jolt that tore His flesh, He was praying, "Father forgive them; they do not know what they're doing." And when they gambled for His garments, He was praying, "Father, forgive them; they do not know what they're doing."

Often it is helpful to go to another gospel writer and discover what He wrote about a particular detail. Interestingly, Matthew doesn't record this particular saying of Christ, but he does tell us that "when they had crucified Him, they divided up His garments among themselves, casting lots" (Matthew 27:35). John also writes that "The soldiers therefore, when they had crucified Jesus, took His outer garments and made four parts, a part to every soldier and also the tunic; now the tunic was seamless, woven in one piece. They said therefore to one another, "Let us not tear it, but cast lots for it, to decide whose it shall be"; that the Scripture might be fulfilled, "THEY DIVIDED MY OUTER GARMENTS AMONG THEM, AND FOR MY CLOTHING THEY CAST LOTS" (John 19:23–24).

As soon as these hardened soldiers finished their gruesome work, they began dividing their spoils—casting dice for Jesus' garments. Then, Matthew tells us something I find rather curious: They sat down and "began to keep watch over Him there" (Matthew 27:36).

Why did they sit down and keep watch? It certainly wasn't necessary to guard the Man on the cross; He wasn't going to escape. And with five soldiers stationed at the cross, only the most fanatical and suicidal from the crowd of onlookers would have attempted a last-minute rescue. I suggest the possibility that when Jesus uttered His prayer of forgiveness for the fourth or fifth time, His words caught the soldiers' attention. Their ears had grown accustomed to the bitter curses of the victims; their hearts were hardened against the cries of dying men. But never had they heard words like this coming from someone dying on a cross: "Father, forgive them."

They stopped gambling. They looked up at Him and continued to watch Him. Not until we are in heaven will we know for certain the fruit of Jesus' prayer, but there is one person we can justifiably speculate about: the centurion. Perhaps "Father, forgive them" offered the first glimmer of hope for that seasoned Roman soldier and ultimately led to his salvation.

FOUR SIGNIFICANT PARTS

Notice that Jesus' prayer has four significant parts: It is addressed to someone; it offers a request; it has a definite object; and it has a reason.

Jesus addresses His prayer to "Father." The next time He addresses His Father from the cross, He will cry out, "My God, My God" as He bears the full weight of the sins of the world. The first time He speaks in love and compassion on behalf of those guilty of putting Him to death; later He calls out in the darkness as the fellowship between God the Son and God the Father is broken by the weight of the sins of the world.

Up to this point, Jesus has never asked the Father to forgive anyone. At certain times, in fact, Jesus himself forgave sins: "And Jesus seeing their faith said to the paralytic, 'Take courage, My son, your sins are forgiven'" (Matthew 9:2b). Jesus' words infuriated the Pharisees. How could any man forgive sin? "But in order that you may know that the Son of Man has authority on earth to forgive sins," He said to the paralytic, "Rise, take up your bed, and go home" (Matthew 9:6).

As long as the Son of God was on earth, He had the authority to forgive sins. But now He had been raised up off the earth so that He might draw others to Him. He was completing the work of redemption, humbling Himself under the authority of God the Father.

The first part of Jesus' prayer is addressed to God the Father, and the second part of the prayer is a specific request for God the Father to "forgive them." That is an amazing request, isn't it? If someone pressed a crown of sharp thorns on your head, if someone stripped you naked for all the world to see, if someone brutally punched you numerous times in the face, drove nails into your hands and feet and lifted you up on a cross to die, be honest now, would you pray that kind of prayer for them? Today, at the slightest offense we are ready to retaliate, defend ourselves, and fight back. Yet at His greatest moment of agony, Jesus sincerely prays, "Forgive them."

No human being could do that, you say to yourself. I thought the same thing myself when I first considered this passage: "I couldn't have done that. No one could!" But look at this account recorded in Acts:

> And Stephen, full of grace and power, was performing great wonders and signs among the people.
>
> Now when they heard this, they were cut to the quick, and they began gnashing their teeth at him.
>
> But being full of the Holy Spirit, he gazed intently into heaven and saw the glory of God, and Jesus standing at the right hand of God; and he said, "Behold, I see the heavens opened up and the Son of Man standing at the right hand of God."
>
> But they cried out with a loud voice, and covered their ears, and they rushed upon him with one impulse.
>
> And when they had driven him out of the city, they began stoning him . . .
>
> And they went on stoning Stephen as he called upon the Lord and said, "Lord Jesus, receive my spirit!"
>
> And falling on his knees, he cried out with a loud voice, "Lord, do not hold this sin against them!" And having said this, he fell asleep.
>
> —Acts 6:8; 7:54–60

A transformed child of God—a man or woman whose life has been changed by the power of God—could pray such a prayer. In fact, saints down through the ages have done so, beginning with Stephen, the first martyr in the history of the church. With rocks and stones pummeling his body, Stephen graciously prayed, "Lord, do not hold this sin against them!" In other words, "Father, forgive them!"

Anyone can love the lovely. Anyone can forgive the forgivable. But Christians are unique. We are called to love the unlovely, to forgive the unforgivable. Jesus' followers have done so for centuries.

God says to us in this passage, "I not only want you to see what My Son prayed in the midst of His suffering; I want you to see what you can pray when you are mistreated and maligned—'Father, forgive them.'" Few acts have a greater impact on those who mistreat us and abuse us than our telling them we forgive them, and we are asking God to forgive them too.

The third part of Jesus' utterance is the object of His prayer. The prayer is addressed to the Father, and the prayer requests forgiveness. Now consider the object of that request: "Father, forgive them; they do not know what they're doing."

Who is the "them"? Who are "they"? In general terms Jesus' request for forgiveness refers to His immediate world. It includes every Jew who planned His death and initiated the trials that were such a sham. It includes every Gentile who had even the smallest part in His crucifixion. But it's broader than that. It includes all of us—the entire world, throughout the sweep of history—for all of us, had we lived then, would have driven the nails into His hands and feet. But at that time, taken specifically and in context, "them" and "they" referred to the Roman soldiers who had just tortured and crucified Him. Is it any wonder that those soldiers stopped and listened when He prayed this prayer?

> And when they came to the place called The Skull, there they crucified Him and the criminals, one on the right and the other on the left. But Jesus was saying, "Father, forgive them; for they do not know what they are doing." AND THEY CAST LOTS, DIVIDING UP HIS GARMENTS AMONG THEMSELVES.
>
> —LUKE 23:33–34

Quite possibly, those soldiers were the death squad, who commonly were in charge of the crucifixion detail. Appointed by their leader, the centurion, these four men, the quarternian, were accustomed to nailing convicted criminals to the cross. To them, one execution was much like another. Criminals were all the same to those men. They did not know the significance of what they were doing or of the person they were putting to death.

And that brings us to the fourth significant part of Jesus' prayer: the reason behind it.

"Father, forgive them." Why? What's the reason for His request? Because "they do not know what they are doing." They don't realize the significance of their act. Today we'd say, "They don't have a clue." It hasn't dawned on them that the hands and feet they have nailed to the cross are the hands and the feet of the Son of God. They haven't the foggiest idea that the body they have nailed to those timbers is the spotless Lamb of God, who is taking away the sins of the world.

"I Crucified Him"

There is another dimension to this that I don't want us to miss. Spiritually speaking, we're in this scene—you and I. Several years later, the Apostle Paul introduced this other dimension to his fellow Christians in the church at Colossae. I urge you to read his words slowly and carefully:

> And when you were dead in your transgressions and the uncircumcision of your flesh, He made you alive together with Him, having forgiven us all our transgressions, having canceled out the certificate of debt consisting of decrees against us and which was hostile to us; and He has taken it out of the way, having nailed it to the cross.
>
> —Colossians 2:13–14

When the Lord Jesus asked the Father to forgive, He also had us in mind!

Did God the Father hear the prayer of the Son? Yes, He did. And did the Father answer the prayer of the Son? Indeed, He did! For every

Jew and every Gentile (including you and me) since then has access to God the Father's forgiveness through the death of Christ the Son.

The Son had prayed, "Father, forgive them." In Colossians 2:13–14, the Holy Spirit, speaking through the pen of the Apostle Paul, confirms that He did just that. He forgave all our transgressions. He canceled our certificate of debt and its hostile decrees against us, having nailed it to the cross.

When a criminal was put to death on a cross, the soldiers scrawled out the identity of his crime on a sign that was then hung around his neck. As he passed through the streets on his way to the place of execution, all could see the crime for which he was being punished: "Insurrection" . . . "Theft" . . . "Murder" . . . or, in Jesus' case, "Treason." Later, this sign was nailed to the cross, above the victim's head. That is why Jesus had the sign nailed over his head, "This is Jesus of Nazareth, the King of the Jews." The Jews charged that He had claimed that title, thus elevating Himself above Caesar.

Paul says that the Lord Jesus took our guilt and nailed it to His cross. He took our sins—yours and mine—the charges that were against us, the handwritten death sentences that belonged around our necks, and carried them with Him as He was nailed to the cross. He died for the very sins that you and I commit.

> And so, as those who have been chosen of God, holy and beloved, put on a heart of compassion, kindness, humility, gentleness and patience; bearing with one another, and forgiving each other, whoever has a complaint against anyone; just as the Lord forgave you, so also should you. And beyond all these things put on love, which is the perfect bond of unity.
>
> —Colossians 3:12–14

Our Savior did not utter hollow words into a meaningless void that dark day He hung on His cross. He did not pray an empty prayer to a silent God. The Son said, "Father, forgive them," and the Father replied, "I forgive them." Since He bore our sins on the cross, we have been fully forgiven. That means we have been empowered to live differently than we did before. We now have the power to put off the sins of the flesh and "put on a heart of compassion, kindness, humility, gentleness and patience; bearing with one another, and forgiving each other."

Look at that list and think back over the past week. Now, answer this question: Have you exhibited a heart of compassion, kindness, humility, gentleness, patience, tolerance, forgiveness, and love?

Our Lord Jesus Christ voluntarily made Himself the sacrificial Lamb of God that He might be slain for your sins and mine. It was for our sakes that He was despised. It was for our sins that He was forsaken. It was because of us, because of what we have done, that He was a Man of Sorrows and acquainted with grief. He who knew no sin went to the cross and became sin on our behalf. He had us on His heart when He asked the Father to forgive, because we didn't know what we were doing. Talk about God's grace! Even though we sinned in utter ignorance, having no idea of the ramifications of our wrongdoing, God graciously forgave and continued to work out His plan of redemption on our behalf.

All this reminds me of the remarkable, true story of how the gospel first came to Korea. In 1886 a Welsh missionary in China, Robert J. Thomas, learned that the Korean language was somewhat similar to Chinese. As he became burdened for the people of Korea, Thomas wondered if, perhaps, they might be able to read the gospel literature he was using in China. He boxed up some Bibles and Christian literature and boarded an American ship, the *General Sherman,* and sailed for PyongYang. Tragically, as the ship approached shore, a serious conflict broke out between the Koreans and the American crew aboard the *Sherman.* In that vicious battle the ship was set on fire, and every person on board died except Robert Thomas, who staggered onto shore, his arms filled with Bibles and other pieces of gospel literature. He dumped them on the sand as the enraged Koreans clubbed him to death. They did not know what they were doing, but the gospel had reached Korea. God forgave them, and today approximately 30 percent of the people of South Korea are Christians.[2]

Thankfully, He still forgives and forgives and forgives.

"Today You Shall Be with Me"

Jesus, pitying the sighs
Of the thief who near thee dies,
Promising him Paradise:
Hear us, holy Jesus.

May we in our guilt and shame,
Still Thy love and mercy claim,
Calling humbly on Thy Name:
Hear us, holy Jesus.[1]

—T. B. POLLOCK, 1870

10
"Today You Shall Be with Me"

The source of the arrangement of the crosses at Golgatha is uncertain. No one knows for sure why Jesus was hung between those two thieves. Perhaps it was Pilate's idea, adding additional insult to injury, since the procurator heard that this would-be Messiah loved sinners so much. Maybe it was ordered by the Jewish officials, desiring to leave a sarcastic impression that these were the only kind of people over whom this imposter-Messiah reigned as king. Or it could have been the centurion's call to place Jesus on the center cross, since He was certainly the most "notorious" of their prisoners that day.

Whoever made the decision, the likelihood is that there was malice in the motive. Yet, above all, there was a Divine purpose at work, and Christ was never one to miss that purpose. In fact, again and again the careful eye of the reader who ponders these last dark scenes discovers deeper meanings and hidden truths in every shred of action, in every random word aimed at Jesus for the purpose of dishonoring or abusing Him—deeper meanings and hidden truths that bring Him honor and intensify our respect.

> As a fire catches the lump of dirty coal or clot of filth that is flung into it, and converts it into a mass of light, so at this time there

was that about Christ which transmuted the very insults hurled at Him into honours and charged even the incidents of His crucifixion which were most trivial in themselves with unspeakable meaning. The crown of thorns, the purple robe, Pilate's Ecce Homo, the inscription on the cross, the savage cries of the passersby and other similar incidents, full at the time of malice, are now memories treasured by all who love the Saviour.[2]

And so, we are not surprised to find a God-ordained and therefore significant reason behind the arrangement of Golgatha's three crosses. It gave Jesus, right up to the very end of His earthly life, an opportunity to reach out in hope and compassion to those desperately in need. But make no mistake: He did so while continuing to endure inexpressible pain.

When a man was hanging on a cross, suspended on iron spikes, he wanted one thing and one thing only: *death*. He thought of one person and one person only: *himself*. Death couldn't come fast enough. That's what makes the seven statements Christ uttered during the six hours He was on the cross so incredible. Unlike all other victims of crucifixion, He was more concerned about others and their needs than He was about Himself.

A Life-and-Death Dialogue

And one of the criminals who were hanged there was hurling abuse at Him, saying, "Are You not the Christ? Save Yourself and us!"

But the other answered, and rebuking him said, "Do you not even fear God, since you are under the same sentence of condemnation?

"And we indeed justly, for we are receiving what we deserve for our deeds; but this man has done nothing wrong."

And he was saying, "Jesus, remember me when You come in Your kingdom!"

> And He said to him, "Truly I say to you, today you shall be with Me in Paradise."
>
> —LUKE 23:39–43

In speaking of the two men crucified with Jesus, Luke uses the common word for an evil-doer as he identifies them as "criminals." Matthew offers another nuance: "At that time two robbers were crucified with Him, one on the right and one on the left" (Matthew 27:38). The word that Matthew uses is a word for "bandits." We could call them "hoodlums." Perhaps they were members of an organized scheme to overthrow the Roman government. There is good reason to believe that these men were partners in crime with Barabbas, who was both an insurrectionist and a murderer. It is likely that these two men were the criminals mentioned in Mark 15:7, which says, "And the man named Barabbas had been imprisoned with the insurrectionists who had committed murder in the insurrection."

Suffice it to say that these two men were not first-time offenders, who had made a couple of slight mistakes in life and gotten caught. They were criminals, thugs, hoodlums. As I suggested above, this was a supreme effort to humiliate Christ, crucifying this innocent Man alongside the worst of evildoers.

Matthew tells us that, initially, both men hurled verbal abuse at Jesus.

> And those passing by were hurling abuse at Him, wagging their heads, and saying, "You who are going to destroy the temple and rebuild it in three days, save Yourself! If You are the Son of God, come down from the cross."
>
> In the same way the chief priests also, along with the scribes and elders, were mocking Him, and saying, "He saved others; He cannot save Himself. He is the King of Israel; let Him now come down from the cross, and we shall believe in Him. "HE TRUSTS IN GOD; LET HIM DELIVER Him now, IF HE TAKES PLEASURE IN HIM; for He said, 'I am the Son of God.' "

And the robbers also who had been crucified with Him were casting the same insult at Him.

—MATTHEW 27:39–44

The word that is rendered "abuse" literally means "blasphemy." The two men shouted harsh, perhaps even obscene statements concerning things sacred and things that Christ embraced as part of His life. In their own dying misery they directed their curses and abuses at the Son of God.

"So you're the great Messiah, the King of the Jews. Well, come on, get us out of this." The operative word here, of course, is "us." They didn't care about Jesus saving himself. They were thinking solely of themselves. *They* wanted release.

Yet, even as these hardened evildoers were shouting at Jesus, something remarkable occurred.

> And one of the criminals who were hanged there was hurling abuse at Him, saying, "Are You not the Christ? Save Yourself and us!"
>
> But the other answered, and rebuking him said, "Do you not even fear God, since you are under the same sentence of condemnation?
>
> "And we indeed justly, for we are receiving what we deserve for our deeds; but this man has done nothing wrong."
>
> —LUKE 23:39–41

The Lord Jesus did not answer the taunting question coming from one of the criminals: "Aren't you the Christ? Save yourself and us!"

Jesus was silent, "but the other answered." In the Greek text the word "other" literally implies "other of a different kind." Originally this man was shouting abuse along with all the others; now he was in the process of being changed. He was different.

"What's the matter with you?" he says. "Don't you even fear God, since you're under the same sentence of condemnation? Don't you realize that we're getting what we deserve, but this man is innocent?"

A CHANGE OF HEART

What suddenly brought about the change in this criminal?

I can think of at least two reasons for the second criminal's change of heart.

First, He noticed the sign above Jesus' head: "THIS IS THE KING OF THE JEWS." This was not intended as a declaration of truth. In fact, the Jewish leaders said to Pilate, "Don't let that sign read 'This is the King of the Jews.'" They wanted it to say, "He *says* He is the King of the Jews." But Pilate, that hard-headed Roman, stood firm. "What I have written, I have written," he said. I'm convinced the second thief looked at the sign, "THIS IS THE KING OF THE JEWS" and began to believe it to be the truth.

The second factor that changed his heart was the silence of Christ—the way He handled all the abuse. I cannot overemphasize the importance of the written Word and the godly life, a combination that can change even a hardened criminal.

> There's a sweet old story translated for men,
> Written in the long, long ago—
> The Gospel according to Matthew, Mark, Luke, and John—
> Of Christ and His mission below.
>
> You are writing a gospel, a chapter each day,
> By deeds that you do, by words that you say.
> Men read what you write, whether faithless or true.
> Say, what is the gospel according to you?
>
> Men read and admire the gospel of Christ,
> With its love so unfailing and true;
> But what do they say, and what do they think
> Of the gospel according to you?
>
> 'Tis a wonderful story, that gospel of love,
> As it shines in the Christ-life divine,

And oh, that its truth might be told again
In the story of your life and mine!

Unselfish mirrors in every scene,
Love blossoms on every sod,
And back from its vision the heart comes to tell
The wonderful goodness of God.

You are writing each day a letter to men;
Take care that the writing is true.
'Tis the only gospel some men will read,
That gospel according to you."[3]

In His silence and control, Jesus offered the good news (the gospel) that has the power to change a life. And the once-hardened criminal responded. He realized the uniqueness of Christ. He saw in Him more than just a man. With a mixture of desperation and faith, he pleads,

"Jesus, remember me when You come in Your kingdom!"
—LUKE 23:42

How did he know Christ had a kingdom? He read the sign: "THE KING OF THE JEWS." Kings have kingdoms. He understood the truth. He realized he was a sinner, unable to change himself. And he understood that this holy Man could determine his eternal destiny. "Remember me when You come into Your kingdom."

This brings me to a very practical point. Don't nit-pick about the words people use to become Christians. Ever find yourself wanting them to use precise, specific words—the "right words?" Do you believe that a person can say, "Remember me when You come into Your kingdom, Lord" and be saved? Obviously, Jesus did!

Luke records a very good reminder. Let God deal with the attitude of the heart. Let the Holy Spirit give the sinner the words to say. Leave it between the sinner and God. Only He can read the attitude of the heart.

One of the most effective evangelists I have ever known was a fellow who ran a filling station in a suburb of Boston. This man had never spent one day in a theological seminary. He'd never even taken a course in a Bible college. But his Bible was well worn, and he kept it open near his cash register. He used to tell me, "Chuck, the gas-pumping business really gives me opportunities for witness."

This man was an effective witness because, in marvelous wisdom and love, he presented the message of eternal life and left the results with God. Through the years, person after person (the Lord keeps the count) came to know Christ in that filling station or sometime after a conversation with my New England friend, thanks to his faithful witness.

Never underestimate the impact of a godly life and the written Message. Never underestimate the power and providence of God. And never overestimate your own part in the process.

God holds us responsible for sharing the gospel—for living out the gospel in word and in deed. But He does not hold us accountable for what somebody else does with the gospel. What someone else does with the message of eternal life is the Lord's business. The way I give the message is between Him and me, and that's often where He and I have our longest talks. But what happens afterward is God's business.

A Personal Turning Point

And he was saying, "Jesus, remember me when You come in Your kingdom!"

And He said to him, "Truly I say to you, today you shall be with Me in Paradise."

—Luke 23:42–43

If ever there was a deathbed conversion, this is it. This man, a sinner who is dying on the cross for the crimes he has committed, calls out, "Lord, remember me." And Jesus says, "Today you shall be with Me in Paradise." Don't pass too quickly past that all-important word: Today. This very day.

The thief on the cross cries out for salvation, and the Lord hears and answers. The petitioner doesn't have to pray or make a sincere promise. Furthermore, he doesn't have to be baptized. He doesn't have to perform six months of good works to earn heaven. He doesn't even have to pass through a one-week probation period where he proves himself worthy of the calling of eternal life. Grace abounds!

On what basis, then, is he accepted into God's kingdom? (Pay close attention, please.) Faith. It's as simple, and as complex, as that. Faith alone in Christ alone. *Sola Fide* . . . period. That's all that God wants. And that's all that we can offer.

Back in the eighteenth century, Augustus Toplady wrote of this in his great hymn, *Rock of Ages:*

> Not the labors of my hands
> Can fulfill Thy law's demands;
> Could my zeal no respite know,
> Could my tears forever flow,
> All for sin could not atone;
> Thou must save, and Thou alone.
>
> Nothing in my hand I bring,
> Simply to Thy cross I cling;
> Naked, come to Thee for dress,
> Helpless, look to Thee for grace;
> Foul, I to the fountain fly,
> Wash me, Saviour, or I die![4]

Why don't I bring something in my hand? Because everything I bring in my hand is contaminated by sin. Before God I am, as the hymn writer describes me, a "naked, helpless, foul" sinner. If I were to bring anything to the Father, it would pollute His holiness. Therefore, the Father says, "You come to Me by faith in My Son, and I promise you instantly that you will be forgiven, cleaned up, clothed in My righteousness, and secure in My place of Paradise."

TIMELESS LESSONS FOR US TODAY

I see four lessons for us in these second words from the cross.

Lesson one: *No one is ever too far gone to become a Christian.*

I would guess that at some time in your life you have written some-one off, thinking, "Oh, that person never will come to know Christ. I've spoken to him and worked on him and I've prayed faithfully. I've tried everything I know and everything's failed. There's no way to soften a heart that hard. That person just can't be reached with the gospel."

Have you ever heard of Mel Trotter? If there was ever a fellow too far gone, it was Mel Trotter. He was an alcoholic who cared only about one thing in life: his next drink. Even the needs of his family meant nothing to him. When his child became deathly ill, and he was given money to get the medicine the child needed, Trotter bought booze instead. The child died. Before the funeral, Trotter stole the shoes from his child's body in the casket to buy more booze. You probably think nobody can get any lower than that, but *he* did. Eventually, bleary-eyed and broken, he slumped down in the back row of a city mission, where the words of a hymn pierced through his drink-fogged brain. That very night Mel Trotter came to know Christ! A revolutionary change took place in his life. As a result, with his leadership, today missions in the hearts of many cities are ministering to broken men and women like Mel Trotter, feeding their bodies and, even more importantly, their souls.[5]

Thank God, Mel Trotter was not too far gone. Neither is that per-son you are thinking of right now. No one is beyond the reach of the gospel. No one is too far gone to become a follower of Jesus Christ. Believe that!

Lesson two: *The printed page and the godly life are the two most effec-tive tools of evangelism.*

The printed page includes both the Scriptures and that which relates to Scripture. It's amazing how God can use Spirit-directed words. I've heard amazing stories of how some have come to Christ after reading just a page that had been torn out of a Bible or a verse of

Scripture written at the bottom of a letter. I can't tell you how many letters I've received since I first began publishing books, from people who read something I wrote, then received Christ. Mothers, dads, salespeople, pilots, students, athletes, prisoners, military personnel, artists, teachers, even a few pastors. Words . . . How powerful!

You don't have to be called into the preaching ministry to be a witness and to be used effectively by God. The real message is your life. And when your life has created a thirst on the part of the interested party, you will have all the words you need to tell him or her about the Savior.

We have a couple in our church who are foster parents. They take children into their home—sometimes for six months, sometimes for two or more years. Often the child has been in an abusive home or is the victim of neglect. This loving couple has found that their lives speak louder and more effectively than their words. Acts of tenderness, kindness, and compassion so impress those little lives that they are changed—truly and permanently changed. Their stories always remind me of Jesus' promise of His prepared kingdom to those who "did it to one of these brothers of mine, even the least of them" (Matthew 25:40). Isn't it interesting? His promise is extended not to those who *say* the right thing but to those who *do* the right thing. Random and gracious acts of kindness will be honored by our God.

Lesson three: *All that God wants and accepts is simple faith.*

The criminal hanging alongside Jesus was not ushered into Paradise on the basis of anything he had done. It was God's grace that opened the door and invited him in.

Anytime you are tempted to believe in a salvation-by-good-works offer, just remember the believing thief on the cross. Helpless, hopelessly lost, totally depraved, guilty of wrong, condemned to die by crucifixion, unable to change any of that on his personal record, with only a few hours to live, he says in simple faith, "Remember me." Nothing has changed. Salvation has not gotten more complicated. Simple faith is still the only way.

Lesson four: *Never doubt your instant acceptance into God's family when you open your heart to Him.*

Jesus told the man on the cross beside him, "Today, you will be with Me in Paradise." Immediately he was forgiven, accepted, and promised heaven. This flies in the face of every humanistic, self-help program you've ever heard of or participated in.

Jesus said, "I am the way, and the truth, and the life; no one comes to the Father, but through Me"(John 14:6).

No twelve-step process required. Simply reach out in faith to the Son of God and make a similar request: "Remember me, Lord."

You may not be as far gone as Mel Trotter was, or you may be worse. It makes no difference. You may have lived a life as blatantly sinful as the thug hanging beside Jesus on the cross, or you may have lived a good and respectable life. It makes no difference. We all approach the throne of God as sinners, and we all are saved by His grace alone. Whatever specific words we might use, our hearts cry out to God: "I'm a sinner. I'm lost. I'm bound for hell. There's nothing I can bring You to merit Your favor, but, Father, I receive Your Son at this moment. By faith, like a child, I ask Christ to be my Lord and Savior. I believe He died as my substitute and was raised for me. I believe He paid the full payment for my sin. And right now I offer myself to You by faith."

As the great nineteenth-century British pastor, Charles Haddon Spurgeon, ended his sermon, "The Believing Thief," he spoke with the passion that every pulpit should possess. His words provide a fitting conclusion here:

> He is able to save to the uttermost, for He saved the dying thief. The case would not have been put there to encourage hopes which He cannot fulfill. Whatsoever things were written aforetime were written for our learning, and not for our disappointing. I pray you, therefore, if any of you have not yet trusted in my Lord Jesus, come and trust in Him now. Trust Him wholly; trust Him only; trust Him at once. Then you will sing with me—

"The dying thief rejoiced to see
That fountain in his day,
 And there have I, though vile as he,
Washed all my sins away."[6]

"Behold, Your Son! Behold, Your Mother!"

At the cross her station keeping,
Stood the mournful mother weeping,
Where he hung, the dying Lord:
For her soul of joy bereaved
Bowed with anguish, deeply grieved,
Felt the sharp and piercing sword
Who, on Christ's dear mother gazing,
Pierced by anguish so amazing,
Born of woman, would not weep?
Who on Christ's dear mother thinking,
Such a cup of sorrow drinking,
Would not share her sorrows deep?[1]

—LATIN, 13TH CENTURY

11

"Behold, Your Son! Behold, Your Mother!"

At the Place of the Skull the Son of God endured six hours of pain before He died. Think of it—six excruciating hours of pain. During those hours when His body hung suspended on the cross, held in place by square iron spikes through His hands and feet, Jesus never once lost control of His emotions, never showed signs of bitterness, never cursed. Furthermore, He thought not of Himself, but of others. First, He thought of the very ones who were crucifying Him, saying, "Father, forgive them." Then He looked across to the thief hanging beside Him and, responding to the man's plea for salvation, promised, "Today, you will be with Me in paradise."

Now we come to the most touching and tender of all the scenes that took place at Calvary. It happened when the Lord Jesus addressed His mother.

THE CONNECTION

The soldiers therefore, when they had crucified Jesus, took His outer garments and made four parts, a part to every soldier and also the tunic; now the tunic was seamless, woven in one piece.

> They said therefore to one another, "Let us not tear it, but cast lots for it, to decide whose it shall be"; that the Scripture might be fulfilled, "THEY DIVIDED MY OUTER GARMENTS AMONG THEM, AND FOR MY CLOTHING THEY CAST LOTS."
>
> —JOHN 19:23–24

Jesus hung naked on the cross. His clothing had been stripped from Him by the Roman soldiers. It was their right, legally, to take the garments. But since there were four soldiers and five garments, they faced a dilemma. (The fifth soldier, the centurion or leader of the execution squad, did not participate in the division of the spoils.)

As I explained earlier, a Jewish man in Jesus' day typically wore five pieces of clothing: a head piece (some type of turban or cloth about the head); sandals; an outer robe (which hung loosely about the body, usually all the way down to the ankles); a girdle (what we would call a belt or a sash, which held the loose-hanging robe close to the body); and an undergarment. The first four were the outer garments: "The soldiers . . . took his outer garments and made four parts." This does not mean they tore them apart. It means that each soldier chose or claimed one of the four pieces.

But there was one piece of clothing left over: the undergarment. The underclothing that a Jew wore was a tunic made of soft material, much like a nightgown. It draped loosely over the shoulders and hung almost to the knees. This garment was called the *chiton* (pronounced ke-tone). Apparently the *chiton* Jesus wore had been woven in one piece—a seamless garment.

Now we come to an interesting point. According to Bible commentator William Barclay, the description of the tunic of Jesus matches the description of the high priest's tunic—which also was woven in one piece from top to bottom. And the word for "priest" in Latin is *pontifex*, which means "bridge-builder." A priest was one who built a bridge between God and man. No one ever did that better than Jesus Christ.

> Since then we have a great high priest who has passed through the heavens, Jesus the Son of God, let us hold fast our confession. For

we do not have a high priest who cannot sympathize with our weaknesses, but One who has been tempted in all things as we are, yet without sin. Let us therefore draw near with confidence to the throne of grace, that we may receive mercy and may find grace to help in time of need.

—HEBREWS 4:14–16

As the great High Priest of the faith, Jesus paved our way to God. Jesus was our *pontifex*—our bridge-builder. Appropriately, He even wore the seamless garment familiar to the high priest of the temple.

Usually the mother of a Jewish boy made the *chiton* for him before he stepped into the real world on his own. When he reached manhood, his mother presented him with the *chiton*. Legend tells us that when Jesus left home to begin His ministry, his mother, Mary, gave Him the *chiton*. And because of the way this section of the story, as recorded in the Gospels, fits together, I rather suspect that legend is true.

They said therefore to one another, "Let us not tear it, but cast lots for it, to decide whose it shall be" . . . Therefore the soldiers did these things. But there were standing by the cross of Jesus His mother, and His mother's sister, Mary the wife of Clopas, and Mary Magdalene.

When Jesus therefore saw His mother . . .

—JOHN 19:24–26A

The four soldiers have to decide who gets the fifth garment. They don't want to tear it into four pieces, thus making it useless. So they cast lots for it. They throw the dice. They gamble. And as they do so, note the flow of the narrative. As the soldiers gamble for the *chiton*, Jesus "therefore saw His mother."

Why now? She's been there all along, watching and weeping. Why hasn't He acknowledged her or spoken to her? Could it be because of the seamless tunic? I think so. His outer garments were insignificant. That was just paraphernalia that had kept Him comfortable during

His earthly ministry. But when they touched the tunic, they touched something very near to His heart—the garment made for Him by His mother. So it stands to reason that, when they began talking about and haggling over the tunic, He would look at His mother.

What a contrast we have at the cross. God's perfect sacrifice—His Lamb—hangs there in agony, giving His life, shedding His blood for the sins of the world. Heaven stands breathless, poised between life and death, as the salvation of the world is being completed. And at the feet of the Lord Jesus, four coarse, sin-hardened soldiers are shooting dice for garments. The study in contrasts is a bit breathtaking.

Lamentations 1:12a says, "Is it nothing to all you who pass this way? Look and see if there is any pain like my pain." What a fitting passage to apply to this moment. "Is it nothing to you who pass by?" Those soldiers casting lots for His garments were more concerned about a seamless tunic than about what was transpiring on the cross above them.

> And, sitting down, they watched Him there,
> The soldiers did;
> There, while they played with dice,
> He made His sacrifice,
> And died upon the Cross to rid
> God's world of sin.
> He was a gambler too, my Christ,
> He took His life and threw
> It for a world redeemed.
> And ere His agony was done,
> Before the westering sun went down,
> Crowning that day with its crimson crown,
> He knew that He had won.[2]

That's it! That's exactly what took place at Calvary. Jesus threw Himself to the world, and in doing so, He knew that He had won. Yet most of those who passed by couldn't have cared less.

The *chiton* has been gambled for and taken by one of the soldiers, but . . .

> When Jesus therefore saw His mother, and the disciple whom He loved standing nearby, He said to His mother, "Woman, behold, your son!"
>
> —JOHN 19:26

In their effort to keep Mary, the mother of Jesus, from being venerated as the intermediary, the patroness for sinners, Protestants have, unfortunately, denied her the rightful recognition she deserves for her faithfulness and quiet heroism. What a courageous woman this beloved mother was. When Jesus saw His mother, she was not a crumpled heap. She was "standing."

Imagine what it must have been like for that mother to watch her dear son being crucified. It is difficult enough to lose a child—to have a child die young. But to watch your adult son brutalized and tortured and hung on a cross? Think of it.

W. Pink describes it much better than I could:

> After the days of His infancy and childhood, and during all the public ministry of Jesus, we see and hear so little of Mary. Her life was lived in the background, among the shadows. But now, when the supreme hour strikes of her Son's agony, when the world has cast out the Child of her womb, she stands there by the Cross! Who can fitly portray such a picture? Mary was nearest to the cruel Tree! Bereft of faith and hope, and baffled and paralyzed by the strange scene, yet bound with the golden chain of love to the Dying One, there she stands! Try and read the thoughts and emotions of that mother's heart. O what a sword it was that pierced her soul then! Never such bliss at a human birth, never such sorrow at an inhuman death.
>
> Here we see displayed the Mother-heart. She is the Dying Man's mother. The One who agonizes there on the Cross is her

Child. She it was who first planted kisses on that brow now crowned with thorns. She it was who guided those hands and feet in their first infantile movements. No mother ever suffered as she did. His disciples may desert Him, and His friends may forsake Him, His nation may despise Him, but His mother stands there at the foot of His Cross. Oh, who can fathom or analyze the Mother-heart.[3]

THE CHARGE

As she stood there, Jesus says to her, "Mother, behold, your Son." And then He addresses the disciple standing near her: John, "the disciple whom He loved."

Then He said to the disciple, "Behold, your mother!" And from that hour the disciple took her into his own household.

—JOHN 19:27

What Jesus says, in effect, is, "John, I charge you to adopt this woman as your mother. You are to take her into your home and into your life. That means you are to love her and care for her as I would, were I to continue to live. She is to become as precious and dear to you as she has been to Me."

Two questions come to my mind as I study these words. First, why didn't Jesus ask His own brothers to take care of Mary, their mother? And second, where was Mary's husband, Joseph?

Some, of course, believe that Mary continued to be a virgin throughout her life. This teaching is called the perpetual virginity of Mary, and it is unbiblical. The Gospel of Matthew verifies the fact that Mary had other children besides the Lord Jesus. Her virginity was preserved until the birth of Jesus, but it did not continue afterwards.

Matthew's record even includes some of the names of Jesus' siblings.

And it came about that when Jesus had finished these parables, He departed from there.

And coming to His home town He began teaching them in their synagogue, so that they became astonished, and said, "Where did this man get this wisdom, and these miraculous powers?

"Is not this the carpenter's son? Is not His mother called Mary, and His brothers, James and Joseph and Simon and Judas?

"And His sisters, are they not all with us? Where then did this man get all these things?"

—Matthew 13:53–56

The account mentions four brothers by name—James, Joseph, Simon, and Judas—as well as "His sisters." So obviously Mary had other children. In fact, the people from Jesus' hometown were amazed when they heard Him teaching in their synagogue. "Where in the world did this Man get such wisdom. Isn't this the carpenter's son? We've known Him all His life, just as we know His brothers and His sisters."

But what interests me here is Jesus' words concerning their unbelief.

And they took offense at Him. But Jesus said to them, "A prophet is not without honor except in his home town, and in his own household."

And He did not do many miracles there because of their unbelief.

—Matthew 13:57–58

I return to my first question: Why didn't He send Mary to His own brothers? Matthew helps us with the answer: because of their unbelief." I believe this indictment of the people in Jesus' hometown includes His own siblings. They had rejected Him. John 7:5 confirms this: "For not even His brothers were believing in Him."

Throughout His earthly ministry, right up to the point of His death, His brothers did not believe in or support Him. His mother did, but not His brothers. And so it stands to reason that, shortly before His death, He puts her in the care of one who would not only love her and care for her as his own mother, but also one who loved Him and believed in Him—one of His closest followers.

But what about Joseph? Where was Mary's husband, while all this was happening?

Did you realize that Joseph is never mentioned again in Scripture after the story recorded in Luke 2:41–51? The last time we see Joseph in the biblical record is when Jesus is twelve years old, and He and His parents are visiting the temple in Jerusalem. This suggests, I believe, that Joseph died sometime after that—probably before the beginning of Jesus' ministry, because Joseph is not even mentioned as being with Mary at the wedding in Cana.

There is every indication, certainly an eloquent hint from the argument of silence, that Joseph was not alive when Jesus was crucified.

THE RESPONSE

Jesus said to His mother, "Woman, behold, your son!" There He hung . . . naked, humiliated, and in horrible pain. The sight for her must have been anguishing beyond description. Then He said to His disciple, "Behold, your mother!" It was a firm and clear charge, yet full of tenderness.

While Mary was not the patroness for sinners and saints, she was, however, a woman of faith, a courageous woman, but a human woman nonetheless. She was dependent and needy and brokenhearted over the death of her Son, and just as much in need of salvation and forgiveness and grace as any person who ever lived. Because of her needs, especially as the years would begin to stack up, Jesus says to the disciple, "Love her. Take her into your own home and care for her."

> . . . And from that hour the disciple took her into his own *household*.
>
> —JOHN 19:27

Notice that the word "household" is in italics. This means that the italicized word is not in the original text, making the literal rendering, *"the disciple took her into his own."* His home, his belongings, his family, his world would now include Mary. In other words, everything that he had became hers to enjoy.

What happened to Mary, we don't know. How long she lived with the disciple, we do not know. When she died, again, we do not know. But however long she lived, there was nothing hidden between the heart of John and the heart of Mary, the mother of his earthly Mentor and Friend, the Lord Jesus.

At the closing moment of His life, in the midst of His indescribable suffering, Jesus took care of His mother. Though His own pain was borderline unbearable, He had her welfare and protection near His heart to the very last.

The Truths

Three wonderful truths can be found in this passage of Scripture related to Jesus, John, and Mary.

First, grace is extended to those who fail.

You may say, where do you see that? I see it in the life of John, the disciple. The night of Jesus' arrest in the Garden of Gethsemane, all of the disciples deserted Him (Mark 14:50). They all fled. That would include John, the beloved disciple. Even His closest companion ran and hid.

But he came back. For here is John, standing at the foot of the cross, identifying himself with the crucified Christ. Exactly when he came back, we do not know. Why he came back, we are not told. But suddenly, as Jesus is hanging on the cross, we find that John is back, once more a devoted disciple. And what does Jesus do? He looks at John and elevates him in grace to a marvelous position. "Take care of My mother. You will be a son to her, and she will be a mother to you." There was no rebuke or warning. Only confidence was extended. The implication is clear: Jesus trusted John.

Grace is extended even to those who fail.

Have you failed in some area of your life? Have you been disobedient? Have you forsaken fellowship with the Lord? Have you gone your own way in sin or selfishness? Of course you have! Maybe it began earlier in the week when something happened, and everything just turned you sour, and you've been hard to live with ever since. You've failed miserably, and you know it. You feel like a total failure. But wait a minute. The grace of God is provided for those who fail, for those of us who are sinners. The solution is found in coming back. He will forgive and reinstate you. If it were not so, we would all despair.

If you have not already done it, lay your failure, your weakness, your sins before the Lord, and then, without hesitation, claim His forgiveness, because the blood of Jesus Christ, God's Son, cleanses us from all sin, even John, the beloved disciple, who earlier deserted Him.

Second, spiritual bonds are stronger than natural bonds.

Jesus had brothers and sisters. Normally you'd expect Him to speak to one of them about caring for their mother. But Jesus had a much closer bond with John than with His own siblings. Spiritually John was on target; He had been instructed and mentored by Jesus. Therefore, we are not surprised to find Jesus entrusting His mother to John's tender care.

How often have you felt a oneness and kinship with other believers, sometimes a far deeper and warmer bond than any you experience with some of your family members?

As a pastor, I've certainly experienced this. Through the years, God has blessed our family with amazingly strong spiritual ties within His family, even with individuals we've not really known that long. That's one of the most marvelous things about the family of God. Roots deepen quickly within the ranks of the faithful. It's as if we've known each other half our lifetime.

Third, the principle of perpetual parental respect is to be obeyed.

Jesus is involved in the final great work of salvation. Suffering and dying, on the verge of passing into the darkness of death. Yet our precious Savior, in His dying moments, concerned Himself with the welfare of His mother. Mary had said little throughout His public ministry; she had been very much in the background. Yet at the time of His death, Jesus challenged John, "Care for her. Love her. Be a son to her."

Solomon wrote, "Listen to your father who begot you, and do not despise your mother when she is old" (Proverbs 23:22).

Are your parents still living? How is your relationship with them? In all honesty, do you make room in your schedule for them? If I were to ask them, "Do you feel honored by your son/daughter?" how would they respond?

As I examine the landscape of life in today's culture, especially our American culture, I witness a lot of loneliness among aging parents and, at the same time, a lot of independence among their adult children. The me-ism of our times has taken a serious toll on the family. Admittedly there are some wonderful exceptions. But therein lies the heartache—they are *exceptions*.

A longstanding principle finds its origin in the pages of the Bible: God rewards those who care. God will honor you if you will honor your parents. You never grow too old to spend time with them, to glean from their wisdom, and to make certain they know how much you love and respect them.

This priority remained near the top of Jesus' list; so the application to our lives isn't difficult to figure out.

And before I close this chapter, a word of encouragement is in order for all you mothers! Your role is, clearly, the single most important in society. Your place in your family's life is absolutely strategic. Those children you are rearing may not stop to tell you, but you need to know—it's worth all the effort, and it will pay enormous dividends as they grow up and become the men and women who will shape our country's future.

Mary had her Son for thirty years. He never forgot her, nor could He. And though she survived Him, she would never forget His compassionate concern and tender courage.

Who knows? He probably learned both from her.

"Why Have You Forsaken Me?"

It was alone the Savior prayed
In dark Gethsemane;
Alone He drained the bitter cup
And suffered there for me.
It was alone the Savior stood
In Pilate's judgment hall;
Alone the crown of thorns He wore,
Forsaken thus by all.
Alone, alone, alone, upon the cross He hung
Forsaken thus by all.
Alone upon the cross He hung
That others He might save;
Forsaken then by God and man,
Alone, His life He gave.
Alone, alone He bore it all alone;
He gave Himself to save His own,
He suffered, bled and died, alone, alone.[1]

—LATIN, 13TH CENTURY

12

"Why Have You Forsaken Me?"

*B*ecause my radio program, *Insight for Living,* is able to find its way into places I cannot go, the mail we receive is often surprising. Occasionally it is downright heartbreaking.

Among the saddest letters are those written by inmates in prison. The stories some of them tell are tragic beyond description; and among the most depressing are the experiences of the men who have spent time in solitary confinement. Removed from all contact with anyone, sometimes for days or weeks, they exist with the barest of essentials: a narrow, hard bed, a toilet, a basin, and darkness. Often there is no light at all—nothing but endless darkness and silence.

The words these prisoners use to describe their feelings while in such abject settings are desperate terms: desolate, maddening, lonely, hopeless, lost, confused, forgotten, abandoned. One man spoke of becoming so totally disoriented that he lost awareness of time, the names of his children, even the location of those few essentials in his cell. He groped on his hands and knees to find the toilet in the darkness. But the most telling of the terms he used to define his feelings when at the bottom of his emotional pit was "forsaken."

You can imagine the chill that went up my spine when I began to do my research on the hours of darkness Jesus endured and I came across that very term, uttered while He was hanging on His cross: "forsaken." Having recently read the prisoner's letter, that word took on a deeper meaning than it ever had before. The enormity of our Lord's anguish cannot even be imagined, as He screamed in His mother tongue: "ELI, ELI, LAMA SABACHTHANI?" That is, "My God, My God, why have You *forsaken* Me?"

Allow me a few moments to review, so as to establish the setting for this epochal gush of emotion.

Jesus had passed responsibility for His mother to His close disciple, John. Now, He remained suspended between earth and sky, barely clinging to life. He was still pushing Himself up against the raw wooden beam, so as to continue breathing, and then slumping back down, hanging from the iron nails in His hands. Up and down . . . up and down. The pain must have been maddening by now.

At first glance, the casual reader of the crucifixion narrative might think that the events on Golgotha lasted no more than an hour . . . perhaps less. Closer examination of the gospel writers' detailed telling, however, reveals that Jesus' death took no less than six hours. His hands and feet were nailed to the wooden beams at nine o'clock in the morning. Sometime during the next three hours He uttered His first three statements: "Father, forgive them, for they do not know what they are doing"; "Today you shall be with Me in Paradise"; "Woman, behold, your son!" Then, at about noon, "darkness fell over the whole land" (Mark 15:33). Darkness dropped like a thick, wet blanket. An eerie silence now surrounded the Place of the Skull.

Historians tell us that it was not uncommon for a man being crucified to curse and rail profanely, as though only foul language was an adequate expression of the foulest of deaths. But, as we have already noted, this was not Jesus' response. Peter, an eyewitness to the crucifixion, tells us that "Christ also suffered for you, leaving you an example for you to follow in His steps, WHO COMMITTED NO SIN, NOR WAS ANY DECEIT FOUND IN HIS MOUTH; and while being reviled, He did not revile in return; while suffering, He uttered no threats, but kept entrusting Himself to Him who judges righteously" (1 Peter 2:21–23).

Jesus did not curse His executioners. He did, however, make seven powerful statements. We have examined three of those "words from the cross." The fourth statement is the most anguishing of all. Appropriately, it has been called the most staggering sentence in the gospel record.

Nature bowed in sympathy as its Creator was put to death. It was as though the light dimmed across the universe as the darkness of death descended upon the earth. How strange it must have seemed to those who stood and stared. From noon until three in the afternoon two things were present: darkness and silence.

Picture it. Right where you're sitting at this moment. Darkness at noonday, and a descending silence. Some of the crowd, at least the curious, have probably left by now; they've seen who the malefactors are, which is all they really wanted to know. Others, frightened by the sudden and unusual darkness, have fled for home. Those who remain murmur and rustle a bit, but, for the most part, watch quietly.

Then, suddenly, out of the depths of that darkness comes the anguished voice of the abandoned Son of God. Listen closely . . . you will hear it again.

> "ELI, ELI, LAMA SABACHTHANI?" that is, "MY GOD, MY GOD, WHY HAST THOU FORSAKEN ME?"
>
> —MATTHEW 27:45–46

THE NEVER-TO-BE-FORGOTTEN SCREAM

What first catches my eye is the intensity with which Jesus made this fourth statement from the cross: "Jesus cried out with a loud voice." The translation "cried out" comes from a combination of two words: one means "to shout," and it is prefixed with the word "up"—"to shout/scream up." In the Scriptures this combination of words is occasionally used for a guttural scream, perhaps more like a deep roar, or a passionate groan.

Notice how Psalm 22, one of the most eloquent and descriptive of all the messianic psalms, uses this word.

> My God, my God, why hast Thou forsaken me?
> Far from my deliverance are the words of my *groaning*.
> O my God, I cry by day, but Thou dost not answer;
> And by night, but I have no rest.
>
> —PSALM 22:1–2, italics added

A messianic psalm is a psalm that looks forward to or anticipates the arrival, the life and/or death of the promised Messiah. Many of the psalms are messianic in nature, but Psalm 22 offers the most vivid account of Jesus' death, centuries before He went to the cross.

> I am poured out like water,
>   And all my bones are out of joint;
>   My heart is like wax;
>   It is melted within me.
>
> My strength is dried up like a potsherd,
>   And my tongue cleaves to my jaws;
>   And Thou dost lay me in the dust of death.
>
> For dogs have surrounded me;
>   A band of evildoers has encompassed me;
>   They pierced my hands and my feet.
>
> I can count all my bones.
>   They look, they stare at me;
> They divide my garments among them,
>   And for my clothing they cast lots.
>
> —PSALM 22:14–18

In the opening line of the psalm we find David prophetically penning the same words the Savior later groaned from the cross: *"My God, my God, why hast Thou forsaken me?* Far from my deliverance are the words of my groaning." A literal rendering of the word *groaning* would be "roaring," not unlike the deep, guttural roaring of a lion.

Job uses the same expression in his anguish to describe the indescribable agony of his own soul: "For my groaning comes at the sight of my food, and my cries pour out like water" (Job 3:24).

That's the word Matthew uses to describe Jesus' sudden, anguished cry. Pause long enough to imagine the sound.

The second thing that catches my eye is that this statement from the cross is first quoted exactly as Jesus said it in Aramaic: "ELI, ELI, LAMA SABACHTHANI?" Why has the Holy Spirit, through the centuries, preserved Jesus' original language here?

We cannot say for sure, but I suggest that it may be because the Savior's birth language captures our attention and comes closest to representing the deepest sense of Jesus' anguish of soul.

One Thanksgiving in the early 1960s when I was in seminary, my wife and I, along with another couple, invited the dozen or more Korean students who were then studying at Dallas Seminary to share the holiday with us. All of these men were married and were pursuing their degrees separated from their families while here in the States.

We had two big turkeys and all the traditional Thanksgiving trimmings. And as we gathered around the table, I asked the men if they would sing their national anthem. They did, and several of them had tears in their eyes by the time they finished. Then I asked one of them to lead in prayer before our meal together. They had, of course, sung their national anthem in Korean, but I thought the man who prayed would pray in English. Instead, appropriately, he prayed in his native tongue.

And you know what? I did not understand the words he said, but I did understand *what* he said. I felt deeply his loneliness and pain of lengthy separation, the absence of his wife and children, in that prayer. I could feel his love for his homeland, his love for family, and his love for God, even though I understood not one word of his birth language. His fellow students, who spoke the same language, "groaned and sighed" in agreement. And somehow those of us who didn't speak that language also comprehended a depth of feeling that another language, foreign to them but familiar to us, would not have conveyed.

God has preserved for us Jesus' words in His mother tongue, exactly as He said it. As we read those words, with feeling, it gives us a sense, even a better understanding, of the isolation of His soul.

The third thing that captures my attention in this statement is the estrangement between the Son and the Father.

Notice the way He addresses the Lord: "My God, my God." Jesus addresses the Father three times in His seven statements from the cross. In two of those statements Jesus calls Him "Father." But not in this statement. Here, alone, Jesus calls Him "God." It's as though you were to walk up to your father and address him as "Mister" rather than "Dad" or "Daddy." There is a distance, even alienation, here. Jesus, a member of the Godhead, addresses the Father as though He is removed from Him, *indeed He is!* He cries out, "My God!" and then, literally, "Why *Me* have You forsaken?"

Jesus had never known a time when He was not the Father's delight (see Proverbs 8:22–31). The Son had never known a time of broken fellowship with the Father. But now, for the first time in all of time, He experiences it.

Notice also the alienation that is conveyed by the word "forsaken": "MY GOD, MY GOD, WHY HAST THOU FORSAKEN ME?" The apostle Paul uses the same word when he refers to Demas, a fellow worker who had deserted him: "for Demas, having loved this present world, has deserted me and gone to Thessalonica" (2 Timothy 4:10). "Demas has deserted me," Paul writes. "He has forsaken me. He has abandoned me." It conveys the same feeling the prisoner had in mind when he wrote me: completely abandoned!

Of course, the question calls for an answer: Why *did* the Father forsake Him? Have you ever wondered that? If ever the Son needed the Father, He needed Him then. Why wasn't He there?

A single statement Paul wrote years later answers the question for us.

> He [God the Father] made Him [God the Son] who knew no sin to be sin on our behalf, that we might become the righteousness of God in Him.
>
> —2 CORINTHIANS 5:21

Learn a vital theological lesson here. God the Father made God the Son, Who was sinless, to be sin on our behalf. At this moment on the cross, God the Father poured on Christ all of the sins of mankind, from the beginning of time to the ending of time. Jesus Christ, who came to earth in human flesh and lived a totally sinless life, suddenly in this moment of time became sin for us. This explains why the fellowship between God the Father and God the Son was broken, leaving Jesus alienated, abandoned, forsaken, dying alone on the cross.

God is *holy;* we are told this over and over again throughout the Scriptures. And *holy* means "separate from sin." It means "absolutely pure." Thus, when the Lord Jesus Christ took our sin on Himself, when the Father laid on the Son "the iniquity of us all," the holy Father could not fellowship with Him. The crushing weight of mankind's sin was borne all alone by Christ, separated from the presence of the Father.

THE NEVER-TO-BE-FORGOTTEN DIFFERENCE

It makes all the difference in the world that Christ bore our sins and was forsaken by the Father, because that was the turning point in our union with Him. Because Christ took our sin upon Himself, paying the penalty for it in full, we no longer dread facing that penalty. In addition, now that He has opened the possibility of instant access to the Father, we can have a relationship that was once impossible.

> By this will we have been sanctified through the offering of the body of Jesus Christ once for all.
>
> And every priest stands daily ministering and offering time after time the same sacrifices, which can never take away sins; but He, having offered one sacrifice for sins for all time, SAT DOWN AT

THE RIGHT HAND OF GOD, waiting from that time onward UNTIL HIS ENEMIES BE MADE A FOOTSTOOL FOR HIS FEET.

—HEBREWS 10:10–13

Christ offered Himself as a sacrifice for our sins, once for all. Never again would the priests have to make sacrifices in the Temple; never again would blood have to be shed for the forgiveness of sins. Christ was God's one, final, acceptable sacrifice. Mission accomplished! Having made that sacrifice, Christ satisfied the Father's demand on sin and opened the way for us to know God intimately. His being "forsaken" by God meant we would now be accepted by God. Grace!

God the Father forsook His Son then, so that He might never have to forsake us now. That, in one sentence, is the answer to the question, "My God, My God, why have You forsaken Me?" God the Father forsook His Son once for all that He might *never* have to forsake His adopted sons and daughters now or evermore. "For He Himself has said, "I WILL NEVER DESERT YOU, NOR WILL I EVER FORSAKE YOU" (Hebrews 13:5b).

Many stories came out of World War II, but one of the most unforgettable is the story of a little lad in the streets of London. German bombs had destroyed his home and killed his family. Orphaned, he wandered through the rubble and destruction of war. This ragged little fellow walked up to the window of a small bakery that was still in business. Drawn by the warm, yeasty smells, he tried to look through the window, but the glass was covered with frost. The boy wiped off a small circle so he could peer inside. It looked as good as it smelled! He pressed his nose against the window and gazed hungrily, longingly at the small display of baked goods displayed there.

A soldier passing by noticed the lad and stepped up beside him. "Would you like to have one of those?"

The little boy nodded his head. So the soldier went inside and bought six freshly baked donuts, then handed the bag to the little boy.

As the lad clutched the warm bag close to his chest, he looked up at the soldier and asked, "Mister, are you God?"

We wander amid the rubble and destruction of a fallen world, standing outside the window, separated from a Holy God and His eternal life. But because the Son of God went inside—as the high priest once went inside the Holy of Holies on the Day of Atonement—and did business once and for all with the Father, who demanded death as the only payment for sin, we can stand before Him and say, "You *are* God." Because of what the Lord Jesus did on our behalf, we recognize Him as our Savior. And when we do, we can feast on what He provides both now and forever.

In addition to all that, we have the unconditional promise: He will never, ever forsake us.

"I Am Thirsty"

Jesus, in thy thirst and pain,
While thy wounds thy life-blood drain,
Thirsting more our love to gain:
Hear us, holy Jesus.

Thirst for us in mercy still;
All thy holy work fulfil;
Satisfy thy loving will:
Hear us, holy Jesus.

May we thirst thy love to know;
Lead us in our sin and woe
Where the healing waters flow:
Hear us, holy Jesus.[1]

—T. B. POLLOCK, 1870

13

"I Am Thirsty"

Maybe it's time for a brief reality check. Our journey with Jesus through the darkness of His passion is neither pleasant nor easy. It wasn't meant to be. This is not virtual reality where everything is based on fantasy and electronically wired into a video game. In this story the people are actual and the pain is real. The plot is not imaginary, and the final results are not temporary.

We're dealing here with a mixture of vital things that make a difference. Taken seriously, they can transform your thinking and they can, in fact, alter your destiny. This is no fun ride entered into with a joystick, designed to entertain and make us smile. The blood is genuine, not artificial; the cross is real wood, not Styrofoam; and the words were literally spoken, not sounds produced by high-tech gear.

And don't be turned off by the time factor. Just because all this happened almost two millennia ago doesn't mean it's irrelevant, dinosaur-like. What occurred back then impacts right now. If that weren't true, believe me, I wouldn't waste your time or mine.

All that to say, it's time to start thinking at a deeper level. Dumbing down solid truth won't cut it on subjects like these. Now, there's no reason for me to bore you with uninteresting theological trivia either. But coming to terms with stuff that matters requires that we concentrate, and I really mean focus. Otherwise, the journey from the darkness to the dawn erodes into a drift that leads nowhere. So let's agree, we're going somewhere with all this. If you stay with me a little while longer, we'll see the purpose of all the sad darkness as it takes us into the bright light of dawn. I promise I'll do my best to keep the theology of all this interesting.

Author Philip Yancey states it well:

> Books of theology tend to use inert words—omniscient, impassible, imperturbable—to describe God's personality, but the Bible tells of a God who is anything but inert. This God enters history, sides with the underdog, argues with people (sometimes letting them win), and may either exert or consciously curb his power. In the Bible life with God reads more like a mystery story, or a romance, than a theology text. What I find in its pages differs markedly from what I expect, and what most people expect, in getting to know God.[2]

He's right. And there's nothing like an author who dulls the edge of this "mystery story" to make folks think it's an uninteresting hodge-podge of unimportant verbiage. (I'm trying hard not to fall into that category!)

So, with all that in mind, let's step back into the darkness in order to grasp an even better understanding of this Person hanging on a cross.

Conservative theologians have a way of describing the person of Christ: the *Theanthropic* Person. This title comes from two Greek words: *theos,* meaning "God," and *anthropos,* meaning "man." Put them together and you have chosen the best title for Jesus Christ: the God-Man. We who love the Lord have no difficulty in believing that before Christ became a baby in the manger, He existed with the Father in eternity past. In fact, there never was a time that He did not exist. The problem comes, however, when He became a man and lived on this earth for thirty-three years, during which time He was engaged in

His earthly ministry. What about those earthly years? Some people have a great deal of difficulty understanding how two natures can dwell in one person, as they did in the Lord Jesus. If He was a man, how could He also be God? Philippians 2 describes the problem:

> Have this attitude in yourselves which was also in Christ Jesus, who, although He existed in the form of God, did not regard equality with God a thing to be grasped, but emptied Himself, taking the form of a bond-servant, and being made in the likeness of men. And being found in appearance as a man, He humbled Himself by becoming obedient to the point of death, even death on a cross.
>
> —PHILIPPIANS 2:5–8

What does it mean that He "emptied Himself"? How can we describe the God-Man as still being God if He "emptied Himself"? How can we really believe He was both God and man in one person since the Scripture says He "emptied Himself"? This is one of the real problems in believing and defending our faith in the Theanthropic Person, Christ Jesus.

The Scripture teaches that even though Jesus did become a man, He never was anything less than God. Yet for a period of thirty-three earthly years He voluntarily gave up the independent exercise of His own rights as God. While on earth He submitted Himself to the Father, so that every word was spoken as God would have Him speak it, and every act was done precisely as God would have Him do it.

For example, as a human being, He was tired and fell asleep in the hold of a ship, but moments later, as God, He was able to still the sea and calm the wind. As a man, He was broken-hearted and wept at the tomb of Lazarus, but as God, He raised Lazarus from the dead. As a man, He suffered a horrible death on the cross, but as God, He was bodily and victoriously raised from the dead.

A GRIM GLIMPSE OF HUMANITY

> After this, Jesus, knowing that all things had already been accomplished, in order that the Scripture might be fulfilled, said, "I am thirsty."
>
> —JOHN 19:28

In reading John's account, we're faced with an undeniable example of our Lord's humanity. Being truly human, existing in bodily form, the God-Man experienced a common bodily need: He became thirsty.

Christ has been hanging on the cross since nine o' clock in the morning; it is now approaching three o' clock in the afternoon. He has been suffering the agony of crucifixion for nearly six hours. Prior to that He prayed in the Garden and then was arrested. Then He was pushed through six trials and was finally scourged. For most of those agonizing hours He has been silent, uttering only four brief statements from His cross, which we have already examined. Now, out of the darkness, He utters a fifth, very human, statement revealing an intensifying of His physical suffering: "I am thirsty."

In writing His gospel under the direction of the Holy Spirit, John prefaces Jesus' statement with these words: "Jesus, knowing that all things had already been accomplished. . . ." Here, the word "knowing" does not mean to know by experience or to come to know something, as in becoming acquainted with a person; rather, it means to know intuitively, innately—to have the facts already logged within one's memory and then to call them to mind.

To me, that is another example of the deity of Christ. In His mind were all the Scriptures, because even though He was man, remember, He was also God. Therefore, as He hung on the cross, reviewing the covenants of God, and one prophecy after another, after another, He "knew" they had all been fulfilled up to that point in time. "All things had already been accomplished."

Over twenty Scriptures from the Old Testament were fulfilled in the last twenty-four hours of Jesus' life on earth. Among them . . .

Sold for thirty pieces of silver. Fulfilled.
Betrayed by a friend. Fulfilled.
Deserted and denied by His disciples. Fulfilled.
Accused by false witnesses. Fulfilled.
Humiliated, wounded, and bruised. Fulfilled.
Stood silent before His accusers. Fulfilled.
His hands and feet pierced. Fulfilled.
And on and on. . . .

In fact, my friend Max Lucado calls our attention to this remarkable observation about Jesus' life in his book, *He Chose the Nails:*

> Did you know that in his life Christ fulfilled 332 distinct prophecies in the Old Testament? What are the mathematical possibilities of all these prophecies being fulfilled in the life of one man?

$$\frac{1}{\begin{array}{c}840,000,000,000,000,000,000,000\\000,000,000,000,000,000,000,000\\000,000,000,000,000,000,000,000\\000,000,000,000,000,000\end{array}}$$

> (That's ninety-seven zeroes!) Amazing![3]

Knowing all these things, Jesus also realizes that it is almost time to complete the final sacrifice. So in order that the Scripture might be fulfilled, He said, "I am thirsty."

Thirst was a major part of the terrible, torturing death by crucifixion. The mouths and throats of all victims hanging on crosses cried for water. The lips cracked and bled as the eyes glazed. The tongues swelled in the mouths and saliva hung like drying glue in the throats.

Thirst is a terrible thing. We can survive much longer without food than without water. And as He hung on the cross, dying, the Son of God, fully human, knew every agony the human body can experience.

When "Jesus, knowing that all things had already been accomplished, in order that the Scripture might be fulfilled," He certainly would have had in mind the passage in Psalm 69:

> Reproach has broken my heart, and I am so sick.
> And I looked for sympathy, but there was none,
> And for comforters, but I found none.
> They also gave me gall for my food,
> And for my thirst they gave me vinegar to drink.
>
> —PSALM 69:20–21

If I may get a little technical with you, when the God-Man, the Theanthropic Person of Christ, says, "I am thirsty," you understand, it is not deity that's thirsty; it's humanity. His body cried out for water, as ours would. The psalmist pens it poignantly: "I am so sick. I looked for sympathy, but there was none. I found no one to comfort me. And when I was thirsty, they gave me vinegar to drink."

This is one of those passages we call messianic, where the psalmist not only describes his own need and hunger, his own thirst and pain, but in so doing also foretells the Savior's need and hunger, thirst and pain. His words provide an accurate, vivid description of Christ at Calvary.

Psalm 69:21 says, "They also gave me *gall* for my food, and for my thirst they gave me *vinegar* to drink."

Matthew 27:48 says, "And immediately one of them ran, and taking a sponge, he filled it with sour wine, and put it on a reed, and gave Him a drink." John 19:29 says, "A jar full of sour wine was standing there; so they put a sponge full of the sour wine upon a branch of hyssop, and brought it up to His mouth."

Now, I want you to notice what it says earlier, in Matthew 27:33–34: "And when they had come to a place called Golgotha, which means Place of a Skull, they gave Him wine to drink mingled with gall; and after tasting it, He was unwilling to drink."

Twice they offered Christ something to drink: The first time it was "wine . . . mingled with gall"; the second time it was "sour wine" or vinegar.

Before Christ was nailed to the cross, He was offered wine mingled with gall. This mixture of wine and gall had a narcotic effect, somewhat dulling the pain. Apparently wine made the bitterness of the gall palatable. They offered Jesus that which would drug Him and take away the raw edge of the pain before they pounded the nails through His hands and feet. But as soon as He tasted it and realized what it contained, Jesus refused to drink it.

The second drink they offered was in response to His statement, "I am thirsty." This time they give Him "sour wine," which the Old Testament called vinegar. This was the cheapest drink available at that time, a common beverage of the soldiers. It was a cheap alcoholic drink, as common as water in our day. A jar of it sat at the crucifixion site, no doubt for two purposes: for the thirsty soldiers and the victims. One of the cruel purposes of crucifixion was a prolonged death, so the offer of sour wine was a sadistic move that might enable the victims to linger even longer in their misery.

When they dipped the sponge in the sour wine and lifted it to Jesus' mouth at the end of "a branch of hyssop," He took a sip of the liquid to find a moment of relief from the burning thirst.

Jesus was ready to die. He knew that "all things had already been accomplished, in order that the Scripture might be fulfilled," surrounding His sacrifice as the perfect Lamb of God. So why would He do anything that would prolong His life?

When He said, "I am thirsty," He was at the end of His life. I believe that Jesus requested and took that drink because He had two more things to say and would have been unable to do that without moistening His throat.

Three Observations with Practical Overtones

I see three practical lessons in this brief passage of Scripture.

First, *I see humanity: Here we witness a very human, suffering Savior.* Realizing that my Savior was genuinely human strengthens my faith. It brings home to me the reality of that verse in Hebrews: "For we do not have a high priest who cannot sympathize with our weaknesses, but One who has been tempted in all things as we are, yet without sin" (Hebrews 4:15). When I go through earthly trials, He fully understands, because He was absolutely and authentically human.

Christ could not be our high priest if He had not been genuinely human. To be our great High Priest, Christ had to be unique: He had to represent both God and man. He had to be the God-Man—undiminished deity and genuine humanity in one person. And those aren't simply "inert words . . . to describe God's personality." That's a wonderful truth. When you go to your Savior in prayer, laying your petitions before Him, you go to One whose heart beats with yours, because He has known pain and discomfort, He has been thirsty, He has been reproached and offended, He has been hated and ignored and rejected.

When Jesus says, "I am thirsty," we have a reminder of reality. He was altogether human. Therefore, He has room in His compassion for very human needs.

Second, *I see a paradox: Jesus began His ministry hungry and ended His ministry thirsty.* When Jesus went into the wilderness, after His baptism by John, He fasted for forty days and was tempted by Satan. At the end of those forty days, God the Father came and ministered to His Son in the presence of angels. Christ began His ministry hungry; He ended His life thirsty.

Merrill Tenney writes, "Paradoxically enough, He who had offered to all men the water of life … died thirsting."[4]

Third, *I see unselfishness: Perhaps the most wonderful truth in this passage is the unselfishness of our Savior.*

After this, Jesus, knowing that all things had already been accomplished, in order that the Scripture might be fulfilled, said, "I am thirsty."

Jesus waits until "after this," until "all things had been accomplished" so that Scripture "might be fulfilled," to say "I am thirsty" when, in fact, He had been thirsty from the beginning. The trials and crucifixion together have lasted more than twelve hours. Jesus has been scourged, buffeted, beaten, spit upon, mocked, humiliated, stripped naked, and nailed to a cross. Throughout all this, no one has offered Him one moment of rest or relief, not one ounce of food or one drop to drink. Yet not until the very end of this ordeal, the very end of His life, does He ask for even the smallest physical comfort. Throughout His life, our Savior thinks only of others and the fulfillment of Scripture.

If we are to be like Him, as His true followers, it is to this kind of unselfishness we are called.

Many years ago my good friend with the Navigators, Dennis Repko, worked in the Middle East with a small group of Lebanese men who were interested in the things of God and especially in maturing in their walk with Christ. During their time together, Denny decided that they needed to do more than just sit around and study the Bible. They needed to be involved together in some life experiences that might bring to the surface any particular areas of weakness in which they would need to mature. A friend of one of the members of the group needed a wall built around his home, so the group undertook the project of building that wall.

"It's an amazing thing how well these fellows did until they got thirsty and tired," Denny told me sometime later, when he recounted the lessons he had learned, "These guys, who thought they were maturing so quickly in the Christian life, became irritable, demanding, and impatient. Why? Hunger and thirst can be very revealing. That's when the real person comes out."

This is the remarkable thing about the death of Christ. He "suffered for you, leaving you an example for you to follow in His steps, Who committed no sin, nor was any deceit found in His mouth; and while being reviled, He did not revile in return; while suffering, He uttered no threats, but kept entrusting Himself to Him who judges righteously" (1 Peter 2:21–23).

The words, "I am thirsty" reveal both God and man. "I am"—the same words the Lord gave Moses when He said, "Tell them I am sent you. I am that I am, the Eternal Son of God sent you." The same words Jesus used when He told the Pharisees, "Before Abraham was, I am." He says, "I am" . . . That's Deity! And then He says . . . "thirsty." And that's Humanity.

Our Savior is the God-Man. Not just God and not just man, but the Theanthropic Person, our priest and our wonderful Lord and Savior.

Do you have a long way to go in your patience, in your grace, in your long-suffering? Do you become irritable when discomforts or deprivations—great or small—emerge? Does a loss of "my rights" become a galling irritation to you? Perhaps your discomfort is the stress of a responsible job or the never-ending demands of a growing family. Maybe your burden is aging and ailing parents, or your own failing health. Perhaps you have begun to drink the bitter gall of suffering.

I understand. Believe me, I too struggle in some of those very same areas. When we do, it's easy to think, "Nobody really understands how difficult these days are for me." It's also easy to forget that because our Lord was fully human, He really does! In fact He "sympathizes with our weaknesses" (Hebrews 4:15). Yet, at the same time, He models enormous unselfishness.

Our Savior thought of Himself last. Not until death was almost upon Him, not until His work was nearly completed, did He even mention His own thirst.

The Savior suffered and died so that we might be reconciled to God. And then we're able to claim "the power of His resurrection" because of "the fellowship of His sufferings." Pause and reflect on those contrasting thoughts: suffering, which makes possible a fellowship with Him we could not otherwise know, and resurrection, which produces a power from Him we would not otherwise have.

Because He became truly human, we're able to connect with Him in ways that could not and would not have happened. How very grateful we are for the reminder that He, like we, experienced pain and heartache . . . that He, like we, felt the sting of insults and loneliness . . . that He, like we, got hungry and thirsty. Before we know it, we're going to find ourselves running toward words like Theanthropic Person, instead of running from them.

And that's exactly what He wants us to do.

But let's not forget—He's both Man *and* God.

Many years ago I learned a poem, which I love to quote around Christmas each year. I've found that it helps everyone see what a great paradox He was—how deity and humanity resided in this One we call Jesus:

The Maker of the universe
As man for man was made a curse;
The claims of laws which He had made
Unto the uttermost He paid.
His holy fingers made the bough
Where grew the thorns that crowned His brow;
The nails that pierced His hands were mined
In secret places He designed.

He made the forests whence there sprung
The tree on which His body hung;
He died upon a cross of wood,
Yet made the hill on which it stood!
The sky which darkened o'er His head
By Him above the earth was spread;
The sun which hid from Him its face
By His decree was poised in space!

The spear which spilt His precious blood
Was tempered in the fires of God;
The grave in which His form was laid
Was hewed in rocks His hands had made!
The throne on which He now appears
Was His from everlasting years!
But a new glory crowns His brow
And every knee to Him shall bow![5]

"It Is Finished!"

"Man of Sorrows!" what a name
For the Son of God, who came
Ruined sinners to reclaim!
Hallelujah, what a Savior!

Lifted up was He to die,
"It is finished!" was His cry;
Now in heav'n exalted high:
Hallelujah, what a Savior![1]

—PHILIP P. BLISS, 1838–1876

14
"It Is Finished!"

*I*t's over. Those words occupy a special place in my heart as a pastor. I have heard that two-word comment, usually by phone, on many occasions for the past forty years. Almost without exception the voice of the caller carries a blend of exhaustion and relief. In virtually every case, there has been a longstanding illness, a dread disease that has lingered, slowly taking its toll on the person's loved one. But now the end has come. Death has won the long, hard-fought battle. Thankfully, the pain is gone and peace has returned to the face of the sufferer.

Those who remain have a whole new group of emotions to handle, but at least the long-awaited relief has arrived, because "it's over." The battle has ended. The bottles of medicine are no longer needed. It is finished. There is finality—a quiet resignation in those few words.

Interestingly, I've never heard the dying use those words, only those who have spent time near the dying, watching over them, ministering to them. Perhaps that is one of the reasons Jesus' words, "It is finished," stay so firmly in our minds. They came from His lips, carried on some of the final gasps of air from His lungs.

But let's understand, Jesus' sixth statement on the cross was not a cry of anguish; it was a declaration of victory. He had reached the goal and was able to say, "It is finished. Mission accomplished. It's over."

As we read through the Gospel of John, we pick up the thread of that goal, time and again:

> Jesus said to them, "My food is to do the will of Him who sent Me, and to accomplish His work."
>
> —JOHN 4:34

> "But the witness which I have is greater than that of John; for the works which the Father has given Me to accomplish, the very works that I do, bear witness of Me, that the Father has sent Me."
>
> —JOHN 5:36

The Father had given Jesus "works . . . to accomplish." He came to earth with a goal, a purpose, a destiny.

Accomplish means "to bring to an end, to complete, to finish." Jesus' entire life was devoted to accomplishing the Father's will. "My very food," Jesus said, "is to finish the Father's work." Everything He did, He did toward that end: "The very works that I do, bear witness of Me."

> "I glorified Thee on the earth, having accomplished the work which Thou hast given Me to do."
>
> —JOHN 17:4

By John 17, the verb tense has changed. Jesus says, "I have accomplished the work. I've completed the task." At this moment Jesus has completed His work, except for the culminating act—His death.

THE SOVEREIGN WILL OF GOD

After this, Jesus, knowing that all things had already been accomplished, in order that the Scripture might be fulfilled, said, "I am thirsty."

A jar full of sour wine was standing there; so they put a sponge full of the sour wine upon a branch of hyssop, and brought it up to His mouth.

> When Jesus therefore had received the sour wine, He said, "It is finished!" And He bowed His head, and gave up His spirit.
>
> —JOHN 19:28–30

Both "finished" and "accomplished" are from the same Greek verb *teleo,* which means "to bring to an end." Jesus' statement on the cross, rendered *tetelestai* in John 19:30, could be translated, "It has been completed." Papyri receipts for taxes have been recovered with this same Greek word, *telestai* written across them, which meant "paid in full."[2]

But the question is: What is finished? To what does "it" refer? In Hebrews 10, the Lord describes His goal.

> For it is impossible for the blood of bulls and goats to take away sins. Therefore, when He comes into the world, He says, SACRIFICE AND OFFERING THOU HAST NOT DESIRED, BUT A BODY THOU HAST PREPARED FOR ME; IN WHOLE BURNT OFFERINGS AND SACRIFICES FOR SIN THOU HAST TAKEN NO PLEASURE.
>
> THEN I SAID, "BEHOLD, I HAVE COME (IN THE ROLL OF THE BOOK IT IS WRITTEN OF ME) TO DO THY WILL, O GOD."
>
> —HEBREWS 10:4–7

Make no mistake about it. Jesus' coming to this planet was no random afterthought on God's part. And what He did once He arrived was never a casual matter. His mission was clear: to do the Father's will. Nothing more. Nothing less. Nothing else.

When He was hanging on the cross and said, "It is complete," He meant He had completed the will of God for His earthly sojourn. More specifically, the will of God in this regard had to be satisfied or "finished" in four areas: the atonement, the Scriptures, the Law, and the devil. And I believe with all my heart that all four things were uppermost in Jesus' mind when He said, "It is finished!"

THE ATONEMENT

Hebrews 10:5 says, "A body Thou hast prepared for Me." God gave the Savior a body. In that body God pitched His tent on earth for thirty-three years, and in that body God found satisfaction for sin. We sometimes refer to this as the "substitutionary atonement of Christ."

Substitutionary obviously comes from the word "substitute." When something or someone is a substitute, that person or thing takes the place of someone or something else. Atonement means "to cover over." So when we speak of the substitutionary atonement, we mean that Jesus' death at Calvary was a complete covering over of sin on our behalf. He died in our place, on our behalf. In His death He covered over our sin.

> And He died for all, that they who live should no longer live for themselves, but for Him who died and rose again on their behalf. He made Him who knew no sin to be sin on our behalf, that we might become the righteousness of God in Him.
>
> —2 CORINTHIANS 5:15,21

He died as our substitute and rose again in our place—on our behalf. The Law said that where there was sin, there must be death. Their own sin drove Adam and Eve from the Garden of Eden, and that original sin became a curse upon them and all mankind. After that, only the blood of animal sacrifices could atone for the sins of the people. But those animal sacrifices could never permanently remove sin. Only the perfect sacrifice—God's only Son—could do that.

When Jesus hung on the cross, He took all the sins of all the people of all time upon Himself. On our behalf, in His human body prepared by the Father, Jesus bore the curse of sin. In that bruised and beaten body our sins were atoned or covered over. When the Savior died at Calvary, He died in your place, in my place. It was effective because He was the perfect sacrifice; therefore, the Father was satisfied in every way.

How do we know that Christ's atonement satisfied God the Father and fully covered mankind's sin? First of all, the veil of the Temple was torn in two.

> And it was now about the sixth hour, and darkness fell over the whole land until the ninth hour, the sun being obscured; and the veil of the temple was torn in two.
>
> —LUKE 23:44–45

The veil of the temple separated the Holy Place from the Most Holy Place, where the presence of God resided. Only the High Priest could enter that small, ultra-sacred room once a year, on the Day of Atonement. But when the veil was split, there was no longer a wall of partition between man and God.

> But when Christ appeared as a high priest of the good things to come, He entered through the greater and more perfect tabernacle, not made with hands, that is to say, not of this creation; and not through the blood of goats and calves, but through His own blood, He entered the holy place once for all, having obtained eternal redemption.
>
> For if the blood of goats and bulls and the ashes of a heifer sprinkling those who have been defiled, sanctify for the cleansing of the flesh, how much more will the blood of Christ, who through the eternal Spirit offered Himself without blemish to God, cleanse your conscience from dead works to serve the living God?
>
> HEBREWS 9:11–14

Second, we know that Christ's death completed the work of atonement because God raised Jesus from the dead. If He had not been satisfied in the death of His Son, the Son would have remained a lifeless corpse in the tomb. When the Father raised the Son, it represented His "stamp of approval" on the whole transaction.

And finally, when the Savior went back to heaven at the Ascension, the Lord seated Him at His own right hand. Had the Father not been satisfied, He would never have welcomed Him back. But in that marvelous epochal moment, the Father said, in effect, "I am satisfied with Your sacrifice." He then sent the Holy Spirit to begin His remarkable work in the church. Jesus had promised His disciples, "When I return to My Father, I will send the Spirit to you," and so the Spirit's arrival on earth was proof that He had entered heaven again.

Now this isn't just a theological truth. These are not inert words. This is a tremendously practical set of facts. As one poet has expressed it:

> Upon a Death I did not die,
> Upon a Life I did not live,
> Another's death—another's life
> I cast my whole eternity.[3]

The only way you are going to be able to enter heaven is upon the life and death of Another, namely, Jesus Christ.

Ian Thomas put it in another way: "The life that Jesus lived qualified Him for the death that He died, and the death that He died qualifies us for the life that He lived!" That's no tongue twister; that's a statement of grand and glorious theology.

When Jesus said, "It is finished," He meant that the sacrifice for sin—the atonement—was complete. Paid in full!

THE SCRIPTURES

God's will concerning the Scriptures was also complete.

> After this, Jesus, knowing that all things had already been accomplished, in order that the Scripture might be fulfilled, said, "I am thirsty."
>
> A jar full of sour wine was standing there; so they put a sponge full of the sour wine upon a branch of hyssop, and brought it up to His mouth.

> When Jesus therefore had received the sour wine, He said, "It
> is finished!" And He bowed His head, and gave up His spirit.
> —JOHN 19:28–30, italics added

The Old Testament frequently speaks of the promised Messiah, offering dozens of Scriptures related to His birth, His life, His death, and His resurrection. If you had been an ancient scholar of the Old Testament scrolls available in the first century A.D., and had examined them exhaustively, you would not have uncovered one prophecy of Messiah's death that had not been fulfilled. Once Jesus had been offered the sour wine, He knew that not one Scripture up to that point in time remained unfulfilled.

If Jesus was so careful to make sure that each passage, each minute prophecy concerning His death was fulfilled, then He is certainly going to keep His word today. He is trustworthy. He did not allow His spirit to depart from Him until every inerrant, inspired messianic Scripture was fulfilled, down to the last detail.

THE LAW

God's will was also completed concerning the Law, for the Law was fulfilled in Jesus' death.

> "Do not think that I came to abolish the Law or the Prophets; I
> did not come to abolish, but *to fulfill.*
> —MATTHEW 5:17, italics added

Jesus said He would fulfill the Law by obeying it perfectly and He would fulfill the prophets' predictions of the Messiah.

Now let me make something very clear. Nothing is wrong with the Law. The Law that God gave to His people, through His servant Moses, is holy and just and good. But there's a lot wrong with those who received the Law: humanity. Because all are born in sin, men and women can never keep the Law. The Law shows man his own sinfulness and need for the Lord. We can never attain to God's righteousness in any energy of the flesh, with the work of our own hands. Only through Jesus Christ can we be justified (declared righteous) before the Father, for only Jesus Christ lived a sinless life, a life of pure righteousness, fulfilling the smallest letter and stroke of the Law.

> Is the Law then contrary to the promises of God? May it never be! For if a law had been given which was able to impart life, then righteousness would indeed have been based on law.
>
> But the Scripture has shut up all men under sin, that the promise by faith in Jesus Christ might be given to those who believe.
>
> But before faith came, we were kept in custody under the Law, being shut up to the faith which was later to be revealed.
>
> Therefore the Law has become our tutor to lead us to Christ, that we may be justified by faith.
>
> —GALATIANS 3:21–24

"Before faith came," before we believed, we were in custody—we were held in bondage, in chains, under arrest. By what? By the Law.

Some will tell you that in order to please God you must keep the Law. Impossible. The words from Galatians tell us that we can't. The Law cannot produce righteousness—it was never meant to. Rather, it was designed to be a tutor to escort us to Christ.

A tutor, in the apostle Paul's day, was not someone who helped you learn math and Greek. A tutor was more like a nanny. Wealthy families would hire a tutor to escort their children to school, to discipline them and mentor them, helping them handle the basics of life. That's the role of the Law. The Law escorts us to Christ. And all along the way it tells us, "You cannot live the life. You cannot fulfill My righteous requirements. You cannot be as holy as God is. That's why I'm here, because I want you to meet One who can provide you with this righteousness." And who is that? Galatians 4:24 tells us: It is Christ.

> But when the fulness of the time came, God sent forth His Son, born of a woman, born under the Law, in order that He might redeem those who were under the Law, that we might receive the adoption as sons.
>
> GALATIANS 4:4–5

We could never, ever work our way into the family of God. But Christ came to lift the curse of the Law so that we might be adopted into His family.

It was this passage of Scripture, and related passages from the Book of Romans, which caused Martin Luther to realize where the teaching of the Roman Catholic Church fell short. For months this devout monk sought in vain to find relief. He tossed and turned on his bed and rolled on the floor in his little cubicle, crying out, "Oh, my sin! My sin! My sin!" At last, through his own careful study of the Scriptures, he realized that Christ had freed him from the curse of his own sin. And that realization changed his words to, "My Savior! My Savior! My Savior!" The Law makes us constantly aware of our sin, our wrongdoing, but the Savior, by faith, declares us righteous before God. Salvation comes to us by faith alone in Christ alone.

With the death of Christ, God's will concerning the atonement was finished, God's will concerning Scripture was finished, and God's will concerning the Law was finished. As a result, we have been escorted into a new way of life: the life of freedom in the Spirit, instead of the life of bondage under the Law.

The righteousness of the Law is fulfilled *in* us by the Spirit who is given to us. That "in" is a tiny but very important preposition. The righteousness of the Law in this age is fulfilled *in* us, not *by* us.

THE DEVIL

When Jesus said, "It is finished," He was also speaking of God's will concerning the devil. Jesus' "It is finished" once and for all sealed Satan's doom.

Since then the children share in flesh and blood, He Himself likewise also partook of the same, that through death He might render powerless him who had the power of death, that is, the devil; and might deliver those who through fear of death were subject to slavery all their lives.

—HEBREWS 2:14–15

What an important statement! The truth of that passage strengthens our spiritual foundation. "He Himself likewise also partook of the same"—that is, flesh and blood, Jesus' physical body—"that through death" (on the cross) "He" (Christ) "might render powerless him" (the devil).

Because of that, I shout, "Hallelujah!" Until the death of Christ, the devil strutted around like a peacock, proud of his grip on helpless and hopeless humanity. Then, through Christ's death at Calvary, the devil is "rendered powerless" as the death of Christ "delivers those who through fear of death were subject to slavery all their lives."

I love to compare the devil and his certain doom to playing chess with a real pro. If you know someone is a real pro at chess, take my advice: Don't waste your time playing against him. You can't win! Nobody knows this better than the devil. He's playing against a pro, and he knows it. He keeps making his moves, but he's already been defeated. So if you want to defeat the devil, you will not do it in the strength of the flesh; you'll do it in the power of the Lord Jesus Christ. His blood will overcome and render powerless the power of the devil.

"It is finished!" It's over! The atonement is complete. The Scriptures are fulfilled. The Law is abolished. The devil is defeated. He's still active, of course, but he knows that he is defeated and doomed.

The practical aspect of all this is very simple: There is nothing left to be finished by man. We can add nothing to the death of Christ. Remember His word *tetelestai*. It is finished.

IT IS FINISHED!

"Father, into Your Hands I Commit My Spirit"

Hail! Thou once-despised Jesus!
Hail, Thou Galilean King!
Thou didst suffer to release us;
Thou didst free salvation bring.

Hail, Thou universal Saviour,
Who hast borne our sin and shame,
By Whose merits we find favor!
Life is given through Thy name.

Paschal Lamb, by God appointed,
All our sins on Thee were laid;
By almighty love anointed,
Thou hast full atonement made.

Every sin may be forgiven
Through the virtue of Thy blood;
Open is the gate of heaven,
Peace is made 'twixt man and God.[1]

—AUTHOR UNKNOWN, circa 1757

15
"Father, into Your Hands I Commit My Spirit"

Christian parents often teach their children certain prayers to use on special occasions. As I was growing up, I learned a prayer to say before eating a meal:

> God, bless the food,
> And make our bodies strong and free,
> That we may use our health and strength
> In service, Lord, to Thee. Amen.

I must have said that prayer thousands of times when I was a child. To this day, those words are etched in the creases of my brain; I can still repeat them effortlessly.

Another prayer, far more familiar to most folks, accompanied me to bed at night when I was a child:

> Now I lay me down to sleep,
> I pray Thee, Lord, my soul to keep.
> If I should die before I wake,
> I pray, Thee, Lord, my soul to take. Amen.

Since earliest days faithful Jewish parents have taught their children prayers to repeat at certain times of the day. Often, these prayers come directly from the Book of Psalms. One such prayer is an evening prayer, lifted from a line out of Psalm 31: "Into Thy hand I commit my spirit" (v. 5a). As the trusting Jew rests his head on his pillow, that prayer is on his lips, commending himself into God's care during the night's sleep.

I wonder if Mary taught her son, Jesus, this very prayer when He was a young boy growing up? I would like to think so. Perhaps He had said it throughout His childhood and teenage years and could repeat it effortlessly. And so, naturally, those familiar words would be on His lips at this final hour of His life, and how appropriate the tender words were! The end had come. He had finished the mission He had been given.

> The cup of suffering which He had to drink to accomplish His work as Savior had been emptied; the penalty for the sins of the world had been paid; the God-forsakenness had ceased. In His soul there reigned a sweet calm. He is ready to yield up His spirit, and He knows God will receive it.[2]

Therefore, His final words are appropriate—not only because His work was done, but also because death must be given permission.

Make no mistake about this: Jesus was not murdered, nor did He die of exhaustion. He did not die involuntarily. He died because He deliberately chose to die. He, Himself, had said,

> I lay down My life that I may take it again. "No one has taken it away from Me, but I lay it down on My own initiative. I have authority to lay it down, and I have authority to take it up again. This commandment I received from My Father."
>
> —JOHN 10:17–18

It is the Lord of life who gives up His life. And in so doing, He commits Himself to the Father, calmly, quietly, confidently. In uttering the familiar words of this lovely Jewish prayer from the Psalms, He releases His spirit as He breathes His last. Mercifully, the excruciating pain will cease. Death will come as a welcome, invited guest.

SOMETHING ADDED . . . SOMETHING OMITTED

It is worth observing how Jesus quoted from the familiar psalm. He added something at the beginning, and He omitted something at the close. At the beginning He added, "Father." This does not appear in David's psalm. It could not have been. In Old Testament days individuals had not yet begun to address God as "Father." While He was called "the Father of the nation" as a whole, such familiarity or intimacy between man and God was foreign to ancient Hebrews.

No longer. This new relationship, which Christ introduced into the lives of the faithful, is embodied in the term "Father." By adding it as a prefix to His final utterance, Jesus gave the verse new depth, new color. This verbal intimacy is highlighted by the fact that, shortly before, He was groaning with enormous passion, "My God, My God!" No longer. Sin has been borne. The desperate loneliness brought on by the holy God's abandonment is over forever. He has turned back *toward* His dear Son. Hence, "Father" is now appropriate. The tender relationship He has always enjoyed has returned. Sin no longer blocks the path of intimacy.

The other change Jesus made was the omission of the second half of David's psalm. If you check the record, you'll find Psalm 31:5 states,

> Into Thy hand I commit my spirit;
> Thou hast ransomed me, O LORD, God of truth.

But when Jesus uttered His prayer, He did not include "Thou hast ransomed me, O LORD, God of truth." The reason is clear when we remember who is quoting the psalm. Jesus, the spotless Lamb, the God-Man, the sinless and sacrificial substitute had no need to be ransomed. The Redeemer need not be redeemed, and so, fittingly, He omitted the closing line in His prayer to the Father.

A QUESTION . . . AN ANSWER

This is a good place to ask: Do you remember another painful, dying moment recorded in Scripture when this prayer was used? Stop and think. If you cannot remember, turn to Acts 7 for the answer, found in the moving account of the first martyr recorded in the New Testament. His name was Stephen. After declaring his faith with confidence and courage, he pointed an accusing finger toward the Sanhedrin council (whom he called "stiff-necked and uncircumcised in heart and ears") and charged them with being guilty of receiving the Law but not keeping it. Incensed and out of control, they lunged at him, dragged him out of the city, and began stoning him.

Just before his death, Stephen "called upon the Lord and said, 'Lord Jesus, receive my spirit!'" (Acts 7:59). The martyr's fight for his faith had ended. Though vicious, cruel men with wicked hearts would finish off his life by hurling stones and crushing his skull, his mind was at rest. He would, in a matter of seconds, fall unconscious and shortly thereafter die, but his spirit would immediately be in the secure hands of his Lord and Master.

Ironically, the one who was standing there, looking on in hearty agreement at the stoning, was "a young man named Saul" (Acts 7:58)—none other than the man who was yet to be remarkably transformed at his own conversion, later called Paul the apostle. We can't help but wonder if Paul had Stephen on his mind when, years afterward, he wrote of death as being "absent from the body and . . . at home with the Lord" (2 Corinthians 5:8).

So it was with Stephen, the martyr, so it is now with Jesus, the Messiah, who has committed His spirit into the Father's hands.

YOUR HANDS . . . MY SPIRIT

During His thirty-three years on earth, Jesus' life has, in a sense, been in the hands of other human beings. His mother and Joseph held Him as a baby and as a boy. Aging Simeon took Him in his arms and blessed

Him when He was eight days old. The teachers at the temple must have placed their hands on Him as they conversed with Him, amazed at His understanding and His questions. John, who baptized Him, held Him close, as did His disciples on numerous occasions. And, as we have seen repeatedly, those who put Him on trial, scourged, mocked, and crucified Him, did so, as Peter later preached, with "the hands of godless men" (Acts 2:23).

Now, at long last, He would be back in the Father's hands. Interestingly, when Dr. Luke records Jesus' final words, the Greek term He uses for "commit" is the word that means, literally, "to place beside." It was commonly used for making a deposit. Thus, the term conveys a secure sense of trust . . . "I entrust My spirit."

The Father's hands were trustworthy. And what was it Jesus placed there? Not His body. That would remain on the cross a little while longer. It would be punctured by a soldier's spear, and would later be taken down, prepared for burial, and placed in a tomb. It was His spirit—the innermost, most sacred part of His being—that He placed in the Father's hands. As James Stalker describes it,

> In the language of Scripture it is distinguished even from the soul as the most lofty and exquisite part of the inner man. It is to the rest of our nature what the flower is to the plant or what the pearl is to the shell. It is that within us which is specially allied to God and eternity .... Jesus knew that He was launching out into eternity; and, plucking His spirit away from these hostile hands [referring to demonic forces] which were eager to seize it, He placed it in the hands of God. There it was safe. Strong and sure are the hands of the eternal.[3]

The darkness is almost over. The dawn will soon appear, as the tragic scenes surrounding the cross are swallowed up in the triumph of His resurrection!

THE ART OF DYING . . . THE SECRET OF LIVING

Two realms of application seem worthy of at least a brief comment. One has to do with how to die; the other with how to live.

First, our Lord has modeled the art of dying for all of us. Though mercilessly mistreated, tortured almost to the point of unconsciousness, He refused to retaliate in any way; though seared by pain from thorns thrust on His head and iron spikes nailed through His hands and feet, He remained emotionally under control. Though cursed and maligned, He never verbally defended Himself. By the time His young life ended, impaled on that rugged cross, His facial features were so swollen and His body so bruised, He scarcely bore the resemblance of a man.

And in spite of all that, in dying He recalled a childhood prayer learned at His mother's knee, and He spoke the words of Scripture with confidence and free of bitterness: "Father, into Your hands I commit my spirit."

What a model for us to follow as we breathe our last! Regardless of our lot—for sure, we all have our own tales of woe and sorrowful memories of offense and mistreatment—*this* is how to die. Is it any wonder that these same last words from our Savior's lips were the ones chosen by Polycarp, Jerome of Prague, Martin Luther, his dear friend Philip Melanchthon, and many others who have died in the Lord, whose lives were anything but pleasant and their treatment anything but fair?

Second, our Lord has modeled the secret of living.

Where could we point to identify any root of bitterness in Him, right up to the last? Not a shred of blame. Not a thought of retribution or a hint of revenge. Instead, He held lines of memorized Scripture in His heart and childhood prayers on His lips. The quiet depositing of His spirit into the tender hands of the Father. The deliberate living of His life with single-minded determination to accomplish His mission, then release His spirit.

I've concluded most of my chapters by addressing those of you who may not have yet come, by faith, to Christ. Here, however, I'd like to write a few words to you who know Him, you who say you believe in Him and wish to follow Him, modeling His example. May I ask you, directly: Are you doing that? Having entrusted your soul to Him at the time of your conversion, have you also deposited your spirit with Him as well? Have you come to terms with your past, all the unfair treatment and the unkind words? Whatever it takes, go there. Don't stop short of fully forgiving those who don't deserve it—just as Christ did. And stay with it until you calmly accept where you are today, all the pain notwithstanding, as Christ did. Remember, He was still hanging on that cross, surrounded by darkness, when He released it all to the Father. As His follower, let it be. Let it be.

A soldier in World War II was fighting his way across a battlefield in France when he stumbled upon an old wooden picture frame. The house in which it once hung was destroyed by fire and the frame was empty and battered. Wiping away the soot and debris, the soldier saw two Latin words carved into the bottom of the frame: *ECCE HOMO.* He had no clue what the words meant, but he thought the frame would make a memorable souvenir from his days of battle in France, so he took it with him and later mailed it back home to West Virginia.

When his mother opened the package and saw the frame, she didn't understand the strange words either. But she held it close to her breast and gave thanks for the continued safety of her son. In a few days she had a mirror fitted and placed within the frame, then hung it up in her son's room in their small country home.

Meanwhile, the battle raged on in Europe and the young soldier, mainly out of a growing fear of dying, began attending the simple worship services led by the army chaplain. Eventually he came to Christ and began to read the New Testament he'd been issued many months earlier in boot camp. The more he read, the more he learned of Jesus Christ, and the more he longed to model his Savior's life. His heart became increasingly tender and, slowly, he dealt with areas of his life that needed attention. Because of his relationship with his new Companion, his fears faded.

When the war ended, the young man returned to his West Virginia home and was warmly welcomed by his family and neighborhood of longtime friends. The first night, when he walked up the stairs to his room and flipped on the light, his eye caught the familiar frame hanging on the wall. His mother had not only put a mirror in it, she had found the meaning of those two words and written them on a small piece of paper, which she'd placed at the corner of the mirror. Referring originally to Christ, the words burned their way into his heart as he saw his own face in the mirror while reading, "Behold the Man." Tears flowed as he pictured himself *in* Christ Jesus as he had never done before.

All the way through our journey of this sacred story, it's as if the Word of God is telling us, "Behold the Man." Behold Him at Bethlehem when He was born. Behold Him in Nazareth where He grew up. Behold Him in Galilee as He taught and worked miracles. Behold Him beside the table in Jerusalem where He had His last meal with His followers. Behold Him in Gethsemane where He agonized in prayer. Behold Him at Golgotha where on the cross He suffered and finally committed Himself into His Father's hands. Behold the Man!

And as you do, pause and consider the reflection in the mirror—it's you, but it bears His name.

> Jesus, Refuge of the weary,
>   Blest Redeemer, whom we love
> Fountain in life's desert dreary,
>   Savior from the world above,
> O how oft Thine eyes, offended,
>   Gaze upon the sinner's fall!
> Yet, upon the cross extended,
>   Thou didst bear the pain of all.
>
> Do we pass that cross unheeding,
>   Breathing no repentant vow,
> Though we see Thee wounded, bleeding,

See Thy thorn-encircled brow?
Yet Thy sinless death hath brought us
Life eternal, peace, and rest;
Only what Thy grace hath taught us
Calms the sinner's stormy breast.[4]

—GIROLAMO SAVONAROLA, 1454–1498

O My Lord and Savior

Thou hast appointed a cross
for me to take up and carry, a
cross before thou givest me a crown.

Thou hast appointed it to be
my portion, but self-love
hates it, carnal reason is
unreconciled to it; without
the grace of patience I cannot
bear it, walk with it, profit by it.
O blessed cross, what mercies
dost thou bring with thee!

Thou art only esteemed hateful
by my rebel will, heavy
because I shirk thy load.

Teach me, gracious Lord and
Savior, that with my cross
thou sendest promised grace so
that I may bear it patiently,
that my cross is thy yoke
which is easy, and thy burden
which is light.[1]

—THE VALLEY OF VISION

16
Lessons in Obedience ... Taught Severely

We began in the darkness. We're still in the darkness. But not for long!

However, before we step out into the sunlight of new life and new hope, there remain a few insights to glean in the shadow of His presence. There are still secret areas to be invaded. There exist carefully guarded rooms we've not yet invited the Spirit of God to enter and expose.

Among them, for sure, are feelings of resistance brought on by our longstanding stubborn wills. We do not want to be submissive. We do not welcome those truths that push us off the throne of our own lives. We certainly do not like the thought of suffering or of anything taught severely. Ease and comfort we enjoy. But hardship, sacrifice, and releasing the controls? Forget it. That's why we need to linger longer near the cross of Christ.

In Eugene's Petersen's fine paraphrase of the Scriptures, *The Message,* here is Luke 9:23–25:

> Anyone who intends to come with me has to let me lead. You're not in the driver's seat—I am. Don't run from suffering; embrace it. Follow me and I'll show you how. Self-help is no help at all.

Self-sacrifice is the way, my way, to finding yourself, your true self. What good would it do to get everything you want and lose you, the real you?

This is not a popular message, but it is the message of truth. To some people it will seem dated and, to a few, masochistic. Please understand, my desire is not that we become extreme and out of balance to the point of fanaticism, but that we become deeper in our devotion. Accepting suffering helps us do that.

Jesus was the first to teach us that each one of us has a cross to bear. We may not necessarily look as if we are bearing one, but we are. Each of us has some area of pain and suffering in life. The world around us would have us run from that burden—to resent it, hate it. Instead, we should—and I know this is tough to hear and believe— embrace it.

Recently I heard about a man who suffered the threat of a detached retina. This man loves to read. So with the possibility of eyesight loss hanging over him, he had to lie very still for two weeks. Imagine two full weeks lying completely still. He said later, "Would I ever want to go through that again? Absolutely not. But would I want to miss the lessons I learned in going through it? Absolutely not." This man embraced his affliction.

The thorns along the pathway of life are many. Pain is a frequent companion. Everything within us wants to run from affliction. We resent it. Truth be known, we despise it. Our culture has learned to dodge it. With the help of drink or drugs, trinkets, toys, and travel, many have discovered that they can dodge pain for awhile, only to find it waiting for them when they return.

As believers, we need to learn how to deal with suffering biblically, to cultivate a theological depth that enables us to look at life through the lens of our Father's perspective rather than our own.

We are, by nature, takers and keepers. We hoard if there is much. We grasp if there is little. But our suffering Savior teaches us to release, to let go, to find lasting joy in a lifestyle of generosity.

Everything within us recoils against the thought of pain. Even as little children we were taught to treat suffering as an unfair intruder, rather than an escort along the path of obedience. J. B. Phillips' paraphrase of James 1:2–3 speaks powerfully of this: "When all kinds of trials and temptations crowd into your lives, my brothers, do not resent them as intruders, but welcome them as friends! Realize that they come to test your faith and to produce in you the quality of endurance."

Who needs such humiliation! Almost sounds like self-flagellation. How dare anyone suggest that such heartaches come from God? Don't they always come from the Enemy of our souls? Once we give ourselves to the Lord Jesus, don't we live happily ever after? Hardly. In fact, not at all.

Our Lord's major pursuit, once we come to know Him, is obedience. He is not the Divine Bellhop, waiting for your phone call, listening for your order, anxious to say, "Whatever you wish, yes! My pleasure. Why of course, yes!" He's not the Divine Genie in the bottle, ready to give you your every wish or smile and grant your every prayer. It is His desire to create within His children a capacity for endurance. And that capacity is cultivated mainly through hardship, disappointment, misunderstanding, as well as physical, and often emotional, pain and heartache.

Wait, you say. Isn't life about being fulfilled? Isn't it about finding that beautiful avenue of satisfaction and laughter and fun and games? Isn't God mainly concerned that we be happy? Just show me the verse where the Bible promises uninterrupted happiness, and I'll be happy to preach it. Well, someone says, "We're to have life and have it abundantly." Ah, but I don't see any mention of happiness there. Certainly there may be occasions of genuine joy, but abundant life has to do with a God-given dimension of living that doesn't come naturally and isn't given permanently.

Remember the response Job gave to his wife after he had lost everything? In case you have forgotten, they had lost their home, their cattle, their sheep and camels, their hired help, their source of income. Worse than that, they had just buried ten children—*all* their children.

It was like one great tornado sweeping through, destroying everything. The final blow was felt when Job lost his health. Bankrupt and bereft, his heart broken in grief and loss, Job sits there on the barren hillside. And his wife looks him in the eyes and says, "Why don't you just curse God and die?" Meaning what? Death is better than this. How often have we thought such things?

I know a family that, in one terrible accident, lost four of their five children. My first thought? I'd have rather died than go through that. I cannot imagine anything more devastating.

Let's not criticize Job's wife. She loved her husband. But she, too, had lost everything, including her ten children. And her response was, "Job, just have Him take you home." And he responds with those unforgettable words: "You speak as one of the foolish women speaks. Shall we indeed accept good from God and not accept adversity" (Job 2:10)?

Though terribly unpopular to preach (and write!) these days, that is great theology. Job dug deeply and pulled that perspective from the reservoir of maturity.

From our selfish standpoint, we desire only what is good and comfortable and easy and pleasant. However, in a fallen world, we must expect adversity. Yet, as Job later affirmed:

> But He knows the way I take;
> When He has tried me, I shall come forth as gold.
>
> My foot has held fast to His path;
> I have kept His way and not turned aside.
>
> I have not departed from the command of His lips;
> I have treasured the words of His mouth more than my necessary food.
>
> —JOB 23:10–12

"I now value the Lord's words more than tomorrow morning's breakfast, or the evening meal when I am physically famished. I esteem the words of His mouth more than all that!" How could a man say such a thing? Because he accepted reality. He didn't fight it. Life is difficult. He didn't deny it.

The psalmist, too, echoes this refrain. Psalm 119 is the longest of all the chapters in the Bible. Tucked away in the center section of this ancient hymnal of God's people are three verses that I call the triad of trials:

> Before I was afflicted I went astray,
> But now I keep Thy word.
> It is good for me that I was afflicted,
> That I may learn Thy statutes.
> I know, O LORD, that Thy judgments are righteous,
> And that in faithfulness Thou hast afflicted me.
>
> —PSALM 119:67,71,75

These are stair steps of growth, each one including suffering. The psalmist begins with his own waywardness. "I went astray," he says. Then affliction came and I learned to obey. I came to the place where I could say, "It is good for me that I was afflicted" because I really learned to walk in Your statutes. Now I have come to the place where I know "that in faithfulness You are the One who afflicted me."

> I understood your faithfulness.
> I learned to walk in your statues.
> I said it was good for me to be afflicted.
> I learned to obey.
> I was afflicted.
> I went astray.

The source isn't blind fate. Time spent behind bars isn't simply the long arm of the law. Calamities aren't from Mother Nature. Take those superficial words out of your vocabulary. Understand that God, in His sovereignty, places His hand over our lives and allows us to pass through painful experiences that we would never choose or want. Yet when we go through them, accepting them and learning from them, we grow deeper in the Christian life. In the final analysis, if we've responded correctly, we become more obedient.

May I confess something to you? I don't think I have ever learned any deep, lasting, life-changing lessons on the crest of success. I have learned very little from winning, but I have learned a great deal from losing. For that is when I pull off my rose-colored glasses, put on my realism spectacles, and say, "This kind of thing could come only from God. I'd better sit up and take notice."

The Apostle Paul prayed three times that the Lord would remove the "thorn in the flesh." Finally (after answering no each time) the Lord said to him, "My grace is sufficient for you." Note Paul's own comments on this important matter:

> Concerning this I entreated the Lord three times that it might depart from me. And He has said to me, "My grace is sufficient for you, for power is perfected in weakness."
>
> Most gladly, therefore, I will rather boast about my weaknesses, that the power of Christ may dwell in me. Therefore I am well content with weaknesses, with insults, with distresses, with persecutions, with difficulties, for Christ's sake; for when I am weak, then I am strong.
>
> —2 CORINTHIANS 12:8–10

"That the power of Christ may rest on me." When? Go back and look. It was when he accepted the thorn.

Now, be careful here. Let's not lose our senses. I'm not suggesting that you should tough out a root canal without a shot to kill the pain! That's not the kind of endurance I'm talking about. I'm talking about the suffering that comes in life which you cannot stop, and you can't dull the pain—at least not appropriately. My point, in all honesty? You should not try. Let it hit full force, just like the cross. We have spent fifteen chapters with Jesus, watching His life climax in a journey of darkness that ended at Golgotha. He didn't run from it; He walked toward it. It was His mission.

Malcolm Muggeridge was among the famous in England during his years as editor of *Punch* magazine, one of those satirical publications that make cynics laugh at most of life and even at God. Late in life, however, Muggeridge converted to Christ. Needless to say, when news of his testimony became public, it shocked his British and American readers. In a book titled *A Twentieth Century Testimony*, Muggeridge wrote of a new perspective on life.

> Contrary to what might be expected, I look back on experiences that at the time seemed especially desolating and painful with particular satisfaction. Indeed, I can say with complete truthfulness that everything I have learned in my seventy-five years in this world, everything that has truly enhanced and enlightened my existence, has been through affliction and not through happiness, whether pursued or attained. In other words, if it ever were to be possible to eliminate affliction from our earthly existence by means of some drug or other medical mumbo jumbo, as Aldous Huxley envisaged in *Brave New World*, the result would not be to make life delectable, but to make it too banal and trivial to be endurable. This, of course, is what the cross signifies. And it is the cross, more than anything else, that has called me inexorably to Christ.[2]

"It is the cross, more than anything else, that has called me inexorably to Christ." I love that statement! And I can say, without a moment's hesitation, that it will be the enduring of your own cross that will draw people to Christ through you, more than anything else in your life. Seeing what has impacted you, knowing that it is not natural for a person to react with acceptance as you are reacting, they will stare in awe and wonder. Some will ask, "How have you been able to do this?" "What is it?" "How could you?" "Tell me the secret." Your testimony can be, "I learned obedience through what I have suffered.

That's how God taught me. They were lessons taught severely, but that helped me learn them well."

And you'll be in good company.

> Although He [Jesus] was a Son, He learned obedience from the things which He suffered.
>
> —HEBREWS 5:8

Do you know how Jesus learned obedience? He learned obedience through lessons taught severely. We have uncovered many examples already. Critics' words, people's actions, six illegal trials, unfair treatment, mockings, scourging, and, ultimately, torturous death—all of those things put together taught the Son obedience.

Throughout His earthly ministry Jesus was verbally assaulted, particularly by the Pharisees. He was called everything from "illegitimate" to "demon-possessed." He was rejected and ignored. When that didn't stop Him, they plotted against Him, so that He lived in the crosshairs of their conspiracy. Even while Jesus was on trial, the same man who found no fault in Him had Him scourged and then released to be crucified. Yet at every turn, Jesus resisted the temptation to retaliate in kind, to hold a grudge, to be defensive or resentful or bitter, to lash out in anger or revenge.

The Son of God came from heaven to earth. "The Word became flesh and tabernacled among us." God became man. That's the Christmas story. Incarnation. Jesus, the Second Person of the Trinity, took upon Himself human flesh. For the first time in all of time, God lived visibly among humanity. During those thirty-three years He was pushed and shoved, mistreated and misquoted and maligned, tortured and scourged and nailed to a cross. His literal flesh was nailed with a Roman spike to the timbers of a cross. Literal blood came from His wounds. Literal life passed from His lips as He said to the Father. "Into Your hands I commit My Spirit."

While on earth, Jesus learned from experience the lessons taught by suffering, which is why He "can deal gently with the ignorant and misguided, since he himself also is beset with weakness" (Hebrews 5:2). He doesn't have to resort to His imagination. He knows what it's like from first-hand experience

When people are suffering, they turn to those they know will understand—those who will deal gently with them because they have been there themselves. That is why it is so important that we understand the suffering of Jesus and the meaning of His death on the cross. Because He was fully human, as well as fully God, He understands God's demanding penalty for sin, just as He understands the pain of our infirmities; He knows exactly what we are thinking and feeling. He knows what we are going through, because He has been there himself.

> Since then we have a great high priest who has passed through the heavens, Jesus the Son of God, let us hold fast our confession.
>
> For we do not have a high priest who cannot sympathize with our weaknesses, but One who has been tempted in all things as we are, yet without sin.
>
> —HEBREWS 4:14–15

He can "sympathize with our weaknesses" because He "has been tempted in all things" just as we are.

I began this chapter by quoting from Eugene Petersen's paraphrase, *The Message.* Let's return to that source for a little clearer understanding of what you just read: "We don't have a priest who is out of touch with our reality. He's been through weakness and testing, experienced it all—all but the sin."

"Wait a minute," you say. "How could the One who is perfect be tempted as we are, yet *without sin?*" Let's see if I can explain it this way. Some people are able to take twenty percent of affliction before they give up, before they react in the flesh. Some can take thirty percent. Some are strong enough to take sixty percent before they break. But Jesus took one hundred percent of the afflictions. And He never broke. That's how He learned obedience, humanly speaking.

Kenneth Wuest writes, "The omniscient God knew what obedience was, but He never experienced it until He became incarnate in human flesh. Before His incarnation, He owed obedience to no one. There was no one greater than He to whom He could have rendered obedience. But now in incarnation, God the Son became obedient to God the Father. He learned experientially what obedience was."[3]

> Although He was a Son, He learned obedience from the things which He suffered.
>
> —Hebrews 5:8

That is how we learn as well.

And this is a good time for me to add a warning: Please, don't try to fix everybody's afflictions. For some of us, that's a tall order, because we're fixers. We like to make things easier for others, like those we love, especially our children. We want to protect them and guard them and keep them free of pain. If there is any way we can take it instead of them, we will. Gladly. But if we try to do that, they learn less and less. We keep learning a lot, but they learn less and less because we protect them. We hold them back from the lessons of life. Let it happen. Let it unfold. For sure, we need to pray for them and stand alongside them, but don't try to fix their situations. Ask the Lord for personal strength not to jump in and try to bring quick relief.

That is not what the Father did for Jesus. The Father, at times, remained absolutely silent. (In fact that's still one of His preferred responses.)

Remember the Garden of Gethsemane? Olive trees still grow at Gethsemane. *Gethsemane* means "press," remember? It's the word for "pressure." Gethsemane was where they pressed out the oil from the olives in Jesus' day. And there He came under the greatest pressure of all: the tight, inescapable grip of the Father's plan. Knowing that the afflictions are upon Him, that the stakes are about to be driven into His hands, and that He will hang naked before heaven and earth and will die, He comes, in His very real humanity, to the secret place of Gethsemane.

And being in agony He was praying very fervently; and His sweat became like drops of blood, falling down upon the ground.

—LUKE 22:44

Why was He in agony—an agony so great that His sweat was like drops of blood? Partly, perhaps, because God was silent. Lessons are taught severely when God remains silent.

When Jesus hung on the cross, He cried, "My God, My God, why have You forsaken Me?" As we learned in chapter twelve, that was when the Father literally turned His back on the Son who bore the sins of the world. Talk about a severe lesson! Talk about loneliness and pain. And let's always keep in mind, He didn't deserve one moment of that pain and suffering.

It is the cross that, inexorably, brings me to Christ. Through hardship, illness, heartache, crippling diseases, and a dozen other dark avenues, growth and maturity emerge. As my mother often said, "The roots grow deep when the winds are strong." Or, as Ted Engstrom describes:

> Cripple [a man], and you have a Sir Walter Scott.
>
> Lock him in a prison cell, and you have a John Bunyan.
>
> Bury him in the snows of Valley Forge, and you have a George Washington.
>
> Raise him in abject poverty, and you have an Abraham Lincoln.
>
> Subject him to bitter religious prejudice, and you have a Disraeli.
>
> Strike him down with infantile paralysis, and he becomes a Franklin Delano Roosevelt.
>
> Burn him so severely in a schoolhouse fire that the doctors say he will never walk again, and you have a Glenn Cunningham, who set the world record in 1934 for running a mile in four minutes and 6.7 seconds.
>
> Deafen a genius composer, and you have a Ludwig van Beethoven.

Have him or her born black in a society filled with racial discrimination, and you have a Booker T. Washington, a Harriet Tubman, a Marion Anderson, a George Washington Carver, or a Martin Luther King, Jr.

Make him the first child to survive in a poor Italian family of eighteen children, and you have an Enrico Caruso.

Have him born of parents who survived a Nazi concentration camp, paralyze him from the waist down when he is four, and you have the incomparable concert violinist, Itzhak Perlman.

Call him a slow learner, "retarded," and write him off as uneducable, and you have an Albert Einstein.[4]

To Ted's list I would add people like Corrie Ten Boom and Dietrich Bonhoeffer, whose schoolrooms were the Nazi concentration camps.

All these fall into the category of lessons severely taught in the schoolroom of pain.

That's why Joni Eareckson Tada can sit in a wheelchair and hold you in her hands, hands which she can scarcely move. As the result of a diving accident in 1967, this charming young woman wound up in a wheelchair for the rest of her life . . . without bitterness!

That brings me back to where I started. We don't like this subject! You and I want our way. We want to be the ones who teach it *our* way because *we* know how to do it. Then God steps in and says, "Wait a minute. If you want to be My vessel, you'll learn from Me." And you'll learn to revere lessons taught severely, because it's on the anvil of pain and illness, mistreatment and unfairness, that great character is forged. Brokenness forms the building blocks of the spiritual life.

> O LORD,
> I am a shell full of dust,
>   but animated with an invisible rational soul
>   and made anew by an unseen power of grace;
> Yet I am no rare object of valuable price,
>   but one that has nothing and is nothing,

although chosen of thee from eternity.
  given to Christ, and born again ...
When thou wouldst guide me I control myself,
When Thou wouldst be sovereign I rule myself.
When Thou wouldst take care of me I suffice myself.
When I should depend on thy providings I supply myself,
When I should submit to thy providence I follow my will,
When I should study, love, honour, trust thee, I serve myself;
I fault and correct Thy laws to suit myself,
Instead of Thee I look to man's approbation,
  and am by nature an idolater.
Lord, it is my chief design to bring my heart back to Thee.
Convince me that I cannot be my own god, or make myself happy,
  nor my own Christ to restore my joy,
  nor my own Spirit to teach, guide, rule me.
Help me to see that grace does this by providential affliction ...
Take away my roving eye, curious ear, greedy appetite, lustful
    heart;
Show me that none of these things
  can heal a wounded conscience,
  or support a tottering frame,
  or uphold a departing spirit.
Then take me to the cross and leave me there.[5]

We all meet on the same level—the foot of the cross. It's there, in the dark shadow of Jesus' suffering and sacrifice, that we learn best.

Some think it is better to live in rebellion and distance than to walk close to Him through suffering; therefore, they defend their own sins and pursue their own selfish pursuits. But those who are drawn by that inexorable magnet called the cross finally walk from the darkness out into the light, leaving their sins there, where the sacrifice was paid once for all by the Lamb, the suffering Son of God, who was "the Man of sorrows and acquainted with grief."

As we leave the sorrowful and tragic scenes of the darkness and prepare to move out into the brilliance and triumph of our Lord's resurrection, I think some quiet moments spent in prayer would be helpful. Wherever you may be, as you are reading these lines, I invite you to pause, bow your head, and follow along as I pray . . .

Thank You, dear Father God, for these days we've spent with Your Son. We're different because of the journey we've taken together. We have a renewed respect for the One who took our place, bearing our shame, and paying the maximum price for our sins. The darkness was darker than we'd ever imagined. The punishment He endured was even worse than we thought possible. And to think He did it all out of love for us. What grace!

May we, in the midst of the glitz and glare of flashing neon lights from our plastic, superficial world, be drawn back to the cross. May it become the anchor that stabilizes us and gives us perspective when the storms howl and the suffering won't go away. Rather than being mesmerized or intimidated by those who are celebrities, may we "behold the Man" and bow before Him who took our sins away.

The pace is fast these days. Guard us from increasing our speed. Rather, may we learn how to be still and accept the silence. Take the focus off ourselves and enable us to reconnect with You, O Lord. For some, that's only a small step; for others, it's a giant leap. Hold us close as we risk the change.

And now, we anticipate moving out into the light of our Savior's triumph over the grave. We ask that it may bring us new hope and fresh encouragement. We need both. Having deepened our lives, we now pray that You will brighten our path. We're ready to go wherever You lead.

Through Christ we pray, amen.

The Dawn

Christ is risen.
He is risen indeed. Allelujah!
Praise the God and Father of our Lord Jesus Christ.
He has made us Easter people by raising Jesus from the dead.
He lived and died in past history.
But He lives today and influences present history.
Christ is risen. He is alive.
We celebrate His triumph.
We recognize His presence.
We applaud His achievements.
We declare our love for Him.
Rejoice, then, even in your distress.
He has called us from darkness into light.
Allelujah!

17
What Is Your Verdict?

Neither could the gates of death,
Nor the tomb's dark portal,
Nor the watchers, nor the seal
Hold Thee as a mortal.[1]

—JOHN OF DAMASCUS, 8TH CENTURY

17
What Is Your Verdict?

*I*magine yourself in a courtroom. You are a member of the jury, preparing to decide one of the oldest cases in the history of jurisprudence: *The People vs. Jesus of Nazareth.*

Basically, the case has to do with what this Jesus of Nazareth claims: namely, that He died and that He subsequently was miraculously and bodily raised from the dead. For centuries, people have been prosecuting this case, basing their prosecution on one of three theories.

First, there is the swoon theory, which claims that Jesus did not actually die on the cross, but He was in such a state of exhaustion due to loss of strength and blood, that He "swooned" into a coma. In that coma-like state, believed to be dead, He was taken down and put into a tomb. In the dampness of the tomb, He revived. Somehow from within His cave-like chamber of death He pushed the stone away from the mouth of the tomb and slipped out into the night, unnoticed by anyone. He then reappeared to His followers, claiming to have been raised miraculously, when actually He had only fallen into a coma; He had not died but had simply been in a swoon.

The second theory is the kidnap theory. This theory says that Jesus did actually die, but in the middle of the night, someone came and took

His body. Unseen by the soldiers who were guarding the tomb, the kidnapper or kidnappers pushed back the stone, stole the body, and hid it where it would never be found. Because the tomb was empty, the disciples claimed that Jesus had been raised from the dead, when all the while His corpse was kidnapped.

The third theory is the hallucination theory. This theory borrows from the kidnap theory, in that it says that Christ died and His body was hidden away. And those disciples who later thought they were seeing the raised Christ were actually seeing an apparition—a phantom—an hallucination. In other words, the person they claimed to have been the resurrected Christ was a figment of their imaginations.

As a juror, you've heard the prosecution's case. Now it's time to hear the defense.

The Whole Truth and Nothing but the Truth

The attorneys in this case are Matthew, Mark, Luke, and John, the four gospel writers. These men also offer eyewitness testimony. Everything in their case begins with the fact that Jesus did actually die. He didn't swoon. He wasn't kidnapped. The disciples weren't hallucinating.

Matthew says, "And Jesus cried out again with a loud voice, and yielded up His spirit" (Matthew 27:50).

Mark says, "And Jesus uttered a loud cry, and breathed His last" (Mark 15:37).

Luke says, "And Jesus, crying out with a loud voice, said, 'Father, Into Thy hands I commit My Spirit.' And having said this, He breathed His last" (Luke 23:46).

John says, "When Jesus therefore had received the sour wine, He said, 'It is finished!' And He bowed His head, and gave up His spirit" (John 19:30).

Four firm statements declare the death of Jesus.

But surely there are many around the world today who would say those testimonies are biased. So let's hear the testimony of others who actually saw Jesus' dead body. The defense calls to the stand the centurion, the Roman soldier who was the officer in charge of the death squad at Jesus' crucifixion.

The centurion says, in effect, "I was standing right in front of Him. I saw the way He breathed His last. Truly this man was the Son of God" (Mark 15:39)!

The centurion was an intelligent man—a Roman soldier and a trusted officer, seasoned from years on the battlefield. He'd had first-hand experience in dealing with death. He was an alert and able man, a military veteran. He was not a man given to hearsay, flights of fancy, or snap judgment. This was the kind of man who stood in front of Christ, watched Him die, and then openly stated, "This man was the Son of God."

Don't miss the verb in the centurion's testimony: "was." Mark uses the past tense as he records the centurion's testimony. "He *was* the Son of God. He's dead."

Now, let's hear from the other soldiers who were on the crucifixion detail.

> The Jews therefore, because it was the day of preparation, so that the bodies should not remain on the cross on the Sabbath (for that Sabbath was a high day), asked Pilate that their legs might be broken, and that they might be taken away.
>
> The soldiers therefore came, and broke the legs of the first man, and of the other man who was crucified with Him; but coming to Jesus, *when they saw that He was already dead,* they did not break His legs; but one of the soldiers pierced His side with a spear, and immediately there came out blood and water.
>
> And he who has seen has borne witness, and his witness is true; and he knows that he is telling the truth, so that you also may believe.
>
> —JOHN 19:31–35, ITALICS ADDED

Why break the legs of these poor tortured creatures? The answer is simple. In order for a person to stay alive on a cross, to breathe, he had to maintain a constant up-and-down motion. He had to move his body up to inhale and down to exhale. Pinned to the timbers by his hands and feet, his legs were his only leverage to lift himself. If the soldiers wanted to hasten a victim's death, they broke his legs. Unable to move and thus to breathe, he would quickly suffocate.

In this instance, however, the beginning of the Sabbath was fast approaching—and not just any Sabbath; this was the Passover Sabbath. The Jewish leaders did not want dying men hanging outside the city gate during their high and holy days. They asked Pilate to order their legs broken so that the executed men would die immediately and be removed for burial.

"Pilate ordered us to break their legs," the four soldiers testify. "But when we came to the center one, the one called THE KING OF THE JEWS, He was already dead."

But just in case they were mistaken, they "pierced His side with a spear, and immediately there came out blood and water."

One medical authority writes that the separation of the dark red corpuscles from the thin, whitish serum of the blood (called "water" in this verse) indicates death. When the soldiers thrust the spear into Jesus' side, this liquid came from His body. That provided physical proof that Jesus hadn't swooned into a coma. He was dead.

But if this isn't sufficient evidence, hear the words of the burial party.

> And after these things Joseph of Arimathea, being a disciple of Jesus, but a secret one, for fear of the Jews, asked Pilate that he might take away the body of Jesus; and Pilate granted permission. He came therefore, and took away His body.
>
> And Nicodemus came also, who had first come to Him by night; bringing a mixture of myrrh and aloes, about a hundred pounds weight.
>
> And so they took the body of Jesus, and bound it in linen wrappings with the spices, as is the burial custom of the Jews.
>
> —JOHN 19:38–40

Two friends of the deceased, Joseph of Arimathea and Nicodemus, are the next two witnesses. Joseph obtained Pilate's permission to remove and dispose of Jesus' dead body. After taking the body off the cross, he and Nicodemus wrapped it with the burial spices. These wrappings were eight-inch to one-foot-width strips of linen that were wrapped tightly around the corpse from the arm pits to the ankles and held in place by the gummy consistency of the spices. During the wrapping, the spices were pushed into the folds, so that ultimately the body was encased in a hardened wrapping of linen, from the shoulders to the ankles. The head was wrapped in a unique fashion in what was called the face cloth or head cloth. This cloth was wrapped about the top of the head and tied under the jaw, to keep the jaw from sagging. The final appearance of the burial-ready body would have been much like the pictures or exhibits we have seen of Egyptian mummies.

If there had been the slightest sign of life, the least sign of movement, not in a thousand years would these two men have continued to wrap Jesus' body in burial cloths and laid Him in the tomb. But He was dead! They knew this full well. They had handled Him and moved Him and turned Him and wrapped Him and covered Him, from head to toe.

As a jury member, you've been listening closely to those on the witness stand. Joseph and Nicodemus convincingly refute the swoon theory. You take note: Jesus was dead when He was taken from the cross and prepared for burial . . . no question.

THE DISPLACED STONE

With His death firmly established, we come to the cornerstone of the defense's case: the resurrection of Jesus. John stands and speaks first . . .

> Now in the place where He was crucified there was a garden; and in the garden a new tomb, in which no one had yet been laid.
>
> Therefore on account of the Jewish day of preparation, because the tomb was nearby, they laid Jesus there.
>
> —JOHN 19:41–42

To appreciate what Joseph and Nicodemus did, you have to understand the tombs in Jesus' day. For our own clarification and understanding, the word "cave" would be more appropriate than the word "tomb." In fact, that is the very word that was used to describe the burial place of Jesus' close friend Lazarus: "Now it was a cave, and a stone was lying against it" (John 11:38).

The rugged land of Israel is pockmarked with caves. Its rocky hillsides include countless natural caves or areas where caves could be carved into the soft limestone rock. If you have ever traveled there, you have seen this evidence firsthand.

Joseph of Arimathea owned just such a burial cave, probably his own family burial plot. Jesus' body would have been laid on a slab within that cave. Then a stone, circular in shape, and weighing at least a ton, was set into an inclined groove leading down to the mouth of this opening. The stone was held in place, away from the opening, by a wedge at the bottom. When the burial preparations were completed, the wedge was removed, allowing the pull of gravity to roll the stone into place, sealing off the opening of the cave. This kept the body safe from would-be robbers or animals.

But in Jesus' case, an additional precaution was taken, at the instigation of the chief priests and the Pharisees. The Romans placed a seal on the tomb and posted a guard, just in case some of His fanatic followers tried to steal the body. The religious leaders did not want an empty tomb, for that would certainly verify Jesus' promise that He would be raised from the dead.

And in that regard, let's call our next witness—another eyewitness. Will Mary Magdalene please take the stand?

> Now on the first day of the week Mary Magdalene came early to the tomb, while it was still dark, and saw the stone already taken away from the tomb.
>
> —JOHN 20:1

"As soon as the Sabbath was over, on the first day of the week, very early in the morning, before the sun had even come up, I went to the place where they buried my Master, Jesus. But when I got there, I was shocked. The stone had been rolled away from the door of the tomb!"

So the first piece of historical evidence for the resurrection is the displaced stone. On at least seven occasions in the Gospels, the displaced stone is mentioned.

Many prosecutors have argued, of course, that the stone was displaced so that Jesus, who was not really dead, could get out. But I firmly believe that Jesus was gone before the stone was ever moved. I think the stone was moved to let the disciples in, rather than let Jesus out. It allowed them entrance so they could discover that the tomb was empty.

Jesus' physically glorified state changed His molecular structure, which gave Him the ability to slip out of the wrappings and away from that solid rock grave. Later, that same glorified condition of His body would allow Him to pass through closed doors. In His resurrected body, the second person of the Trinity was once again unhindered by mass and matter, time and space. All those barriers that natural, earth-bound bodies must contend with were no longer of any concern to Him. Clearly, the stone was pushed aside so that witnesses could enter and see that the tomb was empty.

THE EMPTY TOMB

This brings us to the second piece of resurrection evidence: the empty tomb. John continues his defense:

And so she [Mary Magdalene] ran and came to Simon Peter, and to the other disciple whom Jesus loved, and said to them, "They have taken away the Lord out of the tomb, and we do not know where they have laid Him."

Peter therefore went forth, and the other disciple [that is, John, who is writing this account], and they were going to the tomb.

And the two were running together; and the other disciple [John] ran ahead faster than Peter, and came to the tomb first; and stooping and looking in, he saw the linen wrappings lying there; but he did not go in.

Simon Peter therefore also came, following him, and entered the tomb; and he beheld the linen wrappings lying there, and the face-cloth, which had been on His head, not lying with the linen wrappings, but rolled up in a place by itself.

So the other disciple [John] who had first come to the tomb entered then also, and he saw and believed.

For as yet they did not understand the Scripture, that He must rise again from the dead.

—JOHN 20:2–9

So here we have at least two more eyewitnesses: Peter and John.

"Ah," says the prosecution, "but what about Mary's comment about the body being taken away—by person or persons unknown?"

This brings us to three possible alternatives in answering the question "Why was the tomb empty?"

Number one: Jesus was really alive and got out of the tomb under His own strength. Stop and think. It would have been a physical impossibility for a man to roll back that immense stone from inside the cave, even for a man in superb physical shape. Consider what Jesus' condition would have been if He had been in a coma and then awakened from it. His was a tortured, beaten-and-bruised body, weakened to the point of death. Consider the condition of His hands and feet, nailed to the cross and bearing His weight there for six hours. Even had He been alive, such a feat performed in His weakened condition would have been a physical impossibility.

Number two: Jesus was dead, and somebody took the body and hid it elsewhere. That's what Mary thought. She came to the tomb, found the stone moved and the tomb empty, and immediately jumped to the conclusion, "Somebody has kidnapped the Lord. They've stolen His body. We don't know where they have put it."

The question is, "Who?" Who would have removed Jesus' body? There are only two possibilities: either His friends or His enemies.

Let's take the enemies first. Let's say that Jesus' enemies, Romans or Jews, wanted the tomb empty. But the question is, "Why?" That's the one thing they did not want. That's the very reason they sealed the tomb and put guards beside it. "For the next several days, especially the third one, we don't want an empty tomb on our hands!"

Furthermore, if these enemies had removed the body, why didn't they produce it when the disciples began to preach the resurrected Christ?

The whole history of Christianity rests on a living Savior, a resurrected Lord Jesus Christ. And when the disciples began to preach, "He's been raised from the dead; we worship a living Savior," surely these enemies would have presented the kidnapped remains to refute them. The corpse of Jesus was all they needed to silence those preachers.

Patrick Fairbairn realized this when he wrote, "The silence of the Jews was as significant as the speech of the Christians." They didn't have the body. Arnold Toynbee, the eminent British historian, adds, "If the body of one Jew, Jesus of Nazareth, can be produced, then Christianity will crumble into a lifeless religion." But they can't find that body.

So if the enemies didn't take it, that leaves only one alternative: It was His friends.

That's exactly what the officials said.

> And behold, a severe earthquake had occurred, for an angel of the Lord descended from heaven and came and rolled away the stone and sat upon it. And his appearance was like lightning, and his garment as white as snow; and the guards shook for fear of him, and became like dead men.
>
> And the angel answered and said to the women, "Do not be afraid; for I know that you are looking for Jesus who has been crucified. He is not here, for He has risen, just as He said. Come, see the place where He was lying. And go quickly and tell His disciples that He has risen from the dead; and behold, He is going before you into Galilee, there you will see Him; behold, I have told you."

And they departed quickly from the tomb with fear and great joy and ran to report it to His disciples. ...

Now while they were on their way, behold, some of the guard came into the city and reported to the chief priests all that had happened.

And when they had assembled with the elders and counseled together, they gave a large sum of money to the soldiers, and said, "You are to say, 'His disciples came by night and stole Him away while we were asleep.'

"And if this should come to the governor's ears, we will win him over and keep you out of trouble."

And they took the money and did as they had been instructed; and this story was widely spread among the Jews, and is to this day.

—MATTHEW 28:2–8,11–15

When the soldiers reported all that had happened at the tomb of Christ, panic set in. "Hey, you'll never guess, but would you believe, *it's empty!*" The religious leaders had no answer for the empty tomb, so they falsified the account and created a story. Then they bribed the soldiers to spread that lie.

"His disciples came during the night, while we were asleep, and stole the body."

Can you imagine Pontius Pilate accepting that excuse? A Roman soldier sleeping on his watch! Heads would surely roll.

"Oh, don't worry about that," said the religious leaders. "If this should come to the governor's ears" (and you can be sure that it would!) "we'll keep you out of trouble."

What amazes me is that these hardened soldiers trusted the chief priests and took the money. These were the same people who had just had one of their own crucified. But the soldiers went right along with the plot.

So the second theory, that Jesus' friends took the body, was a story fabricated by Jesus' enemies.

As a member of the jury, you're beginning to piece together the setting in your mind. The displaced stone and the empty tomb are significant. No question about that. But what about the body itself? And what about those wrappings? The defense now addresses that.

THE GRAVE CLOTHES

We have seen exhibits numbers one and two—the displaced stone and the empty tomb. It is now time to consider exhibit three: the grave clothes, the most tangible, material evidence.

> Peter therefore went forth, and the other disciple, and they were going to the tomb.
>
> And the two were running together; and the other disciple ran ahead faster than Peter, and came to the tomb first; and stooping and looking in, he saw the linen wrappings lying there; but he did not go in.
>
> Simon Peter therefore also came, following him, and entered the tomb; and he beheld the linen wrappings lying there, and the face-cloth, which had been on His head, not lying with the linen wrappings, but rolled up in a place by itself.
>
> —JOHN 20:3–7

Here again are our eyewitnesses, Peter and John. They heard Mary Magdalene's astonishing announcement: "The tomb is empty. Someone has taken the Lord's body away," and they set off running. John got there first, looked in the tomb, and saw the discarded burial wrappings, "but he did not go in."

You've got to appreciate John to appreciate these words. John loved the Savior, and the Savior loved Him. The Savior loved all the disciples, of course, but there appears to have been a special bond between Jesus and John. So close were they that at the cross Jesus left His mother in John's keeping. All this explains why John calls himself "the disciple whom Jesus loved." So when John came to that hallowed place and saw what was inside, he just couldn't walk right in.

Three times in this account the word "saw" appears. And in each case, it's different in the original Greek text, which helps explain the whole story to us.

The first "saw" is in verse five: "He saw the linen wrappings lying there." This is from the Greek word *blepo*, which indicates a casual glance. John came to the tomb, looked in, and saw. But he was just casually looking.

The next is in verse six: "Simon Peter … beheld the linen wrappings lying there." Peter, in his inimitable way, crawls right into the tomb and beheld what was there. This term is from the Greek word *theoreo*, which suggests deeper thinking, or making a careful observation. It's the word from which we get our word "theorize." Peter stood over those grave clothes and gazed at them carefully, theorizing about what had occurred as he tried to put it all together.

From the original text, it seems that the hardened mummy-like wrappings were still intact. They gave the appearance that a body was still within the wrappings, revealing the contour of Jesus' body, but they were like a hollow cocoon. Furthermore, the head cloth was shaped as though still wrapped around a head, but there was no head. Merrill Tenney writes with keen insight,

> "The word used to describe the napkin or head cloth does not connote a flat folded square like a table napkin, but a ball of cloth bearing the appearance of being rolled around an object that was no longer there. The wrappings were in position where the body had lain, and the head cloth was where the head had been, separated from the others by the distance from armpits to neck. The shape of the body was still apparent in them, but the flesh and bone had disappeared.[2]

That's what Peter couldn't figure out. To him, it seemed a puzzle. The wrappings were all intact, even the face-cloth, but there was no body! I have a feeling that things felt a little eerie in there all of a sudden.

Now comes the third "saw," in verse eight: "So the other disciple [that's John again] who had first come to the tomb, entered then also, and he saw and believed." This verb, translated "saw," is from a Greek word, entirely different from the other two. This is *oida,* which means to form a mental perception, to understand, to realize in the mind what has taken place.

John pushes Peter aside and looks in once more and, suddenly, everything clicks into place. John "sees" it all. He understands what has happened! He believes, even though the next verse tells us, "For as yet they did not understand the Scripture, that He must rise again from the dead" (John 20:9).

"He believed." Isn't that beautiful? We read so much theology into the disciples. We portray them as men with halos and immaculate garments and folded hands, walking around like robed clerics, piously quoting the Apostles' Creed. But that's not who they were. To the *last* they were doubting. They didn't even understand the resurrection. And yet John walked into that tomb and "saw and believed."

The abandoned grave clothes at which he and his companion were staring provided tangible evidence. To those who were there in that tomb, Christ had been released from the jaws of death.

THE DEFENSE RESTS

We've heard from eyewitnesses who were present at the crucifixion, the death, the burial, and the discovery of the empty tomb. But now comes the clincher: those who actually saw Jesus after He had been raised from the dead.

Jesus appeared to more than five hundred eyewitnesses, including the apostles, before He ascended into heaven. That would make quite a witness list for the defense, wouldn't it?

The Apostle Paul writes this:

For I delivered to you as of first importance what I also received, that Christ died for our sins according to the Scriptures, and that He was buried, and that He was raised on the third day according to the Scriptures, and that He appeared to Cephas, then to the twelve.

After that He appeared to more than five hundred brethren at one time, most of whom remain until now, but some have fallen asleep; then He appeared to James, then to all the apostles; and last of all, as it were to one untimely born, He appeared to me also.

—1 CORINTHIANS 15:3–8

The defense rests its case not only on the testimony of the eyewitnesses recorded in God's Word, but on the testimony of countless men and women down through the ages, like Frank Morison.

Morison, a British attorney, was an unbeliever, determined, with his legal skills and what he considered to be hard facts, to disprove the resurrection of Christ. But the more he studied, the less he believed his own thesis. He admits this in the preface of his book, *Who Moved the Stone?*

[This] is essentially a confession, the inner story of a man who originally set out to write one kind of book and found himself compelled by the sheer force of circumstance to write quite another.

It is not that the facts themselves altered, for they are recorded imperishably in the monuments and in the pages of human history. But the interpretation to be put upon the facts underwent a change. Somehow the perspective shifted—not suddenly, as in a flash of insight or inspiration, but slowly, almost imperceptibly, by the very stubbornness of the facts themselves.

The book as it was originally planned was left high and dry, like those Thames barges when the great river goes out to meet the incoming sea. The writer discovered one day that not only could he no longer write the book as he had once conceived it, but that he would not if he could.

Slowly but very definitely the conviction grew that the drama of those unforgettable weeks of human history was stranger and deeper than it seemed. It was the strangeness of many notable things in the story which first arrested and held my interest. It was only later that the irresistible logic of their meaning came into view.[3]

This is the testimony of an honest man. "I've examined the facts. In fact, I was biased in the other direction ... no faith in Jesus Christ. I've gone to the New Testament and related historical documents. I've examined the evidence. I've put it all together, and I now realize I was going in the wrong direction." That's the testimony of Frank Morison.

YOUR VERDICT, PLEASE

Down through the centuries, that empty tomb has transformed countless lives. Not by trials or by scientific studies, but by the simple faith of an honest heart. This is, as Josh McDowell says, "Evidence that demands a verdict." A verdict of the heart: false or true?

Ladies and gentlemen of the jury, this is the most important verdict you will ever decide. For your decision will determine your eternal destiny. Will you remain in the darkness or step out into the dawn of new hope?

Your verdict, please.

A Sunday Morning Miracle

Low in the grave He lay—Jesus my Saviour!
Waiting the coming day—Jesus my Lord!
Up from the grave He arose,
with a mighty triumph o'er His foew;
He arose a victor from the dark domain,
and He lives forever with His saints to reign.
He arose! He arose!
Hallelujah! christ Arose![1]

—1st Stanza and chorus
Christ Arose
ROBERT LOWRY, 1826–1899

18
A Sunday Morning Miracle

*I*t happens every Friday evening, almost without fail, when the sun resembles a giant orange and is starting to dip into the blue ocean. Old Ed comes strolling along the beach to his favorite pier. Clutched in his bony hand is a bucket of shrimp.

Ed walks out to the end of the pier, where it seems he almost has the world to himself. The glow of the sun is a golden bronze now. Everybody's gone, except for a few joggers on the beach. Standing out on the end of the pier, Ed is alone with his thoughts . . . and his bucket of shrimp.

Before long, however, he is no longer alone. Up in the sky a thousand white dots come screeching and squawking, winging their way toward that lanky frame standing there on the end of the pier. Before long, dozens of seagulls have enveloped him, their wings fluttering and flapping wildly. Ed stands there tossing out shrimp to the hungry birds. As he does, if you listen closely, you can hear him say with a smile, "Thank you. Thank you."

In a few short minutes the bucket is empty. But Ed doesn't leave. He stands there lost in thought, as though transported to another time and place.

Invariably, one of the gulls lands on his sea-bleached, weather-beaten hat—an old military hat he's been wearing for years. When he finally turns around and begins to walk back toward the beach, a few of the birds hop along the pier with him until he gets to the stairs, and then they, too, fly away. And old Ed quietly makes his way down to the end of the beach and on home.

If you were sitting there on the pier with your fishing line in the water, Ed might seem like "a funny old duck," as my dad used to say. Or "a guy that's a sandwich shy of a picnic," as my kids might say. To onlookers, he's just another old codger, lost in his own weird world, feeding the seagulls with a bucket full of shrimp.

To the onlooker, rituals can look either very strange or very empty. They can seem altogether unimportant . . . maybe even a lot of non-sense. Old folks often do strange things, at least in the eyes of Boomers and Busters. Most of them would probably write Old Ed off, down there in Florida. That's too bad. They'd do well to know him better.

His full name: Eddie Rickenbacker. He was a famous hero back in World War II. On one of his flying missions across the Pacific, he and his seven-member crew went down. Miraculously, all of the men survived, crawled out of their plane, and climbed into a life raft.

Captain Rickenbacker and his crew floated for days on the rough waters of the Pacific. They fought the sun. They fought sharks. Most of all, they fought hunger. By the eighth day their rations ran out. No food. No water. They were hundreds of miles from land and no one knew where they were. They needed a miracle.

That afternoon they had a simple devotional service and prayed for a miracle. Then they tried to nap. Eddie leaned back and pulled his military cap over his nose. Time dragged. All he could hear was the slap of the waves against the raft.

Suddenly, Eddie felt something land on top of his cap.

It was a seagull! Old Ed would later describe how he sat perfectly still, planning his next move. With a flash of his hand and a squawk from the gull, he managed to grab it and wring its neck. He tore the feathers off, and he and his starving crew made a meal—a very slight meal for eight men—of it. Then they used the intestines for bait. With it, they caught fish, which gave them food and more bait . . . and the cycle continued. With that simple survival technique, they were able to endure the rigors of the sea until they were found and rescued.

Eddie Rickenbacker lived many years beyond that ordeal, but he never forgot the sacrifice of that first lifesaving seagull. And he never stopped saying, "Thank you." That's why almost every Friday night he would walk out to the end of that pier with a bucket full of shrimp and a heart full of gratitude.[2]

ANALYZING EASTER

Eddie's weekly ritual reminds me of our yearly Easter Sunday celebration. We get up before dawn, dress in our Sunday best, and gather—sometimes outside on a cold, windswept hilltop—for a sunrise service. Think how weird that must look to many people. And then, in our fashionable new outfits, we fight the crowd for a seat at another church service. Often those onlookers are actually in the service, of course. Once a year, on Easter Sunday morning, we look out across the church and, with sincerity and prayer, we toss out terms like "reconciliation" and "redemption," "resurrection" and "forgiveness."

For some who have been celebrating Easter most of their lives, this message has long since lost its edge. They've heard the words over and over again, but tradition has dulled the impact. I never really understood what Easter was all about until I was in junior high school, and then, frankly, I didn't care. I'd heard the same words every Easter for fourteen years.

For those to whom the message is unfamiliar, the words really don't mean much. To them Easter is colored eggs and bunnies and Spring Break in Daytona or Palm Springs. Yet we who are "in the know" assume that everybody speaks our language.

So what in the world is Easter all about? If I were to distill the Easter message into one sentence, it would be this: Jesus came back to life after He died. I could even put that message into one word: "resurrection."

"Resurrection" comes from *resurge* or *resurgence,* in the sense of "coming back" or "renewing" or "rising up." In other words, Jesus Christ, who was once down, dead, laid aside, crucified, later stood up miraculously and bodily. He "resurged." He came back to life, never to die again.

Most religions, and the world is filled with them, are built on philosophies. The four major world religions, however, are built on personalities, and of those four, only Christianity claims that its founder is still alive, having been resurrected from the dead.

Judaism, the oldest of the four, teaches that its founder was Abraham, and that is true. But historians tell us—in fact, the biblical record states, and Jews agree—that Abraham is dead. Around 1900 B.C., he died at "a ripe old age" and was buried by his sons, Isaac and Ishmael (Genesis 25). Abraham is still dead.

Buddhism was founded by Buddha himself. The most ancient reliable piece of literature I could find regarding Buddhism says this of his death: "When Buddha died it was with that utter passing away in which nothing whatever remains behind." That pretty well seals the deal. No disciple of Buddha can declare, "I've seen the founder. He's been raised from the dead. I've spoken with him. He has appeared." Why? Because he is dead. Buddha is still dead.

Islam is founded on Mohammed and his teachings. Professor Childers, who has written a classic work on the subject of Islam entitled *The Light of Asia and the Light of the World,* writes this: "There is no trace of this founder having existed after his death or appearing to his disciples. Mohammed was born about A.D. 571 and died in A.D. 632 at the age of 61, at Medina, where his tomb is annually visited by thousands of devout Mohammedans." Not one follower of Islam could declare with proof that he has seen the risen Mohammed. Why? Because Mohammed died. He is still dead.

Unlike the founders of those three major world religions, the founder of Christianity, Jesus Christ is alive . . . and is still alive. His tomb is empty. He is risen. He is risen indeed!

His life was the watershed of history. His death and resurrection are the cornerstone of Christianity.

Wilbur Smith says, "The central tenant of the church is Christ's resurrection."

Robertson Nicoll writes, "The empty tomb of Christ has been the cradle of the church."

Michael Green, in his book *Man Alive,* states, "Without faith in the resurrection there would be no Christianity at all. The Christian church would never have begun; the Jesus Movement would have fizzled like a damp squib with His execution. You see, Christianity stands or falls with the truth of the resurrection. Once disprove it, and you have disposed of Christianity."[3]

What Bethlehem was to Jesus of Nazareth, the empty tomb is to Christianity. It's the keystone, the capstone, and the foundation of our faith. If He were still dead, we would have no living Savior, no living message. We would have only a series of dogma. But He is risen indeed.

After the horror of that crucifixion afternoon, darkness must have descended upon the hearts of the disciples as it had descended around the cross at Golgotha. Darkness, disillusionment, and great sorrow. Even the thought of a dawn of new hope seemed an eternity away to those depressed and confused disciples.

EASTER'S FIRST DAWN

Early Sunday morning, just as the sun was rising, three women made their way through the mist to the tomb where Jesus had been buried. They weren't on their way to a sunrise service. They weren't on their way to worship and sing songs of praise. They weren't excited about what the future held. Their world had dropped out from under them. En route, they were wondering how they would ever get the stone rolled away from the tomb so they could enhance embalming the body of their crucified Master by adding fresh spices.

> And when the Sabbath was over, Mary Magdalene, and Mary the mother of James, and Salome, bought spices, that they might come and anoint Him.

And very early on the first day of the week, they came to the tomb when the sun had risen.

And they were saying to one another, "Who will roll away the stone for us from the entrance of the tomb?"

—MARK 16:1–3

But they worried unnecessarily. When they arrived the stone was rolled back, and an angel was sitting on it. Their worry was replaced with wonder. Have you ever done that? You worried about something, only to find that the problem was already solved, and a solution even better than you could have imagined had occurred?

The Apostle John, writer of the fourth gospel, had sixty years to ponder what had happened that bright and glorious morning. He wrote his gospel late in the first century about events that had happened about A.D. 35; so he'd had a long time to think about Jesus' ministry and all the events surrounding it. In the process, the Holy Spirit led him to write what is known today as the Gospel of John. Because he was an eyewitness to many events, John wrote with additional authority.

I think of that often when I read the accounts of the resurrection of Christ. What must it have been like to actually be there? What if I had come to that garden tomb in the misty morning hours, burdened with sorrow and loss, only to find the huge stone pushed aside and the tomb empty? What would my reaction have been? How would I have assessed the situation had I been one of His disillusioned disciples?

As we mentioned in the previous chapter, Jesus' disciples and other followers did not yet understand the resurrection. Then, they have their first encounter with the risen Savior.

But Mary was standing outside the tomb weeping; and so, as she wept, she stooped and looked into the tomb; and she beheld two angels in white sitting, one at the head, and one at the feet, where the body of Jesus had been lying.

And they said to her, "Woman, why are you weeping?" She

said to them, "Because they have taken away my Lord, and I do not know where they have laid Him."

When she had said this, she turned around, and beheld Jesus standing there, and did not know that it was Jesus.

Jesus said to her, "Woman, why are you weeping? Whom are you seeking?" Supposing Him to be the gardener, she said to Him, "Sir, if you have carried Him away, tell me where you have laid Him, and I will take Him away."

—JOHN 20:11–15

Peter and John had hurried to the tomb after Mary had alerted them to the disappearance of Jesus' body, and they had seen the evidence of the displaced stone, the empty tomb, and the disturbed-but-empty grave clothes. Not fully understanding how such things could have happened, the disciples had returned to their homes. But the men left too soon. Mary stayed, and because she did, she saw something much better than the lifeless evidence in and around the empty tomb.

UNFORGETTABLE DIALOGUE

Mary was weeping, overwhelmed with sorrow and grief and the reality of the events of the past few days. Once again she stooped to look into the tomb. Could it really be empty? Not only was her beloved Master dead, but now someone had desecrated His tomb. They had even stolen His body!

But when she peered inside the dark cave this time, she saw something even more startling: two angels in white. One was perched at the head of the burial slab, and one was perched at the foot. We're not told whether or not she recognized them as angelic beings, but my guess is that she did. How could she not? Considering their location and their appearance, it would seem obvious that Mary realized they were more than mere men. However, their presence was not as alarming to her as the Master's absence.

"Woman, why are you weeping?" they asked.

"Because they have taken away my Lord, and I do not know where they have laid Him."

Isn't it astonishing that Mary responded so matter of factly to a question from angels in white sitting inside an empty tomb? She was not blown away. She simply answered their question. Apparently, she was so preoccupied with the emptiness of the tomb that their identity meant little at that moment.

As soon as she said this, she turned around and saw another man standing there. It was the resurrected Jesus, but she did not recognize Him. The record states that she thought He was the gardener (v. 15).

He asked her the same question the angels had just asked: "Woman, why are you weeping?"

Why didn't she know who He was? First, it was dark. Second, she was deeply troubled, her eyes blinded with tears. Third, she had no expectation of ever looking into Jesus' face again. He was the last person she expected to see. Fourth, He did not call her by name; He called her "woman," as though He did not know her or what had recently happened. "Whom are you seeking?" It's not surprising she didn't know who He was.

And so, thinking Him to be the gardener, she continued, "Sir, if you are the one who has taken Him away, tell me where you have taken Him."

And then He called her by name.

> Jesus said to her, "Mary!" She turned and said to Him in Hebrew, "Rabboni!" (which means, Teacher).
>
> —JOHN 20:16

"Mary!" Jesus said. And that's all He had to say. She had heard Him call her name many times before. She knew that voice! And she immediately recognized Him. "Teacher!"

As you would expect, she embraced Him. She reached over and embraced Him. She clung to Him. Some translations suggest that she merely "touched" Him. But the original Greek term that John uses means "to cling to." That becomes clear when we read Jesus' reaction:

> Stop clinging to Me, for I have not yet ascended to the Father; but
> go to My brethren, and say to them, "I ascend to My Father and
> your Father, and My God and your God."
>
> —John 20:17

That is the whole point of Jesus' response to her: "Stop clinging to Me." Why would He say that if Mary were just touching Him? "Stop clinging to Me, for I have not yet ascended to the Father."

In this exchange, it seems clear that Jesus was establishing a new relationship with His followers. He wasted no time instructing Mary to carry that message to the other disciples. He was establishing a spiritual relationship, a relationship not based on touch and sight but on faith.

"Go to my brethren," He told her. Not only was He establishing a new *relationship* by calling His disciples His "brothers," He was also implying that they were now new *relatives*.

> Earlier He had said they were friends: "I no longer call you ser-
> vants ... instead, I have called you friends" (15:15). Believers in
> Jesus become a part of Jesus' family with God as their father . . .
> Mary's new responsibility was to testify to His risen presence.[4]

He went on to say, "Tell them that I will ascend to My Father and your Father, My God and your God."

> Mary Magdalene came, announcing to the disciples, "I have seen
> the Lord," and that He had said these things to her.
>
> —John 20:18

After the disciples left the tomb they could say, "I have seen the evidence." But after Mary left the tomb she could say, "I have seen the Lord Himself, and He has said these things to me."

Now you would expect that those men who heard Mary's testimony would have said, "Tell us where He is. We want to see Him." You would expect them to rush out the door to meet the Savior, wouldn't you?

But Mark tells us they didn't do that.

> She went and reported to those who had been with Him, while they were mourning and weeping.
> And when they heard that He was alive, and had been seen by her, they refused to believe it.
>
> —MARK 16:10–11

How could they deny what she had seen and refuse to believe what she had said? Some chauvinist might say, "Because it came from the lips of an hysterical woman . . . you can't trust the words of a woman when she's excited." But that is simply not true.

> And after that, He appeared in a different form to two of them, while they were walking along on their way to the country.
> And they went away and reported it to the others, but they did not believe them either.
>
> —MARK 16:12–13

They refused to believe any of these eyewitnesses because they had thrown up a wall of rejection around their hearts and minds. People can hear one piece of evidence after another, but if the heart is not prompted to faith, they will not believe, no matter how clear and convincing the evidence. The hammer of truth may strike blow after blow to that wall of rejection, trying to remove one stone after another, and yet the wall stands fast. Candidly, some of you who are reading this book are saying, "I've never believed it, never will, never plan to. Trot out as many eyewitnesses as you want: I just *do* not and *will* not believe it."

My answer to you? Well, maybe *not yet*. Someday, I'm praying, you will.

> And afterward He appeared to the eleven themselves as they were reclining at the table; and He reproached them for their unbelief

and hardness of heart, because they had not believed those who had seen Him after He had risen.

—MARK 16:14

Finally Jesus Christ Himself stood in the presence of the eleven disciples and "reproached them for their unbelief and hardness of heart." Their unbelief was illogical and their hard hearts inexcusable. Eyewitnesses had come to tell them of the risen Christ, yet they had not believed.

INDISPUTABLE EVIDENCE

That brings us to one of the most remarkable proofs of the power of Christ's resurrection: the transformation of the disciples.

The church has had centuries to deal with the fact of His resurrection from the dead. But imagine what it must have been like for Jesus' disciples and followers, who had just seen His bruised and broken dead body taken from the cross and buried. Even though Jesus had said, "When I die, I will come back again; and because I live, you will live also," they didn't understand what He meant. So unbelievable was it, that, when the disciples first heard that Jesus was alive again, from eyewitnesses, they did not believe it. But when they finally did believe, they were transformed.

We have immortalized the disciples as men of incredible courage and remarkable understanding. But they were not always that way. When Jesus Christ breathed His last gasping breath on the cross, these men returned to their homes and their former lives, the fishermen returned to their nets, sorrowful and totally disillusioned. Before they were apprehensive, now they were scared, because each one of them could be identified with the Jewish insurrectionist who had just been crucified. They denied, they doubted, and they fled. And yet, by the middle of the Book of Acts—no more than thirty years later—these same disciples and their converts were described as "these that have turned the world upside down" (Acts 17:6 KJV).

The beginning of their transformation can be traced to that Sunday-morning miracle of Jesus' resurrection. He had been changed to a "glorified state," and they were now changed in their outlook.

Our physical bodies are "fearfully and wonderfully made." Entire books have been written about the wonders of the human body. But what about the supernatural body?

Phillip Keller, in his book *Rabboni,* talks about the supernatural body of Christ after resurrection.

> His body was utterly unique, diametrically different from anything that had ever been present before amongst men. He was no longer restricted in any sense by the time/space concepts of earthmen. He could appear and disappear at will. He could pass unhindered through the rock walls of a tomb or through the stone walls of a house. He did not depend on earth's environment for nourishment. Yet He could eat and relish bread, honey, and fish. He could appear as an apparition, unknown and unrecognized by his former intimates. Or He could speak in His old familiar tones and present Himself as their dearly beloved friend, marked with all the scars of the cross. Distance was of no consequence In an instant His spiritual body could be here, then suddenly gone. Likewise, the reverse was true.
>
> They were totally unprepared for it. It was impressive, somewhat disturbing, even frightening at times, and certainly almost unbelievable.[5]

Imagine it. Just a few days before they had walked with Him and eaten with Him and slept beside Him and talked with Him. Then came that horrendous betrayal in the darkness of Gethsemane—that turning point, after which nothing was ever the same again. Death—the most horrible form of death—came between them and their beloved Master. All they had hoped for and planned were lost. Their dreams were dashed, leaving them frightened and filled with doubt, until . . .

In a flash, as though time and space have been suspended, He has come back, bringing all sorts of new dimensions to their attention, as the power of God is unleashed in His new body. It was unbelievable.

PERSONAL EMPOWERMENT

This dramatic performance of God's power is a preview of coming attractions. "Because I live, you will live also," Jesus had told them. And now, from that empty tomb, God begins to announce, "All is forgiven! Wrath is removed! There is hope!" These men are about to be empowered by the resurrected Christ. "Despair no longer."

And since Mr. and Mrs. Average Citizen don't know what to do with that message, they misread it.

No one ever said it in more simple terms than John Stott in his excellent little book, *Basic Christianity:*

> It's no good giving me a play like *Hamlet* or *King Lear,* and telling me to write a play like that. Shakespeare could do it; I can't. And it is no good showing me a life like the life of Jesus and then telling me to live a life like that. Jesus could do it; I can't. But if the genius of Shakespeare could come and live in me, then I could write plays like that. And if the Spirit of Jesus could come and live in me, then I could live a life like that . . . To have Him as our example is not enough; we need Him as our Saviour.[6]

That's it! Christ came back from the dead so we might live as He lived and claim the triumph He has provided. He didn't die just to be studied and oohhed and aahhed over; He died and rose again to offer, through His blood and His life, new life—transforming power to live beyond the dregs of depravity's leftovers. And the first evidence we see of this is in the lives of Jesus' once frightened and disillusioned followers.

One of the most outstanding examples is Peter, a man we looked at earlier in chapter four, who denied his Lord three times on the night He was being tried. Yet when the barriers of denial and remorse had finally been broken down in his own heart, when grace gave him his new standing in Christ, Peter became the first spokesman to declare the message of the resurrection to the world. Do you remember his words? Talk about empowered!

> Men of Israel, listen to these words: Jesus the Nazarene, a man attested to you by God with miracles and wonders and signs which God performed through Him in your midst, just as you yourselves know—this Man, delivered up by the predetermined plan and foreknowledge of God, you nailed to a cross by the hands of godless men and put Him to death.
>
> And God raised Him up again, putting an end to the agony of death, since it was impossible for Him to be held in its power.
>
> This Jesus God raised up again, to which we are all witnesses.
>
> Therefore let all the house of Israel know for certain that God has made Him both Lord and Christ—this Jesus whom you crucified.
>
> —ACTS 2:22–24,32,36

Peter, one of the eyewitnesses to the empty tomb and the resurrected Christ, had been transformed from a brash young fisherman into an articulate, stalwart man of faith and a fiery evangelist for the Lord. His transformed life began as a result of one great event: his Lord's triumphant resurrection. That became the turning point for Peter's survival and later success.

WE ARE HIS WITNESSES

The resurrection of Christ is based on historical evidence—not on emotion, but on evidence.

I once knew a man who was studying law at Stanford University. Being an unbeliever, he determined to study the case for the resurrection of Christ as his dissertation topic. He was a brilliant man and a thorough scholar. He read shelf after shelf of books on the resurrection, studying all angles and aspects of the case. Then, in his own words, "Late one night I turned out the lights in my study, and I got down on my face beside my desk and said, 'Oh, God. I believe it.'" Why? Because he was an honest, intelligent searcher who could no longer deny the facts. The weight of the evidence finally crushed his stubborn will, and he surrendered in faith.

"No weapon has ever been forged, and none ever will be, to destroy rational confidence in the historical records of this epochal and predicted event," writes Wilbur Smith. "The resurrection of Christ is the very citadel of the Christian faith. This is the doctrine that turned the world upside down in the first century and that lifted Christianity preeminently above Judaism and all the pagan religions of the Mediterranean world."[7]

The tomb of Abraham is occupied. The tomb of Buddha is occupied. The tomb of Mohammed is occupied. But the tomb of Jesus Christ is empty.

Christianity alone is based on a living Person—the resurrected Son of God. And this resurrected Christ offers sufficient power to transform our lives.

As a result, like Old Ed used to do on the end of that pier every Friday evening, we spend the rest of our lives saying, "Thank You. Thank You."

19
Curing the Plague of Death

Bold shall I stand in thy great day;
For who aught to my charge shall lay?
Fully absolved through these I am
From sin and fear, from guilt and shame.

When from the dust of death I rise
To claim my mansion in the skies,
Ev'n then this shall be all my plea,
Jesus hath lived, hath died, for me.[1]

—COUNT NIKOLAUS LUDWIG VON
ZINZENDOR, 1739
Translated by John Wesley, 1740

19
Curing the Plague of Death

The Great Plague of London in the seventeenth century was known to the people of that time as the "Black Death." This epidemic crept through the dark streets of that vast city, an ugly, sadistic killer wreaking its havoc. In May 1664, when it claimed its first few victims, it was observed and ignored. By May of the next year 600 had died. By June it was 6,000. By July it was 17,000. By August 31,000 died in that month alone. People fled the city like rats from a sinking ship. By then, however, the vicious disease was already crawling across Europe. When it was over, about 70,000 people had died.

This great plague was called the "Black Death" for two reasons: One, the victims were marked with large black splotches across their body; and two, the blackness of ignorance surrounded the cause of the plague. Many people at that time thought that the plague was caused by the polluted air that smothered the city of London. Today, we know that rats and fleas from the rats carried the disease. But in those days people believed it was caused by polluted air, and so the physicians devised a strange ritual to bring about a cure.

They would take the victims outside to a bed of roses. There, the patients would form a circle around the roses, holding hands. Then they would all walk around the circle, breathing in the fragrance of the blossoms, believing that this would flush the disease from their lungs. The fragrant air of the flowers would replace the diseased air. For those who were too ill to go outside, the physician would stuff rose petals in their own pockets, and as they made their calls, they would sprinkle petals around the patients in an almost liturgical fashion. For those who were near death, the physicians would burn the petals and bring the ashes up near the noses so the victims could breathe the ashes, hoping this would make them sneeze, and in that way flush out the old, diseased air.

Of course, none of the superstitious rituals worked; people with the plague died . . . thousands upon thousands of them. But this ritual gave birth to a rhyme that was first sung by the man who pushed the death cart. As he loaded the bodies high on the cart and made his way to the cemetery, he could be heard chanting,

> Ring around the roses, a pocket full of posies,
> Ashes, ashes, we all fall down!

Isn't it strange that what we know as an innocent little nursery rhyme would begin in such a way? And yet the truth in that one line is as real for us today as it was then: "We all fall down."

THE INESCAPABLE PLAGUE

Listen to what God says:

> By the sweat of your face
> You shall eat bread,
> Till you return to the ground,
> Because from it you were taken;
> For you are dust,
> And to dust you shall return.
>
> —GENESIS 3:19

Therefore, just as through one man sin entered into the world, and death through sin, and so death spread to all men, because all sinned—

—ROMANS 5:12

"We all fall down." God doesn't soften the blow; He allows the hammer of reality to hit hard. God doesn't threaten; He promises. The theme threaded from Genesis to Revelation is the plague of death, and all humanity has the disease. Being the fallen creatures that we are, we don't want to face it. We try to anesthetize ourselves against it by giving it another name.

Tennyson calls it "crossing the bar." Shakespeare refers to it as "that knell that summons us to heaven or to hell." Browning calls it "that pale priest of the mute people." Pope says it is "the grim tyrant." Byron dubs it "that dreamless sleep." Euripedes calls it "the debt we all must pay."

Our initial response to death and dying is denial and isolation. Our very first response is, "It won't happen to me."

In my introduction to this book I mentioned the heart scare I went through in the Fall of 2000. I can testify to the reality of my own denial. Understand, during my almost four decades in various pastoral ministries, I have visited with, ministered to, and stood alongside the dying. My file folder marked "Funerals" is thick with messages I've brought, obituaries and eulogies I've read, and tender correspondence with grieving families I've sent and received. Like all pastors, dealing with death and the dying became a part of my calling that was as familiar as sermon preparation and as frequent as weddings.

Don't misunderstand. Although I was often engaged in this role as a shepherd of a flock, I never did so in a perfunctory manner. On the contrary, I found myself moved with compassion and even brought to tears on occasion. But I must confess, I did not ever think, *Some day this could be me.* Not until that early-morning episode I experienced with my heart. Not until then did the reality of my own mortality become a serious, conscious thought. And, truthfully, I don't think I'm that different from most people.

Death is real. "We all fall down." So our attempts to deny it, avoid it, or ignore it are as useless and meaningless as joining hands in a circle and singing "Ring around the roses, a pocket full of posies."

Satan lied to Adam and Eve in the Garden of Eden, telling them, "You shall surely not die" (Genesis 3:4)! And his great lie is perpetuated today in many forms.

Six Philosophies of Death

The Book of Ecclesiastes reveals six of the ways that mankind deals with death, or tries to *avoid* dealing with it. These six have become major philosophies, or systems of beliefs by which people live, and by which they try to make death seem as harmless as a nursery rhyme. As we consider these philosophies set forth in this ancient book written by Solomon, let's remember that he is writing strictly from the human perspective. He is helping the reader realize how those who attempt to conduct their lives without God think. Solomon himself went through a period of time when he thought this way. The confusion, the turmoil, and the misery he endured is not hidden from us when we read his lines in Ecclesiastes.

Fatalism

There is an appointed time for everything. And there is a time for
    every event under heaven—
A time to give birth, and a time to die;
A time to plant, and a time to uproot what is planted.
A time to kill, and a time to heal;
A time to tear down, and a time to build up.
A time to weep, and a time to laugh;
A time to mourn, and a time to dance.
A time to throw stones, and a time to gather stones;
A time to embrace, and a time to shun embracing.

A time to search, and a time to give up as lost;
A time to keep, and a time to throw away.
A time to tear apart, and a time to sew together;
A time to be silent, and a time to speak.
A time to love, and a time to hate;
A time for war, and a time for peace.
What profit is there to the worker from that in which he toils?

—ECCLESIASTES 3:1–9

In the first nine verses of Ecclesiastes 3, we find the philosophy of fatalism—perhaps the bleakest of all philosophies. People who embrace it occasionally call it "the doctrine of despair."

Fatalism says this: Events are fixed in advance—there is a time for everything. These events follow a blind, irrational pattern, and man has no responsibility. We are like leaves in the wind, blowing about without significance. We are not unlike a little tin soldier with a spring in his back. This spring is wound up tightly when he's born, and he marches through life with a meaningless walk until, finally, the spring winds down to a meaningless death, and that's life.

The fatalist says, "What's the purpose for living? Why go on? My generation, along with the hundreds of generations before me and after me, have gone through and will go through this same meaningless circle of time. What profit is it? It's all an exercise in futility."

What good does it do to get involved in life—to care about anything—when there's nothing to face but an inevitable fate that has neither meaning nor purpose?

SKEPTICISM

If you buy Fatalism, you aren't very far from the philosophy of Skepticism.

I have seen the task which God has given the sons of men with which to occupy themselves.

> He has made everything appropriate in its time. He has also
> set eternity in their heart, yet so that man will not find out the
> work which God has done from the beginning even to the end.
>   —ECCLESIASTES 3:10–11

Skepticism says, with a frown and a curled lip, "Nothing can be known for certain." This philosophy reaches its pinnacle in agnosticism, which proclaims, "No one can know anything for sure. The man who accepts anything as *the* final word cuts his head off, committing intellectual suicide."

This is the philosophy of the intelligentsia of our day: Keep searching, but don't reach any firm and final conclusion. They say, "Those who are dogmatic are the most ignorant. Those who admit their ignorance and keep searching are the most intelligent."

The skeptic says, "We'd like to know more about God, but we cannot. We simply cannot know Him. It's as though God is the great sadist, sitting in the shadows of heaven, every once in a while popping out and bludgeoning man with an unfair blow from His hand. Nobody can understand a God like that." All evil proves there is no such thing as a good God.

EPICUREANISM

If you buy Skepticism, you're primed for the philosophy of Epicureanism.

> I know that there is nothing better for them than to rejoice and
> to do good in one's lifetime; moreover, that every man who eats
> and drinks sees good in all his labor—it is the gift of God.
>   —ECCLESIASTES 3:12–13

"Life's just a cabaret, old chum. Have a good time! Live! Let live! That's all there is." This hedonistic philosophy says, "Forget about tomorrow! Eat, drink, and be merry! Today is all you have."

Oliver Wendell Holmes put it well when he said, "There is that glorious Epicurean philosophy uttered by my friend, the historian, in one of his flashing moments: 'Give us the luxuries of life, and we will dispense with its necessities.'"

Just bring us what is fun, and we'll escape the things that hurt.

A number of years ago, comedian Jerry Lewis was interviewed by reporters in his Las Vegas dressing room. At one point they asked him, "Mr. Lewis, what's your philosophy of life?"

"You see that motto on the wall?" he answered. "That's it."

He pointed to a well-worn quotation that he carried with him whenever he traveled and entertained. In bold print it read: "There are three things that are real: God, human folly, and laughter. Since the first two are beyond our comprehension, we must do what we can with the third."

"You really believe that?" the reporters asked.

"I *live* by that" was the comedian's response.

Two things are beyond our comprehension: God and human folly—God and sin. So? So let's kick back, relax, and have a great laugh. That's the essence of Epicureanism.

DEISM

Man can't do without religion. Our very nature compels us to believe something. Augustine said that our hearts are restless until they find their rest in God. And so, to add a consoling touch of religion, man adds the philosophy of Deism.

> I know that everything God does will remain forever; there is nothing to add to it and there is nothing to take from it, for God has so worked that men should fear Him.
>
> That which is has been already, and that which will be has already been, for God seeks what has passed by.
>
> Furthermore, I have seen under the sun that in the place of justice there is wickedness, and in the place of righteousness there is wickedness.

> I said to myself, "God will judge both the righteous man and the wicked man," for a time for every matter and for every deed is there.
>
> —ECCLESIASTES 3:14–17

In this philosophy, God is present, but man's reasoning is believed to be superior to divine revelation. Deism says, "There is no place for miracles. Everything that happens, happens by human explanation. The highest point in this existence on earth is the mind of man. Yes, there's a God, but He doesn't interrupt. He may judge, but in the end we'll all come out all right." Thomas Paine embraced Deism, as did Thomas Jefferson and several of our nation's founding fathers. Deism has a long tradition in our land.

EVOLUTIONISM

Occasionally, Deism gives birth to Evolutionism.

> I said to myself concerning the sons of men, "God has surely tested them in order for them to see that they are but beasts."
> For the fate of the sons of men and the fate of beasts is the same. As one dies so dies the other; indeed, they all have the same breath and there is no advantage for man over beast, for all is vanity.
>
> —ECCLESIASTES 3:18–19

Solomon observes the very thing that Darwin developed as a *theory*, then later saw as *reality*. From man's finite perspective, we are passing along through a process that's gradual, but constant—from the primordial ooze of the past to our present condition. And if you trace the process back far enough, you'll link us with the "beasts."

"What difference is there between man and beast? None. Why worry about today when you'll die like a dog? The beast in the field is no better or worse off than man when death comes. And that's the way I handle it," says the evolutionist.

This is as meaningless as grabbing hands with another plague victim and singing that nursery rhyme, walking around the circle of life, thinking somehow the scent of roses is going to preserve us from death.

The genius of a philosophy is not in the living of it, but in the dying with it. That's where it must stand the test.

UNIVERSALISM

And so man waves his arms in the presence of God and says, "There's one final answer: Universalism."

> All go to the same place. All came from the dust and all return to the dust.
>
> Who knows that the breath of man ascends upward and the breath of the beast descends downward to the earth?
>
> And I have seen that nothing is better than that man should be happy in his activities, for that is his lot. For who will bring him to see what will occur after him?
>
> —ECCLESIASTES 3:20–22

This offers the ultimate well-being of all persons. "We all *began* the same and we'll all *end* the same. God will embrace all people, saying, 'Ah, how wonderful to people heaven with individuals like you.'" Universalism says, "Be sincere. You'll be able to make it."

Hemingway, Wells, Huxley, Voltaire, Ingersoll, Durant, James. Name them! You will find them all woven like threads through the tapestry of Ecclesiastes 3. All these philosophies have by now been refined and perfected. They have found their way into books, which people believe makes them "fact"; they have been publicized and embraced. Yet, no matter how sensible they sound, no matter how much they tout the dignity, worth, ability, well-being, and power of mankind, these humanistic philosophies are no more effective than walking in a circle and singing, "Ring around the roses, a pocket full of posies," because "we all fall down."

Fatalism. Skepticism. Epicureanism. Deism. Evolutionism. Universalism. What is God's appraisal of all these?

Proverbs 14:12 tells us: "There is a way which seems right to a man, but its end is the way of death."

The word "right" comes from a Hebrew word that means "smooth, agreeable, or acceptable."

There is a way that seems agreeable and acceptable to man. It seems plausible. It makes good sense. It smoothes everything out. But it ends in death. We're back where we started: "We all fall down."

The Bible has two major themes from beginning to ending. One is the tragic truth about the plague: That is, man will die. The other is the glorious news of the cure: There is hope beyond the grave.

The Ultimate Cure

As the death cart rolls relentlessly through the city of humanity, the philosophers wail, "This will get you through." But God says, "I've got a better plan. As a matter of fact, I've got the *only* plan, the ultimate plan. It, alone, will save you."

We find that plan spelled out clearly in Romans 5, a magnificent chapter of hope.

> Therefore, just as through one man sin entered into the world, and death through sin, and so death spread to all men, because all sinned.
>
> —ROMANS 5:12

Because of Adam ("through one man") sin came into the world. With sin came death, which "spread to all men." Here, again, is the black plague of death—"we all fall down."

Humanity + iniquity = depravity. That's the formula for the plague of death. It's not polluted air; it's polluted souls. It's not the atmosphere around us; it's the nature within us. But God doesn't abandon us in our need. He comes to our rescue.

For while we were still helpless, at the right time Christ died for the ungodly.

For one will hardly die for a righteous man; though perhaps for the good man someone would dare even to die.

But God demonstrates His own love toward us, in that while we were yet sinners, Christ died for us.

Much more then, having now been justified by His blood, we shall be saved from the wrath of God through Him.

For if while we were enemies, we were reconciled to God through the death of His Son, much more, having been reconciled, we shall be saved by His life.

—ROMANS 5:6–10

As you read those lines, you realize this is no humanistic philosophy, hoping to help you feel better. God describes man in three words, none of which sound very attractive or appealing. Man without Christ: helpless. Man without Christ: sinful. Man without Christ: an enemy.

But, God says, having laid the truth on us, "There's hope!" Sure you have the disease. Sure you have the plague. And don't kid yourself, you will never be cured by singing the songs of the humanists of our era or those past. There is only one sure cure for the plague of death:

For if by the transgression of the one, death reigned through the one, much more those who receive the abundance of grace and of the gift of righteousness will reign in life through the One, Jesus Christ.

So then as through one transgression there resulted condemnation to all men, even so through one act of righteousness there resulted justification of life to all men.

For as through the one man's disobedience the many were made sinners, even so through the obedience of the One the many will be made righteous.

And the Law came in that the transgression might increase; but where sin increased, grace abounded all the more, that, as sin reigned in death, even so grace might reign through righteousness to eternal life through Jesus Christ our Lord.

—ROMANS 5:17–21

Think in terms of two contrasts. On one side are Adam and death. On the other are Christ and life. If you are without Jesus Christ, you live in the realm of sin and under the reign of death. If you know the Lord Jesus, you're living in the realm of grace and under the reign of life.

Adam & Death	Christ & Life
Sinfulness	Righteousness
Condemnation	Justification
Disobedience	Obedience
Death	Eternal life

Several times in this book I have included Eugene Petersen's helpful paraphrase of various sections of Scripture. Once again, for the sake of clarification, let's get a better understanding of all this from a section of Romans 5 taken from *The Message:*

The verdict on that one sin was the death sentence; the verdict on the many sins that followed was this wonderful life sentence. If death got the upper hand through one man's wrongdoing, can you imagine the breathtaking recovery life makes, sovereign life, in those who grasp with both hands this wildly extravagant life-gift, this grand setting-everything-right, that the one man Jesus Christ provides?

Here it is in a nutshell: Just as one person did it wrong and got us in all this trouble with sin and death, another person did it right and got us out of it. But more than just getting us out of trouble, he got us into life! One man said no to God and put many people in the wrong; one man said yes to God and put many in the right.

All that passing laws against sin did was produce more lawbreakers. But sin didn't, and doesn't, have a chance in competition with the aggressive forgiveness we call grace. When it's sin versus grace, grace wins hands down. All sin can do is threaten us with death, and that's the end of it. Grace, because God is putting everything together again through the Messiah, invites us into life—a life that goes on and on and on, world without end.

What a marvelous message! Sinful through Adam. Righteous in Christ. Condemned without Christ. Justified by Christ. That's the hope. Best of all, that's the cure for the plague: "A life that goes on and on and on, world without end."

We don't have to face death unprepared. As a matter of fact, the cross of Christ prepares us to die. Put another way, we are not really ready to live until we're ready to die. And in the hope of this great plan that God has laid out, there is the Lord Jesus Christ, available, ready, willing to accept those who will call upon Him.

Mankind is divided into two camps—not into six or nine or twelve philosophies, but only two camps: lost and saved. We are either *in* Christ or *out* of Christ.

On the lefthand side we have the person without the Lord Jesus. That individual, according to the Scriptures, is in Adam. Sin has entered, and with sin came death. We are helpless, sinners, and enemies. And the result is clear: That person exists in the darkness of condemnation and death.

But on the righthand side, in Christ, that person is declared righteous. He has peace. Because of God' grace he is saved from wrath and, therefore, lives in the bright new dawn of life, righteousness, and grace.

Those who are in Christ need not fear death and the grave. The sting has been taken from it. There is now only hope and victory.

"But wait a minute," says the philosopher. "How can we say that the man who lives by the philosophies of Ecclesiastes 3 is not ready to die? How do we know it doesn't take him throughout time and on into a blissful tomorrow?"

Good question. Perhaps we should allow a few of those who have embraced such thinking to answer, rather than putting words into their mouths.

Voltaire was, in his day, called Europe's greatest cynic. He took delight in shooting holes in what he called the most foolish religion of all time—Christianity. Yet his biographer said that Voltaire's last utterance on earth was an empty groan.

Anatole France was the famous rationalist of modern France, perhaps the most brilliant literary genius France ever produced. In his memoirs, France states the real condition of his soul: "In all the world the unhappiest creature is man! Enough! Enough! Ah, if you could read in my soul you would be terrified! There is not in all the universe a creature more unhappy than I. People think me happy. I have never been happy for one day, not for a single hour."[2]

H. G. Wells, the apostle of modernism, wrote similar words of his skeptical life when he approached death: "The time has come for me to reorganize my life, my peace—I cry out. I cannot adjust my life to secure any fruitful peace. Here I am at sixty-five, still seeking for peace . . . that is a dignified peace . . . a hopeless dream."[3]

Ernest Hemingway, who had rejected the Christianity of the home in which he had been raised, eventually took his own life. He had written, "There is no remedy for anything in life. . . . death is a sovereign remedy for my misfortunes. I live in a vacuum that is as lonely as a radio tube when the batteries are dead and there is no current to plug into."[4]

Will Durant, American educator and prolific writer, said, "There's nothing in life that is certain except defeat, death, and despair, a sleep from which it seems there is no awakening. Faith and hope disappear. Doubt and despair are the order of my day. It is impossible to give life any meaning any longer." Two weeks later, he died.[5]

Robert Ingersoll, a nineteenth century dramatic lecturer, lawyer, and ungodly skeptic, took delight in attacking Christianity from one end of America to another. Standing at the grave of his brother, these words fell from his lips: "Life is a narrow vale between the cold and barren peaks of two eternities. We strive in vain to look beyond the heights. We cry aloud and the only answer is the echo of our wailing cry."[6]

"Ring around the roses, a pocket full of posies, / Ashes, ashes … " *A sneeze,* and eternity comes. And the philosopher without Christ faces nothing … nothing but death.

One moment a young husband and father, a devout believer, is alive and well. The next moment his heart fails and he is gone, leaving a wife and two young sons. "It is impossible to face a time like this without being secure in my faith," says the young widow. No empty philosophy. No sprinkling of rose petals in the room of the dying. Only the reassuring words of hope.

That's the way to die. Not walking around in a circle, mumbling something we wish were true, but standing firm and secure on the truth of the cross and the empty tomb: "Because He lives, I too shall live."

Outside of Christ, there is no cure for the plague of death. There is only emptiness and superstition and hopeless despair.

In Christ, through His death and resurrection, there is life with God throughout eternity.

We stake our lives not on nursery rhymes or human-viewpoint philosophies, but on His death and resurrection. Rather than trying hard to grope our way through the maze of manmade ideas and opinions, through Christ we find ourselves empowered by the tragedy and triumph of the cross.

Breaking Death's Jaws

Thou has conquered in the flight,
Thou hast brought us life and light:
Now no more can death appall,
Now no more the grave enthrall;
Thou hast opened paradise,
And in Thee Thy saints shall rise.[1]

—LATIN, 1632

20
Breaking Death's Jaws

Let's stay with the subject of death a little while longer. I believe it will help us appreciate all the more the dawn that awaits us.

And speaking of death, I shall never forget the day my father died, shortly after the turn of the decade, in 1980. It was very late on a Wednesday night—in fact, it was already the early hours of Thursday morning. Cynthia and I were in bed when the shrill ring of the telephone by our bed awoke us. "You should come right away," said the nurse at the convalescent home. "Your father is dying."

When we arrived at Room 337, the nurse was cranking down the head of the bed. "He just died," she said. "Just seconds ago."

An eerie chill went up my back. I felt strangely orphaned as I walked to my father's bedside. Even though I had been preparing myself for this moment for several months, I wasn't ready for it.

I looked at the body of the father I had known for almost five decades. His eyelids were open, so I closed them. His hair was disheveled, so I stroked it back on his head. His life was gone, so I whispered, probably for my own benefit, "I love you, Dad. I really needed you. Good-bye."

After kissing him on the forehead, I turned around. Cynthia

reached out her arms and held me tenderly as I wept. Then we walked out into the cold night air.

Death had never been more real to me than it was that night . . . never.

And I thought of two things. First, I remembered the familiar line I've often quoted, from Euripedes, the Greek poet: "Death is the debt we all must pay." My dad had just paid that debt. But the word "all" also seemed to bounce around in my head. "We *all* must pay." Every person must pay the debt, every one of *us*.

And then, strangely, I recalled a recent newscast I had seen about a breed of dog called a pit bull. This breed has an unusual characteristic. When it fights and bites, its bite is so fierce, so strong, that sometimes they have to break the animal's jaw to release its grip. And I thought that night: *If I had one of those dogs, the perfect name for it would be Death.* Talk about a permanent grip and our inability to release it! No matter how hard the physicians and nurses and members of our family tried, there was no way that we could loosen death's grip on my father.

Death is a frightful thing. Life can be difficult enough, but death? We don't know what to do with it. We try to ignore it, but it won't go away. It visits our family and friends with heartbreaking regularity. Furthermore, we can't seem to soften it, even though we try to by softening the vocabulary that surrounds it. We don't say that someone "has died." We say that they are "resting," or that they have "passed on," or "passed away," or "gone to glory."

Some try to laugh at death. Woody Allen joked in one of his films, "It's not that I'm afraid to die. I just don't want to be there when it happens."

But jokes and euphemisms cannot soften the bite of Death. It is inevitable, inescapable, solitary, universal, permanent. Once its jaws tighten, it does not let go. We cannot escape.

In the 1980s, educators attempted to dull the sting of death by making it part of the curriculum in high schools and universities. Those who specialize in "thanatology" are called "thanatologists," from the Greek word for death, *thanatos*. The first time thanatologist Edwin

Snideman taught a course on death at Harvard, two hundred students showed up in a classroom that would seat only twenty. Since then, colleges and universities across the country offer courses and seminars on death and dying, grief and immortality.

In his book *Death of Man,* Snideman writes, "We must face the fact that death is the one act in which man is forced to engage. The threat of being erased is the most treacherous of forced punishment." Strong words, aren't they? "The threat of being erased."

"Into the jaws of death rode the six hundred," penned Tennyson in his *Charge of the Light Brigade.* The jaws of death are firm and final.

THE PERVASIVENESS OF DEATH

The first mention of death in the Bible is in Genesis 2. Interestingly, it is a prediction. Man is still in a stage of innocence. Adam and Eve are in a perfect environment, innocence prevails, but God warns them of the possibility of death.

> And the LORD God commanded the man, saying, "From any tree of the garden you may eat freely; but from the tree of the knowledge of good and evil you shall not eat, for in the day that you eat from it you shall surely die."
>
> —GENESIS 2:16–17

That's a prediction and a promise. We could also call it the first prophecy of the Scriptures. The day you sin, God says, you will die. If sin comes, death comes. The two cannot be separated. Where there is sin, there will be death, which is exactly what happened. When Adam and Eve sinned, they immediately died spiritually, and they both began to age and die physically. That set in motion an uninterrupted cycle of birth, life, and death. It continues to this day.

> So all the days that Adam lived were nine hundred and thirty years, and he died.

Then Seth lived eight hundred and seven years after he became the father of Enosh, and he had other sons and daughters. So all the days of Seth were nine hundred and twelve years, and he died.

Then Enosh lived eight hundred and fifteen years after he became the father of Kenan, and he had other sons and daughters. So all the days of Enosh were nine hundred and five years, and he died.

Then Kenan lived eight hundred and forty years after he became the father of Mahalalel, and he had other sons and daughters. So all the days of Kenan were nine hundred and ten years, and he died.

Then Jared lived eight hundred years after he became the father of Enoch, and he had other sons and daughters. So all the days of Jared were nine hundred and sixty-two years, and he died.

And Enoch lived sixty-five years, and became the father of Methuselah.

Then Methuselah lived seven hundred and eighty-two years after he became the father of Lamech, and he had other sons and daughters. So all the days of Methuselah were nine hundred and sixty-nine years, and he died.

—GENESIS 5:5–27

Adam and Eve sinned, and from then on the record is clear: he died . . . he died . . . he died . . . died. They all died. Even Methuseleh, after living 969 years on earth—almost a thousand years—died. Can you imagine being sentenced to earth for 969 *years!* And even then he didn't escape the curse of death.

Speaking of escape, it is a simple fact that many people believe that death provides escape—escape from reality, escape from pain, escape from judgment. Listen! Death is not only inevitable; it is inescapable. But it is not an escape. Death is like a narrow tunnel that leads into eternity. And yet every day people either attempt or manage to succeed in taking their own lives. In fact, suicide among teenagers has become of intense concern in our day, due to the increasing number of young people who take their own lives each year.

Comedian Freddie Prinze was the darling of television in his day. *Chico and the Man* was the number one sitcom and Freddie won our hearts. At age twenty-two, he performed at the presidential inaugural ball as the most sophisticated and influential people in the nation watched and applauded. Billy Graham, in his book *How to Be Born Again,* traces the story of Freddie's tragic ending.

> A close friend [of Prinze], comedian David Brenner, explained to *Time* magazine, "There was no transition in Freddie's life. It was an explosion. It's tough to walk off a subway from the ghetto at age 19 and step out of a Rolls Royce the next day." Producer James Komack, also a close confidant, said, "Freddie saw nothing around that would satisfy him. He would ask me, 'Is this what it is? Is this what it's all about?'" Mr. Komack said, "His real despondency, whether he could articulate it or not, concerned the questions: 'Where do I fit in? Where's my happiness?' I would tell him, 'Freddie, this is happiness right here. You're a star!' He would say, 'Naw. Naw, that's not happiness for me anymore.' As *Time* magazine lamented at the end of the story, 'For one of the most singular escape stories in ghetto history, escape was not enough.'"[2]

Death is not an escape. It's an open door that says, "Welcome to eternity!" It is inevitable. It is universal. It is inescapable. Yet psychologists tell us that the one place people cannot envision themselves is in a casket at a funeral service. It represents a darkness few can bear to imagine.

In one of the oldest books of the Bible, the Book of Job, the suffering protagonist cries, "If a man dies, will he live again" (Job 14:14)? In the midst of the pain that God chose not to end, Job began to question things beyond life. Death must have looked pretty comforting to him at that point. "If I die, will I live again? Just tell me straight."

But Job asked the wrong question, because it isn't a question of *if* a man dies; it's a question of *when.* "When I die, will I live again?"

John 11 provides us with a very personal answer to Job's question. Though the setting is quite different, the subject of life beyond the grave is the same. Let's fast-forward to the first century when Jesus walked among His friends in Galilee and Judea.

THE PAIN OF GRIEF

In the little hamlet of Bethany, about two miles outside Jerusalem, lived three of Jesus' closest friends: Martha, Mary, and Lazarus. When the press of the public was too great, and He needed a place to rest and relax, Jesus retreated to their home. One day, however, He receives word that His friend Lazarus is ill.

> The sisters therefore sent to Him, saying, "Lord, behold, he whom You love is sick."
>
> But when Jesus heard it, He said, "This sickness is not unto death, but for the glory of God, that the Son of God may be glorified by it."
>
> Now Jesus loved Martha, and her sister, and Lazarus. When therefore He heard that he was sick, He stayed then two days longer in the place where He was.
>
> —JOHN 11:3–6

Mary and Martha don't ask Jesus to come; they just assume He will. But Jesus does not drop everything and hurry to their home. Instead, He waits, saying that His friend's sickness is "for the glory of God." He waits for *days,* in fact. And Lazarus dies!

Too often Christians try to take the hideousness out of death. In doing so, however, we cut short the grieving process. We're so eager to rush to the end and show the hope beyond the grave that we don't deal adequately with the pain that accompanies death. For there is no denying it: Death is an ugly thing! Jesus says it is an enemy that He will ultimately destroy.

Joe Bayly, in his book *A View from the Hearse,* tells of how he lost three of his sons to death. One of his sons died of leukemia when he was five years old. It wasn't a pleasant or serene death. He didn't just fall asleep. It happened at two-thirty in the afternoon. "The boy was violently hemorrhaging, screaming for a bedpan," Bayly says. "I couldn't talk about it for two years."

At another time and place, at a memorial site on the rim of the Grand Canyon, a group of people met to honor those who had died in a mid-air collision. Suddenly a man in the group cried out in anger: "Where was God when this happened?" His words echoed down through the vast canyon and back into everyone's ears: "Where was God when this happened? Where was God when this happened? Where was God when this happened? Where was God? Where was God?"

Wisely, the young minister who was leading the service was honest enough to admit his own inadequacy in explaining the unfathomable. After the man's words had finally echoed into silence, the minister quietly responded, "Where was God when this happened? I have only one answer. God was in the same place He was when men took His Son and crucified Him on a cross."

Mary and Martha ask a similar question. "Where is Jesus? Where was He when our brother was sick? Where was He when our brother was dying? We told Him that His friend was sick. We thought He loved Lazarus. Now our brother is dead. Where is He?"

Jesus finally makes His way to Bethany, but before He gets to their home, Martha confronts Him on the road.

> Martha therefore said to Jesus, "Lord, if You had been here, my brother would not have died."
>
> —JOHN 11:21

Implied in that strong rebuke is, "It's Your fault! Here we were, ministering, doing all we could, without the power of God, and You stood away from us, at a distance, and You waited and You delayed. Even though we notified You, You didn't come to help. Where were You when we were hurting?"

And then follows a dialogue that has become one of the most significant dialogues in the Scriptures—certainly one of the most significant dialogues in the life of Jesus.

Martha adds a comment designed to soften the blow of her earlier outburst:

> "Even now I know that whatever You ask of God, God will give You."
>
> Jesus said to her, "Your brother shall rise again."
>
> Martha said to Him, "I know that he will rise again in the resurrection on the last day."
>
> Jesus said to her, "I am the resurrection and the life; he who believes in Me shall live even if he dies, and everyone who lives and believes in Me shall never die. Do you believe this?"
>
> —JOHN 11:22–26

"Don't give me theological facts," says Martha. "I know that there will be a resurrection, and I know my brother will rise from the grave. But I want him here . . . *now!*"

"I am the resurrection and the life," says Jesus.

Don't miss the pronoun "I" here. Jesus doesn't say to her, "Look, you've got your theological facts correct. You're on target. You're safe, Martha." Instead, He says, "Martha, look at *Me!* Martha, look up! Martha, *I* am God. I have the power over death. I've broken the jaws of the grave. Martha, *I* am the resurrection. If you know Me, you know resurrection. He who believes in Me, even though he dies, will live."

In human terms, we are absolutely helpless in the face of death. I walked out of my father's room that early Thursday morning back in 1980 knowing that I had absolutely no power to bring life back—none whatsoever. And I drove away grimly accepting the inevitable. Of course I was rejoicing that my father was with the Savior, but I also knew that earthly finality—there was nothing I could do to draw him back.

Martha was grieving over the same thing. And Jesus said, "Oh,

Martha, it isn't theology that I'm testing you on; it's faith. I am the resurrection. I am the life. Believe in *Me,* Martha!"

But what about her sister, Mary?

> Therefore, when Mary came where Jesus was, she saw Him, and fell at His feet, saying to Him, "Lord, if You had been here, my brother would not have died."
>
> —JOHN 11:32

Another family member, but the same rebuke. Burdened with grief and disbelief, Mary also implies that her brother's death is Jesus' fault—if He had only been there, Lazarus would not have died. "Where were You, Lord?"

Have you ever asked that question? Yes, you probably have. Remember when? When you reached the end of your rope? When you lost a loved one? When you were going through severe suffering? When your child's fever kept rising? When your marriage partner rejected you for someone else?

Where was God when the bottom dropped out? He could have changed things.

Where was He? Call to mind the young minister's words at the canyon: God was at the same place He was when His Son was crucified—in full control, omnipresent.

"Where were You, Lord?" Mary asks. And Jesus is now overwhelmed with grief.

> When Jesus therefore saw her weeping, and the Jews who came with her, also weeping, He was deeply moved in spirit, and was troubled, and said, "Where have you laid him?" They said to Him, "Lord, come and see."
>
> Jesus wept.
>
> —JOHN 11:33–35

Take note of Jesus' response. When you counsel the grieving, you don't need a lot of words. When Jesus saw them weeping, He grieved with them. He wept. The great Conqueror of death Himself was grieved by the enemy's ugly power over life.

Ah, but not for long. What a change when He, shortly thereafter, stared death in the face!

> Jesus therefore again being deeply moved within, came to the tomb. Now it was a cave, and a stone was lying against it.
>
> Jesus said, "Remove the stone." Martha, the sister of the deceased, said to Him, "Lord, by this time there will be a stench, for he has been dead four days."
>
> Jesus said to her, "Did I not say to you, if you believe, you will see the glory of God?"
>
> And so they removed the stone. And Jesus raised His eyes, and said, "Father, I thank Thee that Thou heardest Me.
>
> "And I know that Thou hearest Me always; but because of the people standing around I said it, that they may believe that Thou didst send Me."
>
> And when He had said these things, He cried out with a loud voice, "Lazarus, come forth."
>
> He who had died came forth, bound hand and foot with wrappings; and his face was wrapped around with a cloth. Jesus said to them, "Unbind him, and let him go."
>
> —JOHN 11:38–44

This is one of those epochal moments recorded in the pages of the Bible. In only a few words, our imaginations are given the room to run free. Please allow me . . .

All eyes in the group surrounding Jesus were fixed on the darkness inside the now-open tomb. An eerie chill ran up their spines as they stood in silence, mouths open. At first, they saw nothing except a black hole where the tight jaws of death gripped its victim. Then, "Look! Look there!" someone said as he pointed toward something moving inside the shallow cave.

A grayish, awkward figure stirred, then rose slowly off the limestone shelf just inside the entrance. Dragging itself upright, the figure turned and shuffled toward the daylight.

Arm in arm, the sisters stared in disbelief. Each could feel the heavy pounding in her chest. They sucked in their breaths, then gasped together, "It's Lazarus . . . he's back . . . he's alive!"

As the tightly wrapped figure of a man began to twist and turn, trying to shake off the grave clothes, Jesus smiled and commanded, "Unbind him. Set him free!"

Both sisters sprang to aid the figure. One grabbed for the head napkin as the other grasped a loose end of one of the strips of cloth and began to pull it away. Quickly they looked into Lazarus' eyes, which were bright and flashing with life. His broad smile reassured them, especially when he said to Mary, "Hurry up and get me out of this mess!" All three were laughing and crying at the same time. "You're alive, you're back!" screamed Martha.

What an awesome experience! Lazarus had died. Make no mistake, the man was actually, completely, thoroughly dead. For four *days* he had been in that grave. But when Jesus said, "Come out!" Lazarus came out. Talk about being empowered! The jaws of death were supernaturally broken by the One who has the power over life's longterm enemy.

Lazarus's resuscitation was only temporary, of course. He still had the same physical body, subject to death and decay. Lazarus would still have to pass through death, that narrow tunnel to eternity.

THE ULTIMATE TRIUMPH

One day, Jesus Christ will once again say to His own, "Come out," and graves all around the world will give up their dead.

I love to tell people at funeral services, when we're standing around the graveside, "All of you should understand, we are standing on resurrection ground."

"'I am the resurrection and the life,'" Jesus says to His friends in Bethany, and to us. "'He who believes in Me shall live even if he dies, and everyone who lives and believes in Me shall never die. Do you believe this'" (John 11:25–26)?

Jesus has broken the jaws of death. He has won the victory beyond the grave. And all those who know Him, who have trusted in Him for eternal life, can anticipate the same triumph.

No one, no matter how successful in this life, can claim victory over death all on his or her own. We may climb our ladders of achievement, of higher education, of financial prosperity, of athletic reputation, of faithful and diligent responsibility, of integrity in business, of high moral standards. But only through faith in Christ do we have the assurance of hope beyond the grave.

Though His resurrection, He offers Himself—not a religion, or a philosophy, or a lengthy period of probation through which we might climb some ladder to perfection. No, He takes us as we are and makes us as He is.

The Essential Redeemer

The great Russian author Ivan Turgenev speaks of the grave in his book *Fathers and Sons.* Specifically, he speaks of a village graveyard in one of the remote corners of Russia. Among the many neglected graves was one "untouched by man, untrampled by beast," writes Turgenev.

> Only the birds rested on it and sang at daybreak. Often from the nearby village two feeble old people, husband and wife, moving with heavy steps and supporting one another, came to visit this grave. Kneeling at the railing and gazing intently at the stone under which their son was lying, they yearned and they wept. After a brief word they wiped the dust away from the stone, set a straight branch of fir tree, and then began to pray.
>
> Can it be that their prayers and their tears are fruitless? Can it be that love, sacred love, devoted love is not all-powerful?
>
> Oh, no! However passionate, sinning, and rebellious the heart hidden in the tomb, the flowers growing over it peep serenely at

us with their innocent eyes. They tell us not of eternal peace alone, but of that great peace of nature. They tell us, too, of eternal reconciliation and of life without end.[3]

Agh! Turgenev, great writing, bad theology! Because the birds sing in the springtime, the grass turns green again, the snow melts, the blossoms return to the branches, and the earth is renewed, will the person underneath the earth have eternal life with God? That's mere emotion. And it won't bring eternal reconciliation and life without end.

Job, however, found the answer. He asked the question we referred to earlier: "If a man dies, will he live again?" And he finally discovered the answer.

And as for me, I know that my Redeemer lives,
And at the last He will take His stand on the earth.

—JOB 19:25

In order to handle death, we don't need university courses or impressive accomplishments. We don't need the naturalist telling us that the snow will melt, the flowers will bloom, the grass will turn green and life will revive. What we need, plain and simple, is a *redeemer*.

The term "redeemer" comes from the Hebrew word *goel*, meaning "defender." We need someone to defend our cause, someone to acquit us of all charges laid against us.

No thanatologist can say, "Your sins are forgiven." But the Lord in heaven can look into my face and say, "You're forgiven. Come into My presence, My son. You have a *goel*. You have a Redeemer."

Who is this Redeemer? Go back to Job's words. According to Job 19:25, He is one who is alive. In other words, for me to have the kind of life that isn't natural with my own human body, I must be rightly connected to the one who has a supernatural life. Furthermore, He must be one who has gone on beyond the grave and can tell me the truth about what I can expect and safely get me there, too. That's the Redeemer. And He lives.

Someday we will stand before God. And when we do, we will need something more than speculative imagination or a warm, fuzzy feeling about nature. When we pass from time into the presence of the Eternal God, we will need more than good medical assistance or the promise of some well-meaning friend. We will need a *goel,* a living Redeemer, whose nail-pierced hands hold our salvation and whose shed blood is the wonderful detergent that can wash away our sins and present us faultless before the presence of God's glory, with exceeding joy.

Because my Redeemer lives, I will live forever!

Soren Kierkegaard, the Danish philosopher, wrote a book entitled *The Sickness Unto Death,* in which he said, "Man is born and lives in sin. He cannot do anything for himself; he can only do harm to himself."

After years of psychological study, Dr. Carl Jung wrote, "All the old primitive sins are not dead but are crouching in the dark corners of our modern hearts, still there, and still as ghastly as ever."

You better believe it.

Today, hearts that are "as ghastly as ever" are seeking a *goel,* but too often they search everywhere but the right place. And where is that? Go to the cross where our Savior died. Go to the grave—to the empty tomb from which He was raised.

The question is not, "Will I live forever?" Everyone lives forever. The soul never dies. The question is, "*Where* will you live forever?" Where will you spend eternity?

In 1757 Christian F. Gellert penned these words:

> "Jesus lives, and so shall I.
> Death! thy sting is gone forever!
> He who deigned for me to die
> Lives, the bands of death to sever.
> He shall raise me from the dust—
> Jesus is my Hope and Trust."[4]

We don't need a thanatologist. We don't need a naturalist. We don't need an out-of-body experience. We don't need a poet or a philosopher. We don't even need a theologian. What we do need, desperately, is the Redeemer who has broken the jaws of death.

The longer I live the more convinced I am that a person is not really ready to live until he's ready to die. Those who live with the greatest assurance and security and with the least amount of panic are those who know how to die, through the Redeemer who lives.

Though grieved because I would never see my father again on this earth, I walked out into the darkness that cold night in 1980 with the calm assurance that I *would* see him again—at the dawn of eternity. What a wonderful hope.

Tell me, is that *your* hope?

Triumph for the Undeserving

Soar we now where Christ has led,
Foll'wing our exalted Head;
Made like Him, like Him we rise,
Ours the cross,
the grave,
the skies.
Alleluia![1]

—CHARLES WESLEY, 1739

21

Triumph for the Undeserving

We've been awfully serious for a long time. I think it's time for a break, and maybe a smile or two.

Down through the years I've collected epitaphs. Messages etched on tombstones are often surprising and sometimes hilarious. I always wish I'd known the deceased better or, perhaps, the one who wrote the message for all to read. Here are a few that will bring a smile.

An old wooden grave marker on Boot Hill:

Here lies Les Moore, shot four times with a forty-four
No Les, No Moore.

In a Ribbesford, England, cemetery:

Anna Wallace
The children of Israel wanted bread;
The Lord sent them manna.
Old Clerk Wallace wanted a wife;
The devil sent him Anna.

Another old grey-slate stone in England:

> Beneath this sod, a lump of clay,
> Lies Arabella Young,
> Who, on the twenty-fourth of May
> Began to hold her tongue.

A lonely widow wrote this epitaph, which appears on an old headstone in a Vermont cemetery:

> Sacred to the memory of my husband,
> John Barnes, who died Jan. 3, 1803.
> His comely young widow, aged 23, has
> Many qualifications of a good wife
> And yearns to be comforted.

In a Silver City, Nevada, cemetery:

> Here lies Butch—we planted him raw—
> He was quick on the trigger
> But slow on the draw.

In a cemetery near the church I used to pastor, this brief warning appears on a granite marker:

> You can't win!

Some epitaphs make us smile. That one makes us wish we knew more, doesn't it? And then there are those that remind us of the spiritual dimension of life, like this one that appears on James Russell Lowell's grave:

> Here lies that part of James Russell Lowell,
> Which hindered him from doing well.

One of my favorites is the epitaph that Benjamin Franklin requested they etch on his stone:

> Like the cover of an old book,
> Its contents torn out,
> And stripped of its lettering and guilding,
> Lies here food for worms.
> But the work shall not be lost
> For it will (as he believes)
> Appear once more,
> In a new and more elegant edition,
> Revised and corrected by the Author.

I am especially fond of that one because it looks beyond the tombstone and focuses on the ultimate triumph that is ours in Christ.

In his classic sixteenth-century *Book of Martyrs,* John Foxe records some of the epitaphs of the ancient martyrs buried in the catacombs beneath the city of Rome. Having been there and seen some of them with my own eyes, I can testify to the moving messages that appear, often accompanied by symbols of vines, ships under full sail, the fish, or a cross. One reads, "Here lies Marcia, asleep in peace." Another, simply, "Victorious in Christ."

What contrasts to the ancient graves of hopeless unbelievers:

> Live for the present hour,
> Since we're sure of nothing else.

> Traveler, curse me not as you pass,
> I am in darkness and I cannot answer you.

What a difference faith makes! What a miserable way to live, without the Light of reassurance. Only darkness.

This is a good time to track that tragic path a little further. What would life be like for us if there were no dawn to anticipate? Let's assume for the next few minutes that there is no resurrection. The Apostle Paul follows that thought in his first letter to the Corinthians, and he comes up with at least six results.

What If . . .?

Let's suppose for a moment that the false is true. If there is no resurrection of the dead, six things result, like dominos pushing against each other, toppling one after another.

> But if there is no resurrection of the dead, not even Christ has been raised; and if Christ has not been raised, then our preaching is vain, your faith also is vain.
>
> Moreover we are even found to be false witnesses of God, because we witnessed against God that He raised Christ, whom He did not raise, if in fact the dead are not raised.
>
> For if the dead are not raised, not even Christ has been raised; and if Christ has not been raised, your faith is worthless; you are still in your sins.
>
> Then those also who have fallen asleep in Christ have perished.
>
> If we have hoped in Christ in this life only, we are of all men most to be pitied.
>
> —1 Corinthians 15:13–19

Count them. If Christ hasn't been raised . . .
our preaching is in vain,
our faith is vain,
we are liars,
we are still in our sins,
the dead have perished forever, and
we are to be pitied more than anyone else.
If there is no resurrection, we live and die in our sins. We are the most pitiful creatures on the face of the earth. Pity Joe Bayly, who

anticipated seeing his three boys someday in heaven. Pity Corrie ten Boom, who awaited being with her sister, Betsy, in glory. Pity the grieving Christians all around the world who have one strand of hope to carry them through today—the hope of the eternal tomorrow. Pity them.

But no, says Paul. A thousand times no! Wrong assumption and, therefore, wrong conclusion. For Christ *has* been raised from the dead!

But Now . . . !

But now Christ has been raised from the dead, the first fruits of those who are asleep.

—1 CORINTHIANS 15:20

We don't use the word "first fruits" today. We use the word "sample." Christ has been raised from the dead, and He is a living, breathing sample of all those who are yet to believe in Him and who will yet, like Him, be raised.

Then Paul writes those thrilling words, so magnificently set to music by the great composer Handel in *The Messiah:*

For since by a man came death, by a man also came the resurrection of the dead.

For as in Adam all die, so also in Christ all shall be made alive.

—1 CORINTHIANS 15:21–22

We need to be changed within and without. That's a major purpose of resurrection. Here on earth we live in fragile, perishable bodies. So if we are to enter an imperishable, permanent heaven, our bodies must change. We have mortal bodies; so if we are to enter into immortality, those bodies must be made immortal.

Behold, I tell you a mystery; we shall not all sleep, but we shall all be changed, in a moment, in the twinkling of an eye, at the last trumpet; for the trumpet will sound, and the dead will be raised imperishable, and we shall be changed.

For, this perishable must put on the imperishable, and this mortal must put on immortality.

—1 Corinthians 15:51–53

That's resurrection in a nutshell. God slips into the grave and miraculously changes the entire structure of the body so that it becomes like His own Son's resurrected body, and thus, we can live forever.

The mystery is that not all are going to pass into the Lord's presence through death. Some will be alive at the time the Lord Jesus Christ returns for His own. And between earth and heaven, in the fluttering of an eye, at the last trumpet, the dead will be raised, the living will be changed, and there will be this magnificent family reunion, and we will be home with Him forever. Though undeserving in and of ourselves, through Christ we triumph. It's enough to make us laugh out loud!

As one American poet writes:

> Let's celebrate Easter with the rite of laughter. Christ died and rose and lives.
>
> Laugh like a woman who holds her first baby. Our enemy Death will soon be destroyed.
>
> Laugh like a man who finds he doesn't have cancer, or he does, but now there's a cure. Christ opened wide the door of heaven.
>
> Laugh like children at Disneyland's gates. This world is owned by God and He'll return to rule.
>
> Laugh like a man who walks away uninjured from a wreck in which his car was totaled.
>
> Laugh as if all the people in the whole world were invited to a picnic, and then invite them.[2]

Come to a picnic! You'll be joined by people who will no longer cry, no longer get sick, never die, and spend eternity in the presence of their

Savior, rejoicing with Him forever as the Lamb of God through whose stripes we are healed, on the merits of the One who takes away the sin of the world.

German theologian Helmut Thielicke wrote:

> The Easter faith, then, is not just an upward glance to satisfy my curiosity. It is a summons of the Prince of Life. . . . Perhaps God will require your soul this night. Who knows? Be supremely careful, then, that your soul is in the one, good hand which can still the waves, open the graves, bind up wounds and cancel guilt. Then the dark companion cannot cross the circle which the Saviour has drawn around you. Then your coffin will be a couch on which you will awaken when the morning of resurrection dawns. Then the burial place, whether at home, or on the high seas, or in a distant land, will be a plot where you will sleep as a seed in the eternal sowing of God, to ripen on the day of harvest.
>
> Therefore, when I die—though now I die no more—and someone finds my skull, may this skull preach to him as follows: I have no eyes, yet I see Him; I have no brain nor understanding, yet I know Him; I have no lips, yet I kiss Him; I have no tongue, yet I praise Him with all you who call upon His name. I am a hard skull, yet I am softened and melted in His love. I lie without in the churchyard, yet I am within Paradise. All suffering is forgotten because of His great love when for us He bore His cross and went to Calvary.[3]

The finest and most fitting epitaph that could ever be put on a gravestone is found in 1 Corinthians:

> But when this perishable will have put on the imperishable, and this mortal will have put on immortality, then will come about the saying that is written,
> "DEATH IS SWALLOWED UP in victory.
>
> "O DEATH, WHERE IS YOUR VICTORY? O DEATH, WHERE IS YOUR STING?"

The sting of death is sin, and the power of sin is the law; but thanks be to God, who gives us the victory through our Lord Jesus Christ.

—1 CORINTHIANS 15:54–57

When the storm gets wild and death is absolutely certain, you will have one Light to get you through it, and that's the Light on the horizon at the dawn of the resurrection.

A Norwegian fisherman and his two sons were out on their daily fishing run. By mid-afternoon a sharp, brisk wind was whipping salty spray into the faces of the rugged man and his teenage boys. As the wind increased, the waves grew into gray-blue giants. The little boat pitched back and forth as the three rowed desperately to get back to shore. The storm was so fierce that it washed out the light in the lighthouse on the shore, leaving the fishermen dependent upon dark, groping guesswork.

Meanwhile, on shore, in their rustic cottage where their wife and mother waited for them, a fire broke out. Unable to put it out, the woman watched as the flames destroyed their home and all their earthly possessions.

When the father and sons finally made it safely to shore, she was waiting for them with the tragic news. Yet even as she told her husband of the terrible fire that had destroyed their home and all their possessions, he seemed strangely unmoved by the loss. It was as though he never heard the news.

"Didn't you hear me, Karl?" she asked. "Our house is gone."

"Yes, I heard you," he said. "But a few hours ago we were lost at sea, fighting fierce wind and high waves. Our only guide to the shoreline was the lighthouse on the cliff, and then it went out. I was certain we would die. Then I noticed a dim, yellow glow in the distance. We turned our boat and rowed toward the light. It grew brighter and brighter, and we followed it safely to the shore."

"You see, Ingrid," he said, "that little yellow glow was the first sight of our house on fire. At the peak of the blaze, we could see the shoreline bright as day. The same fire that destroyed our house created a light that saved our lives."[4]

We're on the sea of life and all the lights are out. Our ship is going down, and the only way to get to shore is the light of the resurrection.

Through the tragedy of a burning house a family was saved. Through the tragedy of a crucified Jesus we have a risen Savior. And because He lives, we also live.

THE LIGHT THAT WILL NEVER GO OUT

The constantly recurring theme and the grand climax in the great symphony of the gospel is the resurrection of our Lord, Jesus Christ. Though we are undeserving, He died for our sins, and He arose from the dead, triumphant over sin and death. His triumph becomes our only hope of victory. If we subtract this from our message of love and hope, then we really have nothing to say, for it is the resurrection of Jesus Christ that assures us of our own personal salvation.

Death is not the end, but the beginning. It is not termination, but promotion. And this we know, because Jesus arose from the dead! We shall indeed be risen again. The perishable shall become imperishable, and the mortal will become immortal on that great day.

This provides all the motivation we need to labor committedly and sacrificially in the purposes of our Lord. Let us be awake and aware always. Even as we rest in what God has done on our behalf, let us be on the tiptoe of expectancy—working, serving, giving, loving, keeping the faith and demonstrating that faith to the world of men and women around us. And dedicating ourselves in loving service to God and humanity. The resurrection is the key to the mystery of eternity—the key to the last things. It's the light in our faith that will never go out.

With her inimitable bravado, the aging actress Katherine Hepburn offered the following comment to an interviewer: "I think we're finally to a point where we've learned to see death with a sense of humor. I have to. When you're my age, it's as if you're a car. First a tire blows, and you go and get that fixed. And a headlight goes out, and you go and get that fixed. And then one day, you drive into the shop, and the man frowns and says, 'Sorry, Miss, they don't have this make anymore.'"

That's what happens when we get older. We realize that death is near, and so some of us joke about it.

But you can laugh at death just so long. For the truth is, most people are scared to death of it (no pun intended).

The Bible calls death, "the king of terrors" (Job 18:14).

In *Pilgrim's Progress,* John Bunyan refers to death as Mr. Fearing. Pilgrim says of him, "He is a most troublesome man, one of the most troublesome pilgrims I have ever met."

Yet some believers possess a faith so strong that they are able to look beyond death. The great preacher Dr. Donald Barnhouse lost his wife when she was only in her thirties. She left him with three children ages twelve and under. Dr. Barnhouse chose to bury his wife and conduct the service himself. While he was driving to the memorial service with his three grieving, heartbroken children staring blankly out the window, a truck passed them on the highway and cast a shadow over their car. Dr. Barnhouse, never losing his brilliant ability to illustrate, paused and thought, *What does a father tell his motherless children at a time like this?* Then he looked at his twelve-year-old daughter and said, "Sweetheart, tell me, would you rather be run over by that truck or by its shadow?" Startled by the question, she said, "Oh, I don't know, Daddy, the shadow, I guess."

"Why?" he asked.

"Because the shadow can't hurt you."

He then said, "Children, listen. Your mother has not been run over by death, but by the shadow of death."

That shadow is going to cross over every one of us, but when we are in Christ, ultimately the shadow can't hurt us.

A major, yet future, event will be the judgment our Lord will conduct, following His return in glory.

But when the Son of Man comes in His glory, and all the angels with Him, then He will sit on His glorious throne.

And all the nations will be gathered before Him; and He will separate them from one another, as the shepherd separates the sheep from the goats; and He will put the sheep on His right, and the goats on the left.

Then the King will say to those on His right, "Come, you who are blessed of My Father, inherit the kingdom prepared for you from the foundation of the world.

"For I was hungry, and you gave Me something to eat; I was thirsty, and you gave Me drink; I was a stranger, and you invited Me in; naked, and you clothed Me; I was sick, and you visited Me; I was in prison, and you came to Me."

Then the righteous will answer Him, saying, "Lord, when did we see You hungry, and feed You, or thirsty, and give You drink?

"And when did we see You a stranger, and invite You in, or naked, and clothe You?

"And when did we see You sick, or in prison, and come to You?"

And the King will answer and say to them, "Truly I say to you, to the extent that you did it to one of these brothers of Mine, even the least of them, you did it to Me."

Then He will also say to those on His left, "Depart from Me, accursed ones, into the eternal fire which has been prepared for the devil and his angels; for I was hungry, and you gave Me nothing to eat; I was thirsty, and you gave Me nothing to drink; I was a stranger, and you did not invite Me in; naked, and you did not clothe Me; sick, and in prison, and you did not visit Me."

Then they themselves also will answer, saying, "Lord, when did we see You hungry, or thirsty, or a stranger, or naked, or sick, or in prison, and did not take care of You?"

Then He will answer them, saying, "Truly I say to you, to the extent that you did not do it to one of the least of these, you did not do it to Me."

And these will go away into eternal punishment, but the righteous into eternal life.

—MATTHEW 25:31–46

Sitting on His glorious throne, Jesus will serve as sovereign Judge.
He will separate the sheep from the goats—not literal sheep and literal
goats, but people. This judgment will include all the nations. People
like us. Including people who are yet to be born. Somehow all nations
will be brought before Him, alive and fully conscious.

Our Lord will demonstrate supernatural discernment. If there is
judgment, then there must be discernment between the destinies of
sheep (those who know Him) and goats (those who do not).

Heaven is something we inherit. We are undeserving, therefore we
do not *earn* heaven; it is a *gift* provided by the One who went before
us. "It is the kingdom prepared for you."

Since the beginning of time, God has anticipated the joy of His
people in His presence throughout eternity.

How do you know a Christian when you see him? You watch his
works. Does that mean that one earns his way to heaven? No, we
inherit heaven. A Christian is able to stand in heaven before the living
God and enjoy His presence forever. It's not because he has earned his
way in, but because he's taken the gift of eternal life that God has
offered and, in proof of that gift, has begun to live before "the least" of
the brothers and sisters on earth, as Christ Himself would.

Heaven. It's the place of eternal bliss; it's the place of God's presence
forever. It's the place of our eternal inheritance and reward, of light and
wholeness, the place without disease or pain. There's no crippling
problems, no death, no tears, no darkness, and no ending. Those former things are all passed away.

A young girl was walking with her father one evening when the rays
of the setting sun were shining gloriously across the skies and lighting
up the fleecy clouds. With more insight than she realized, she said to
her father, "Daddy, if the wrong side of heaven is so beautiful, what do
you think the right side will look like?"

We can't even imagine. We hear "heavenly" music today, and we think it's going to be like that in heaven. But actually, the most beautiful music on earth sounds like *Chopsticks* when placed alongside real heavenly music. Handel's *Hallelujah Chorus* will be nothing compared to the myriad of angels who will sing in antiphonal voice as we join them in praises to the Lamb of God.

But eternity is not just heaven. For "He will say also to those on His left, 'Depart from Me, accursed ones, into the eternal fire which has been prepared for the devil and his angels.'"

Hell. We don't like the thought of it, but we dare not ignore it. This is literal hell. But there is a difference here. Hell is not inherited. Hell is the place originally prepared for the devil and his demons. But because of mankind's sin, God has had to enlarge the space of hell. More than the devil and his angels will be there. The "accursed ones" will be there as well—those who have lived and finished their earthly lives without Christ.

Hell is a place of eternal, literal torment. It is a place where the living God is absent. He is not in hell. It is a place of sorrow, pain, darkness, memory, loneliness, remorse, and never-ending misery.

Jonathan Edwards, the great early American preacher known for his sermons on the subject of hell, said, "The corruption of the heart of man is immoderate and boundless in its fury; and while wicked men live here, it is like fire pent up by God's restraints, whereas if it were let loose, it would set on fire the course of nature; and as the heart is now a sink of sin, so, if sin was not restrained, it would immediately turn the soul into a fiery oven, or a furnace of fire and brimstone."

Thomas Hooker, the Puritan clergyman who founded Connecticut, wrote, "Conceive this much, if all the diseases of the world did seize on one man, if all the torments that all the tyrants in the world could devise, were cast upon him; and if all the creatures in heaven and earth did conspire the destruction of this man; and if all the devils in hell did labor to inflict punishments upon him, you would think this man to be in a miserable condition. And yet all this is but a beam of God's indignation. If the beams of God's indignation be so hot, what is the full sum of His wrath when it shall seize upon the soul of a sinful creature."

Charles Haddon Spurgeon, the great nineteenth-century pastor in London, proclaimed, "There is a real fire in hell, as truly as you have a real body—a fire exactly like that which we have on this earth, except this: It will not consume though it will torture you. You have seen asbestos lying amid red hot coals, but not consumed. So our bodies will be prepared by God in such a way that they will burn forever without being consumed. With your nerves laid raw by searing flame, yet never desensitized, and the acrid smoke of the sulfurous fumes searing your lungs and choking your breath, you will cry out for the mercy of death, but it shall never, never, no never bring relief."

Such suffering is beyond our comprehension.

To summarize, death is real; it's the beginning of all that we shall face. Judgment is sure; it is inevitable. Hell must be reckoned with by every one of us, but heaven is available to all who believe. And resurrection is our glorious hope—the light of our future that escorts us from time to eternity.

Let's suppose a person is very sick with a rare disease. The doctors tell him that his disease is inoperable and will be terminal. But, he says, there is a certain remarkable medicine—expensive, but it is life-saving. "I'm writing a prescription for you, and this prescription will save your life. Just get it and take it. And never stop taking it." A month later, the man calls back and says, "You have to do something, Doc. The pain is unbearable. I'm not gonna make it. It's your fault."

"Did you take the medicine?" the doctor asks. "Did you take the remedy?" If the person says no, he has no one to blame but himself.

No one will ever be able to point an accusing finger in the face of God and say, "It's Your fault!" He has given us the remedy, the guaranteed prescription: Believe on the Lord Jesus Christ. Believe that when He died at Calvary, He died for you. Believe that when He came back from the grave, He emptied the tomb for you. He is alive. And those who believe in Him will never perish.

What good news! Do you believe it? Have you personally embraced it? If you have, even when you die, you can anticipate your final moment of triumph when He raises you from the grave and calls you home.

But wait. I need to cover one more base. It occurs to me that some who are reading this book may need a little extra reassurance. Perhaps not so much for yourself as for someone you love. What if that person died a tragic death—in an explosion, let's say, or a drowning at sea—and the body was never found. Or your loved one was burned beyond recognition. Is he or she guaranteed the same hope as those who died in their beds? Can we say for sure that all who die in the Lord will be raised and given new, eternal bodies?

Absolutely.

Those saints who became martyrs, torn apart by beasts or beheaded or tortured beyond recognition, will be equally given new bodies. In fact, all who die in the Lord will be raised in new bodies, fit for heaven. To borrow from Ben Franklin's epitaph, all will "appear once more, in a new and more elegant edition, revised and corrected by the Author."

The One who created us from nothing will have no difficulty recreating us, and "we shall all be changed" as "death is swallowed up in victory" (1 Corinthians 15:52,54).

This is *wonderful* news, especially for people like Roger Williams, founder of the Rhode Island colony. Do you know what happened to his body after he died? Many years later it was exhumed for reburial. When that occurred, a surprise awaited those who dug him up.

> It was found that the root of an apple tree had penetrated the head of the coffin and had followed down Williams' spine, dividing into a fork at the legs. The tree had absorbed the chemicals of the decaying body and had transmuted them into its wood and fruit. The apples, in turn, had been eaten by people, quite unconscious of the fact that they were indirectly taking into their systems part of the long-dead Williams.[5]

Our hope of resurrection removes all concerns over such complicated and complex problems. He who made us is well able to make us anew.

For years I've loved the words of Samuel Stennett, who, upon realizing the enormous benefits we derive from Christ's resurrection, wrote this:

> To Him I owe my life and breath,
> And all the joys I have;
> He makes me triumph over death,
> And saves me from the grave,
> And saves me from the grave.[6]

When life hurts and dreams fade, nothing helps like hope.
Without hope, prisoners of war languish and die.
Without hope, students get discouraged and drop out.
Without hope, athletic teams slump and keep losing.
Without hope, fledgling authors run out of determination.
Without hope, addicts return to their habits, married couples decide to divorce, inventors, artists, entertainers, entrepreneurs, even preachers, lose their creativity.[1]

—Charles R. Swindoll, *Hope Again*

22
Hope for the Unforgiven

*H*ope is our lifeline, keeping us engaged in the struggle. Marathoners press on to the finish line as long as they have hope. Nothing—virtually *nothing*—is able to defeat us if our hope stays alive.

Just last evening, my wife and I watched another example of this. The American Olympic gold-winning cyclist and *Tour de France* champion, Lance Armstrong, was featured on a televised documentary. What a story! He was struck down by testicular cancer. Multiple malignant tumors appeared on his lungs and in his brain. One of his testicles was "the size of a large lemon" (his words) when he finally went to see his physician. The treatment that followed his surgery included massive doses of radiation and chemotheraphy, leaving him bald, listless, and jobless . . . but not hopeless. In fact, if there was one word that resurfaced in that interview more than any other, it was hope. "I never lost hope," was Armstrong's recurring theme. It was hope that kept him exercising; it was hope that got him back on his bike; it was hope that prompted him to return to racing (without a sponsor!); it was hope that pushed him ahead of all the others the day he achieved his dream: the undisputed champion of his sport.

But what about folks like us? What about common, ordinary, non-Olympic, relatively unknown men and women, who aren't all that gifted, don't feel very significant, and have to work hard to make a living; then, on top of that, we can't seem to get past the daily challenges connected to just plain living? We not only struggle to get ahead, we often blow it and find ourselves lacking the ability to measure up spiritually. In a word, we're unforgiven.

Unforgiven. That's the title of one of the major films of 1992 and one of the stars in Clint Eastwood's Hollywood crown. Directed by and starring Eastwood himself, it won four academy awards, among them Best Supporting Actor, Best Director, and the most coveted award, Best Film.[2]

The same year that *Unforgiven* won the Academy Award for Best Picture, I took a trip with the pastoral interns and a couple of men on our pastoral team from the church I was then pastoring in Fullerton, California. Once a year our pastoral team and interns took a trip like this, visiting twelve to fifteen churches and talking to pastors, pastoral staffs, and laypeople, informing ourselves about other church settings. We called it the "thousand-mile conversation," as we traveled in a van from the southern end of California up to the Bay area and back.

About halfway through this particular trip, we realized that we had a few hours of time one evening when we had nothing scheduled, so we decided it would be good for us to take a break. "Let's go to a movie," someone said. Several of the guys immediately thought of the movie that had just won the Academy Award, *Unforgiven.* We all agreed that a Clint Eastwood film would be our kind of film—kind of a guy thing—tough, rugged, unshaven, hard-knuckled stuff. This was gonna be terrific.

Well, guess what? I hated it. I *hated* it! I sat there thinking, *This is the worst movie I've ever seen.* I almost walked out two or three times. I thought the screenplay was terrible, the characters were despicable, and the language at times was really raunchy. Every time I thought it might get better, it only got worse.

Basically the plot boils down to this: The character Clint Eastwood plays the part of a man who returns to the gunslinging life he had left and blows the bad guys away. When he's finished, he returns to his little farm, where he and his two unhappy children stand by the grave of his dead wife. Some inane comments are made, and the credits start rolling. I wanted my money back.

Walking out of the theater I groused about the film. Getting into the van, I fussed about the way it started, the plot, and how it ended.

The guys listened patiently to my complaining. Then, as we were driving back to the hotel, Paul Sailhamer said, "Did you ever think, Chuck, that's really the way life is when there isn't forgiveness?"

Of course! Dumb me. What I really had hoped to see was *Forgiven*. But the movie was *Unforgiven*. It was about life without hope—*the worst kind of existence.*

If you have been in the Christian life so long that you've forgotten what life is like without hope, you need a good dose of the message in that film. It is as pointless, meaningless, empty, and torturous as you can imagine, and then some. Anger, ugliness, and sadness prevail. Then there's the grave scene at the end, and the credits roll. There's no joy, no relief, no rewards—no hope!

Let's Pretend . . .

As I thought about that, I thought, *wouldn't it be great to make our own film: A Tale of Three Men, three vignettes, directed by Clint Easterless.*

Let's go there.

Unforgiven: Act I

Scene 1: The first man is Little Joe, the youngest in a large family, and his older brothers hate him because he's the favored son. Daddy loves Little Joe so much that he buys him a special coat. He never buys the other boys anything. The older brothers resent Little Joe, and their resentment soon turns to hatred.

One day the brothers go on an overnight campout. While they are away from home, one of the brothers says, "Now's the time to get rid of Little Joe." So they tie him up and drop him in a pit.

"Let's let him die there," they say. "The animals will eat him. Good riddance."

So they take Little Joe's coat, smear it with the blood of a wolf they've killed, and then they plot to tell their daddy that Little Joe was killed by a vicious wild animal.

Then one of the boys gets a better idea. Spotting a camel caravan in the distance, he says, "Why should we leave him to die? Let's sell him and make some money." So they hail the caravan, which is on its way to Egypt, and they sell their brother into slavery for twenty bucks.

As the scene fades out, Little Joe is watching his brothers walk away laughing, counting their money.

Scene 2: In the land of Egypt, Little Joe is nothing more than chattel—a piece of flesh to be bought and sold. He becomes a slave in the household of a government official, and there he becomes a favorite of the owner of the house. Unfortunately, he also becomes the favorite of the wife of the owner of the house. Little Joe is tall, dark, and handsome, and she wants him. But she stands against everything he stands for, and he resists her advances.

Angered by his rejection, the wicked mistress of the household gets her revenge by crying "Rape!" Her husband believes her and throws Little Joe in jail, leaving him imprisoned there for years for a crime he didn't commmit.

Eventually, through an interesting chain of events, the king of the land hears that Little Joe can interpret dreams. The king has an audience with Little Joe, who tells him the future of the land of Egypt. Almost overnight Little Joe is promoted to a place of authority and soon becomes prime minister.

Scene 3: Meanwhile, back on the ranch, Little Joe's brothers are raising their own families and doing well, despite the fact that their father has never stopped mourning for the youngest son he believes is dead. Then a recession hits. The brothers lose their jobs. Word reaches them that someone in Egypt has a storehouse of food and that he is willing to provide a handout to those who are homeless or needy. The brothers make their way to Egypt, not knowing that they will be asking help from their long-lost brother.

This is a great moment in the film, and director Clint Easterless makes the most of it. The brothers don't know who the prime minister is, but he recognizes them. He has them imprisoned and tortured, then condemns them all to terrible deaths.

UNFORGIVEN. ACT II.

Scene 1: The next scene introduces us to a character named Sammy. His parents are devout people, and God tells them, through the words of an angel, that their son will be special to God. Not only will he become a judge—the most prominent position among their people—but he will be a powerful force to slay the enemies of their people and Almighty God. He will be the mightiest and strongest man in the land. He won't have to lift weights or train at the local fitness center. He will be strong because God will make him strong.

The secret of Sammy's strength lies in the special vows that he must take. Mainly, he must never cut his hair. Furthermore, he must never imbibe in strong drink. He must be careful about what he eats and steer clear of dead carcasses.

Scene 2: When Sammy becomes a man, however, his private battle with lust begins to control him. He does become a judge, but he also falls in love with a girl named Lila, from among the enemy of his people. He becomes more intimate with Lila than he had ever been with his own God and he tells her the secret of his life. With his head in her lap, he mumbles, "My strength is in my hair." Then he falls asleep. Because he has entered the city of the enemy, he is an easy target. They cut off his hair, down to the scalp.

When Sammy awakens, he's bald as an egg and has no strength. Worse than that, he has no God.

His enemies blind him, and he spends the rest of his days as a grinder in the prison house, walking mindlessly around and around, pushing the huge wheel that grinds the grain.

Easterless concludes the scene with a final shot of despair, showing Sammy slumped on his knees, facedown in the mud and manure as he breathes his last—a blind man caught in the tentacles of his own lust.

Unforgiven. Act III.

Scene 1: The final act opens with a bang as the lens focuses on the third character, a young "rebel without a cause." We first see him when he tells his father, "I'm through with this family. I don't want to spend another night under this roof. Just give me what I've got coming, and I'm out of here."

His father writes him a check, and the boy slams the door behind him.

Scene 2: The teenager is riding high—from Reno to Vegas he's on a roll. He skis through Colorado and roars on to Chicago and New York. He's got a whole gang of fast friends who want to be with him, because he's the boy with the bucks. He can get whatever he wants: drugs, booze, women—lots of women.

But suddenly he runs out of bucks. And when you're out of bucks, you're out of buddies. His friends pull out. The women walk away. He can't even win the lottery.

He rides the rails back across the country. When he gets to Iowa, he gets off and takes a walk down a country road. He meets a pig farmer, and before nightfall he's knee-deep in swine slop. At night he slumps into a cold dirty bunk—that night and the next night and the next, until he realizes that every single thing he wants is really back home with his dad.

Early the next morning, he washes himself off as best he can and hitchhikes the rest of the way home.

Scene 3: But in an Easterless film, you can't go home again. When his father answers the door, he says bitterly, "What do you want?"

"I . . . I'm . . . I'm back," says the thin-and-dirty kid.

"You're back? There's no place for you here. Listen, you got what you wanted, now live with it. Look at what you've done with yourself! You're a miserable wreck. You stink. Get out of my life!" The door slams, and the boy has nowhere to go but down.

The final scene shows the boy sitting in a seedy room on Skid Row, holding a pistol to his head. As the scene fades, there's a gunshot. And the credits roll.

THE END.

HOLD IT! THERE'S MORE

When there is no resurrection, there is no Easter. When there is no resurrection, there is no forgiveness. And when there is no forgiveness, you don't have time for returning sons or repentant brothers. Your life revolves around you. You don't forgive. You hold grudges. You get even!

Fortunately, that is not the way the real stories end. Some of you who are reading this know what really happened. In the real stories, Little Joe is really Joseph. And when Joseph finally realizes that his brothers are standing before him, he says to them, "I know what you did to me. You meant it for evil, but God meant it for good. When you sold me into slavery, God broke my stubborn will. When I was accused of rape by Potiphar's wife, God taught me to submit. In the prison house, I praised God for what I learned about humility and patience. I grew up in there. And when I finally was promoted to this place of honor I realized what an opportunity I had been given." Joseph didn't take revenge. He didn't torture anyone or break anyone's bones or end anyone's life. In fact, he fully forgave his brothers. He said, "Go get our father and your families and let's live together." That's how the story really ends! Why? Because Joseph forgives. Because life is full of hope when there is a resurrection.

How about Sammy? Well, he's really Samson. And when his hair begins to grow again, it's a wonderful proof of God's mercy and grace. Before long, he could run his fingers through his hair. And before long he could again accomplish the mission God gave him: He could slay the enemies of the Lord. Samson's final act of courage was the greatest act of his life. He used his strength for God's glory, not as a lustful pastime. He killed more in the fulfillment of his purpose on earth than he had killed throughout his days on earth as he pushed those columns apart.

But I think my favorite of the three stories is the prodigal son. In the true story, the father welcomed his son back with open arms. In fact, the son didn't have to come all the way to the door; the father went running down the road to meet him.

Every morning that father stared out toward the dawn, wondering, *Is this the day my son comes home? Is this the day he comes to the end of himself and realizes that everything he wanted is here in my love and my forgiveness?* And as soon as he saw his son's gaunt silhouette on the horizon, the father ran and threw both arms around his son's neck and kissed him repeatedly and said, "Quick, bring out the best robe and put it on him! Put a ring on his hand! Bring out the best food and let's celebrate, because this son of mine that was lost has been found."

That's how the story ends when there's forgiveness. That's how the story ends when there's an Easter. Hope returns and hearts are changed.

Since He is risen, we're forgiven. Remember that! I wrote that in my Bible back in 1993, the year that Clint Eastwood film started me thinking about this. "Easter, 1993: Since He has risen, I'm forgiven."

Do you have this hope? Can you go to sleep tonight knowing that your sins have been forgiven? As we've seen all the way through this book, it's because Christ died and has been raised that He has washed you free of the hatred, revenge, lust, resentment, rebellion, and selfishness. If you can say that, you have a reason to sleep well. If you cannot, may God keep you awake, make you miserable, and give you no peace until you turn your heart over to Him.

God isn't roaming across heaven, carrying a club, looking down on earth for people to strike down. God's wrath has been satisfied. The resurrection was God's "Amen" to Jesus' "It is finished!" The death of the Savior paid the complete penalty for sin. His death built the bridge that was needed between you and God. His resurrection opened the door, welcoming you home. When God is the director, you can come home!

There's hope because you're forgiven. The darkness has passed. Look! The dawn has arrived. Come on home. He's left the light on for you.

Conclusion
Do You Believe in Easter?

*I*t is one thing to write about being empowered by the tragedy and triumph of the cross. It's another thing to read about it. When you write about it, thinking through the issues and doing the research that helps illustrate and verify the truth, it stretches you. But when you read these things, not having been exposed to many of the details before, it deepens you. I hope this book has deepened you.

I'll admit that it has stretched me. The work involved in examining the evidence and then expressing those things has forced me to discipline myself in the process. From the first chapter to the last, I've prayed that all who read of both the darkness and the dawn of our Savior's earthly experience will enter into those scenes personally, rather than stay at a safe distance and explore them in an uninvolved, calculated manner.

But to be completely candid with you, there's a third level to which both writer and reader must go with a book like this, if either of us hopes to glean the maximum benefit. It's more valuable than being stretched, and it's more vulnerable than being deepened. I'm referring to being changed. If the kind of things I've been writing about and you've been reading about don't change us, you and I have missed the message the old rugged cross and the empty tomb were preserved to convey.

The question is not merely, "Have I been significantly stretched in the writing of this book?" Nor is it simply, "Have you grown deeper in the reading of it?" The crucial question is, "Are we different, now that we have come to terms with what our Lord endured in His agony at the cross and with what He accomplished in His triumph over the grave?" Have those things changed us? Do we *truly* believe them? Only time will tell.

Many months ago a friend of mine sent me a story I've deliberately saved until the end. Because it illustrates so perfectly what I'm getting at, I'll simply pass along the story and let you draw your own conclusions.

Do You Believe in Easter?

Edith Burns was a wonderful Christian who lived in San Antonio, Texas. She was the patient of a doctor named Will Phillips, a gentle physician who saw patients as people. His favorite patient was Edith Burns.

One morning Dr. Phillips went to his office with a heavy heart, however, and it was because of Edith Burns. When he walked into the waiting room, there sat Edith with her big black Bible in her lap, earnestly talking to a young mother sitting beside her.

Edith Burns had a habit of introducing herself in this way: "Hello, my name is Edith Burns. Do you believe in Easter?" Then she would explain the meaning of Easter, and many times people would be saved.

Dr. Phillips walked into his office area and said good morning to his office nurse, Beverly. Beverly had first met Edith when she was taking her blood pressure.

Edith said to her, "Hello, my name is Edith Burns. Do you believe in Easter?"

Beverly said, "Why, yes I do."

"Well, what do you believe about Easter?"

"Well," said Beverly, "it's all about egg hunts, going to church, and dressing up."

Edith kept pressing Beverly about the real meaning of Easter, and finally led the nurse to a saving knowledge of Jesus Christ.

That morning, Dr. Phillips said, "Beverly, don't call Edith into the office quite yet. I believe there's another delivery taking place in the waiting room."

After being called to the doctor's office, Edith sat down, and when she took a look at the doctor, she said, "Dr. Will, why are you so sad? Are you reading your Bible? Are you praying?"

Dr. Phillips said gently, "Edith, I'm the doctor and you're the patient." And then with a heavy heart he said, "Your lab report came back, and it reveals you have cancer, and, Edith, you're not going to live very much longer."

"Why, Dr. Phillips," said Edith, "shame on you! Why are you so sad? Do you think God makes mistakes? You have just told me I'm going to see my precious Lord Jesus, my husband, and many of my friends. You have just told me that I am going to celebrate Easter forever. And here you are having difficulty giving me my ticket!"

Dr. Phillips thought to himself, *What a magnificent woman this Edith Burns is.*

Within a few weeks, Edith had reached a point in her illness where she needed to be hospitalized. "Dr. Will, I'm very near home now," she said, "so would you make sure that they put women in the room with me who need to know about Easter?"

Well, they did just that, and one patient after another shared the room with Edith. Many of them gave their hearts to Christ. Everybody on that floor, from staff to patients, were so excited about Edith that they started calling her Edith Easter—that is, everybody except Phyllis Cross, the head nurse on the floor.

Phyllis made it plain that she wanted nothing to do with

Edith because, "She is a religious nut." Phyllis had been a nurse in an army hospital; she'd seen and heard it all. She was the original G. I. Jane. She had been married three times. She was hard, cold, and did everything by the book.

One morning the two nurses who were to attend to Edith were sick. Edith had gotten the flu, so Phyllis Cross had to go in and give her a shot. When she walked in, Edith had a big smile on her face as she said, "Phyllis, God loves you, and I love you, too. I've been praying for you."

The head nurse frowned. "Well, you can quit praying for me. It won't work. I'm not interested."

"Well, I will pray," responded Edith, "and I have asked God not to let me go home until you come into the family."

"Then you will never die," snapped Phyllis, "because that will never happen," and she curtly marched out of the room.

Every day when Phyllis Cross walked into the room, Edith would smile and say, "God loves you, Phyllis, and I love you too . . . and I'm still praying for you." Finally, one day, Nurse Cross found herself being literally drawn into Edith's room like a magnet would draw iron. She sat down on the side of the bed and Edith said, "I'm so glad you have come, because God told me that today is your special day."

"Edith, you have asked everybody here the question, 'Do you believe in Easter?' but you've never asked me," said Phyllis.

"I wanted to many times, but God told me to wait until you asked, and now that you have asked. . . ." And then Edith took her Bible and shared with Phyllis Cross the Easter story of the death, burial, and resurrection of Jesus Christ.

Then Edith said, "Phyllis, do you believe in Easter? Do you believe that Jesus Christ is alive and that He wants to live in your heart?"

"Oh, I want to believe that with all of my heart," said Phyllis. "And I do want Jesus in my life." And right then and there Phyllis prayed and invited Jesus Christ into her heart.

For the first time Head Nurse Phyllis Cross did not march out of the hospital room, she was carried out as if on the wings of angels.

Two days later Edith said to Phyllis, "Do you know what day it is?"

"Why, yes, it's Good Friday."

"Oh, no," said Edith. "For you every day is Easter. Happy Easter, Phyllis!"

Two days later, on Easter Sunday morning, Phyllis stopped at the hospital flower shop before she went to her desk. She wanted to take a bouquet of Easter lilies up to Edith and wish her a Happy Easter.

When Phyllis walked into Edith's room, Edith was lying still in her bed. Her big black Bible was open on her lap and her hands were on her Bible. She had a sweet smile on her face.

When Phyllis reached over to pick up Edith's hand, she realized Edith was gone.

Her left hand rested on John 14:2–3: "In my Father's house are many mansions: if it were not so, I would have told you. I go to prepare a place for you. And if I go and prepare a place for you, I will come again, and receive you unto myself; that where I am, there ye may be also."

Her right hand was on Revelation 21:4: "And God shall wipe away all tears from their eyes; and there shall be no more death, neither sorrow, nor crying, neither shall there be any more pain: for the former things are passed away. "

Phyllis Cross took one look at that dead body, then lifted her face toward heaven, and, with tears streaming down her cheeks, said, "Happy Easter, Edith. Happy Easter!"

Then Phyllis left Edith's body, walked quietly out of the room and over to a table where two student nurses were sitting. She smiled and said, "Hello, my name is Phyllis Cross. Do you believe in Easter?"

Appendix

- Chronology of Events

- The Trials of Jesus Christ

Chronology of Events

Event	Approximate Time
Prayer and agony at Gethsemane (Matthew, Mark, Luke)	1:00 A.M.
Betrayal by Judas and arrest of Jesus (Mark 14:43–46; John 18:12)	1:30 A.M.
Irregular, unauthorized inquiry at Annas' residence (John 18:13–23)	2:00 A.M.
Unofficial trial at Caiaphas' residence (Matthew 26:57–68; John 18:24)	3:00 A.M.
Formal, official trial before Sanhedrin in their chamber to confirm capital sentence (Mark 15:1; Luke 22:66–71)	6:00 A.M. ("when it was day")
First interrogation by Pilate at official residence (Matthew 27:1–2, 11–14; Luke 23:1–7; John 18:28–38)	6:30 A.M. ("when morning had come . . . and it was early")
Audience/mockery before Herod (Luke 23:8–12)	7:00 A.M.
Final judgment of Pilate (All Gospels)	7:30 A.M.
Scourging in Praetorium (All Gospels)	8:00 A.M.
Nailing of hands and feet to the cross (All Gospels)	9:00 A.M. ("it was the third hour")
Darkness (Matthew, Mark, Luke)	12:00 Noon ("when the sixth hour had come, darkness fell")
Death of Jesus (All Gospels)	3:00 P.M. ("and at the ninth hour")

In less than twenty-four hours, Jesus goes from arrest to execution.

THE TRIALS OF JESUS CHRIST

Trial	Officiating Authority	Scripture	Accusation	Legality	Type	Result
1	Annas, ex-high priest of the Jews (A.D. 6–15)	John 18:13–23	Trumped-up charges of irreverence to Annas.	ILLEGAL! Held at night. No specific charges. Prejudice. Violence.	Jewish and religious	Found guilty of irreverence and rushed to Caiaphas.
2	Caiaphas—Annas' son in-law—and the Sanhedrin (A.D. 18–36)	Matthew 26:57–68 Mark 14:53–65 John 18:24	Claiming to be the Messiah, the Son of God—blasphemy (worthy of death under Jewish law).	ILLEGAL! Held at night. False witnesses. Prejudice. Violence.	Jewish and Religious	Declared guilty of blasphemy and rushed to the Sanhedrin (supreme court).
3	The Sanhedrin—seventy ruling men of Israel (their word was needed before He could be taken to Roman officials.	Mark 15:1a Luke 22:66–71	Claiming to be the Son God—blasphemy.	ILLEGAL! Accusation switched. No witnesses. Improper voting.	Jewish and Religious	Declared guilty of blasphemy and rushed to Roman official, Pilate.
4	Pilate, governor of Judea, who was already in "hot water" with Rome (A.D. 26–36).	Matthew 27:11–14 Mark 15:1b–5 Luke 23:1–7 John 18:28–38	Treason (accusation was changed, since treason worthy of capital punishment in Rome).	ILLEGAL! Christ was kept under arrest, although He was found innocent. No defense attorney. Violence.	Roman and Civil	Found innocent. . . . but rushed to Herod Antipas; mob overruled Pilate.
5	Herod Antipas, governor of Galilee (4 B.C.–A.D. 39).	Luke 23:8–12	No accusation was made.	ILLEGAL! No grounds. Mockery in courtroom. No defense attorney. Violence.	Roman and Civil	Mistreated and mocked; returned to Pilate without decision made by Herod. Herod.
6	Pilate (second time).	Matthew 27:15–26 Mark 15:6–15 Luke 23:18–25 John 18:29–19:6	Treason, though not proven (Pilate bargained with the mob, putting Christ on a level with Barrabas, a criminal	ILLEGAL! Without proof of guilt, Pilate allowed an innocent mand to be condemned.	Roman and Civil	Found innocent, but Pilate "washed his hands" and allowed Him to be crucified..

Endnotes

Chapter One
The Suffering Savior

1. Dorothy Sayers, as quoted by Barbara Brown Taylor, *God in Pain,* in *Christianity Today,* April 3, 2000, page 71.
2. Amy Carmichael, "No Scar?" from *Toward Jerusalem* (Fort Washington, Penn.: Christian Literature Crusade, © 1936 The Dohnavur Fellowship).
3. John Piper, *The Pleasures of God* (Sisters, Ore.: Multnomah Press, 2000), pp. 161–162.

Chapter Two
The Cup of Sacrifice

1. Isaac Watts, *When I Survey the Wondrous Cross,* 1st stanza.

Chapter Three
Midnight in the Garden

1. Jennie Evelyn Hussey, *Lead Me to Calvary,* 1st stanza and refrain.

CHAPTER FOUR
THREE O'CLOCK IN THE MORNING

1. Johann Heermann, *Ah, Holy Jesus, How Hast Thou Offended,* 2nd stanza.
2. William Barclay, *The Gospel of Matthew, Vol. 2* (Philadelphia, Penn.: The Westminster Press, 1975), pp. 346–347.
3. Elizabeth Clephane, *Beneath the Cross of Jesus,* 2nd stanza.

CHAPTER FIVE
THE SIX TRIALS OF JESUS

1. Philip P. Bliss, *Hallelujah, What a Savior,* 1st stanza.
2. Alexander Whyte, *Bible Characters* (Grand Rapids, Mich.: Zondervan Publishing House, 1952), p. 81.
3. Merrill C. Tenney, *The Gospel of John: The Expositor's Bible Commentary* (Grand Rapids, Mich.: Zondervan Publishing House, 1981), p. 176.

CHAPTER SIX
THE MAN WHO MISSED HIS CROSS

1. Cecil F. Alexander, *There Is a Green Hill Far Away* (1848), 4th stanza.
2. James Stalker, *The Trial and Death of Jesus Christ* (Cincinnati, Oh.: Jennings and Graham, 1894), p. 87.
3. William Riley Wilson, *The Execution of Jesus* (New York, N.Y.: Charles Scribner & Sons, 1970), p. 141.
4. Ibid., pp. 141–142.
5. William Barclay, *The Gospel of Mark* (Philadelphia, Penn.: The Westminster Press; Edinburgh, Scotland: The Saint Andrew Press, 1975), p. 356. Used by permission of The Saint Andrew Press.
6. A. T. Robertson, *Word Pictures in the New Testament, Vol. II,* "The Gospel According to Luke" (Nashville, Tenn.: Broadman Press, 1930), p. 284.

CHAPTER SEVEN
THE WAY OF THE CROSS

1. Peter Abelard (12th century), 1st stanza.
2. Os Guinness, *The Call* (Nashville, Tenn.: Word Publishing, 1998), p. 79.
3. Jim Bishop, *The Day Christ Died* (New York, N.Y.: International Creative Management, 1957), p. 303. Used by permission.
4. Barclay, *The Gospel of Mark,* pp. 360-361. Used by permission.
5. Arthur Bennett, ed., *The Valley of Vision: A collection of Puritan prayers and devotions,* (Carlisle, Penna.: The Banner of Truth Trust, 1975), p. 172.

CHAPTER EIGHT
THE DARKEST OF ALL DAYS

1. Bernard of Clairvaux, *O Sacred Head, Now Wounded* (12th century), 1st stanza.
2. Bishop, *The Day Christ Died,* pp. 320–321. Used by permission.
3. Merrill F. Unger, Unger's Bible Dictionary (Chicago, Ill.: Moody Press, 1957), p. 229.
4. Wilson, *The Execution of Jesus,* p. 152.
5. Bishop, *The Day Christ Died,* pp. 325–326. Used by permission.
6. Harvie Branscomb, *The Gospel of Mark* (1937), p. 292; as quoted in Wilson, The Execution of Jesus, p. 153.
7. Bernard of Clairvaux, *O Sacred Head, Now Wounded,* 2nd and 3rd stanzas.

CHAPTER NINE
"'FATHER, FORGIVE THEM'"

1. Frederick W. Faber, *St. Cross* (1849), 3rd stanza.
2. Based on Kenn Gangel, *Coaching Ministry Teams* (Nashville, Tenn.: Word Publishing, 2000), pp. 43–44.

CHAPTER TEN
"'TODAY YOU SHALL BE WITH ME'"

1. Thomas Benson Pollock, *Jesus, Pitying the Sighs* (1870), 4th and 5th stanzas.
2. Stalker, *The Trial and Death of Jesus Christ*, p. 199.
3. Author unknown, "The Gospel According to You," as found in Al Bryant, *Sourcebook of Poetry* (Grand Rapids, Mich.: Zondervan Publishing House, 1968), p. 207.
4. Augustus M. Toplady, *Rock of Ages, Cleft for Me* (18th century), 2nd and 3rd stanzas.
5. Based on Walter B. Knight, "The Little Baby's Shoes," as quoted by Paul Lee Tan, ThD., in *Encyclopedia of 7,700 Illustrations: Signs of the Times* (Chicago, Ill.: R. R. Donnelley and Sons, Inc., 1979), p. 122.
6. Charles Haddon Spurgeon, *The Treasury of the New Testament, Vol. VI,* (Grand Rapids, Mich.: Baker Book House, 1981), p. 186.

CHAPTER ELEVEN
"'BEHOLD, YOUR SON! BEHOLD, YOUR MOTHER!'"

1. Author unknown, *At the Cross Her Station Keeping,* (Latin, 13th century), 1st and 3rd stanzas.
2. Studdert Kennedy, as quoted by William Barclay in *The Gospel of John,* Volume Two (Edinburgh, Scotland: The Saint Andrew Press, 1955), p. 295.
3. Arthur W. Pink, *The Seven Sayings of the Saviour on the Cross* (Grand Rapids, Mich.: Baker Book House, 1958), pp. 49–50.

CHAPTER TWELVE
"'WHY HAVE YOU FORSAKEN ME?'"

1. Ben H. Price, *Alone* (circa 1900); 1st, 2nd, 3rd stanzas, and refrain.

Chapter Thirteen
"'I Am Thirsty'"

1. Pollock, *Jesus, Pitying the Sighs* (1870), 12th–14th stanzas.
2. Philip Yancey, *Reaching for the Invisible God,* (Grand Rapids, Mich.: Zondervan Publishing House, 2000), p. 113.
3. Max Lucado, *He Chose the Nails* (Nashville, Tenn.: Word Publishing, 2000), p. 96.
4. Merrill C. Tenney, *John: The Gospel of Belief,* (Grand Rapids, Mich.: William B. Eerdmans Publishing Company, 1948), p. 267.
5. F. W. Pitt, "The Maker of the Universe," in Henry Gariepy, *100 Portraits of Christ* (Colorado Springs, Colo.: Victor Books, 1987), pp. 21–22.

Chapter Fourteen
"'It Is Finished!'"

1. Bliss, *Hallelujah, What a Savior,* 1st and 4th stanzas.
2. John F. Walvoord and Roy B. Zuck, ed. *The Bible Knowledge Commentary* (Wheaton, Ill.: Victor Books, 1983), Vol. 2, p. 340.
3. As quoted by Pink, *The Seven Sayings of the Saviour on the Cross,* p. 114.

Chapter Fifteen
"'Father, into Your Hands I Commit My Spirit'"

1. Author unknown, *Hail, Thou Once-Despised Jesus* (circa 1757), 1st and 2nd stanzas.
2. William F. Arndt, *The Gospel According to St. Luke* (St. Louis, Mo.: Concordia Publishing House, 1956), p. 473.
3. Stalker, *The Trial and Death of Jesus Christ,* p. 275.
4. Girolamo Savonarola, *Jesus, Refuge of the Weary* (1454–1498), 1st and 2nd stanzas.

CHAPTER SIXTEEN
LESSONS IN OBEDIENCE . . . TAUGHT SEVERELY

1. Bennett, *The Valley of Vision,* p. 172.
2. Malcolm Muggeridge, *A Twentieth Century Testimony* (Nashville, Tenn.: Thomas Nelson Publishers, 1978 Evangelische Omroep), n.p.
3. Kenneth S. Wuest, *Hebrews in the Greek New Testament* (Grand Rapids, Mich.: William B. Eerdmans Publishing Company, 1947), p. 101.
4. As quoted by Ted W. Engstrom, *The Pursuit of Excellence* (Grand Rapids, Mich.: The Zondervan Corporation, 1982), pp. 81–82.
5. Bennett, *The Valley of Vision,* p. 91.

CHAPTER SEVENTEEN
WHAT IS YOUR VERDICT?

1. John of Damascus, *Come, Ye Faithful, Raise the Strain* (8th century), 2nd stanza, lines 5–8.
2. Merrill C. Tenney, *The Reality of the Resurrection* (New York, N.Y.: Harper & Row Publishers, 1963), p. 119.
3. Frank Morison, *Who Moved the Stone?* (London: Faber and Faber Limited, March MCMXXX), pp. 5, 10.

CHAPTER EIGHTEEN
A SUNDAY MORNING MIRACLE

1. Robert Lowry, *Christ Arose,* 1st stanza and chorus.
2. Max Lucado, *In the Eye of the Storm* (Nashville, Tenn.: Word Publishing, 1991), pp. 221, 225–226.
3. Michael Green, *Man Alive* (Downers Grove, Ill.: InterVarsity Press, 1968), n. p.
4. John F. Walvoord, Roy B. Zuck, eds., *The Bible Knowledge Commentary,* (Colorado Springs, Colo.: Victor Books, 1983), Vol. 2, p. 343.

5. W. Phillip Keller, *Rabboni* (Old Tappan, N.J.: Fleming H. Revell Company, 1977), pp. 288–289.
6. John R. W. Stott, *Basic Christianity* (Downers Grove, Ill.: InterVarsity Press, 1958), p. 102.
7. Wilbur M. Smith, "Scientists and the Resurrection," in *Christianity Today*, April 15, 1957.

Chapter Nineteen
Curing the Plague of Death

1. Count Nikolaus Ludwig Von Zinzendor, 1739, translated by John Wesley, 1740.
2. Anatole France, in Leroy Brownlow, *Better Than Medicine* (Fort Worth, Tex.: Brownlow Publishing Company, 1995), p. 66.
3. H. G. Wells, in Brownlow, *Better Than Medicine*, p. 66.
4. Ernest Hemingway, in Billy Graham, *World Aflame* (New York, N.Y.: Pocket Books, division of Simon & Schuster, Inc., 1965), p. 51.
5. Will Durant, source unknown. Public domain.
6. Robert Ingersoll, in Tan, *Encyclopedia of 7,700 Illustrations*, p. 308.

Chapter Twenty
Breaking Death's Jaws

1. Author unknown, *At the Lamb's high feast we sing*, (Latin, 1632), 3rd stanza, lines 3–8.
2. Billy Graham, *How to Be Born Again* (Nashville, Tenn.: Word Books, 1977), pp. 106–107.
3. Ivan Turgenev, *Fathers and Sons* (1862), n.p.
4. Christian F. Gellert, *Jesus Lives, and So Shall I*, (1757), 1st stanza.

Chapter Twenty-One
Triumph for the Undeserving

1. Charles Wesley, *Christ the Lord Is Risen Today* (1739), 4th stanza.

2. Joseph Bayly, *Psalms of My Life* (Colorado Springs, Colo.: Cook Communications, 1973), n.p. Used by permission of the Bayly family.

3. Helmut Thielicke, in Clyde E. Fant, Jr., and William M. Pinson, Jr., *20 Centuries of Great Preaching, Volume Twelve* (Nashville, Tenn.: Word Books, 1971), p. 276.

4. As quoted by Charles A. Allen, *You Are Never Alone* (Old Tappan, N.J.: Fleming H. Revell Company, 1978), pp. 126–127.

5. Tenney, *The Reality of the Resurrection,* p. 120.

6. Samuel Stennett, *Majestic Sweetness Sits Enthroned,* 4th stanza.

Chapter Twenty-Two
Hope for the Unforgiven

1. Charles R. Swindoll, *Hope Again,* (Nashville, Tenn.: Word Publishing, 1996), p. xii.

2. *Forgiven* film review and awards, as posted on the Amazon.com web site.

Chapter Twenty-Three
Conclusion

1. Author unknown. *Do You Believe in Easter?*

DAY BY DAY WITH CHARLES SWINDOLL

Condensed from the *Finishing Touch*, this devotional provides 365 daily readings, which highlight Swindoll's masterful storytelling ability, his insights into Scripture, and his down-to-earth style. *Day by Day with Charles Swindoll* will inspire, challenge, comfort, and even humor readers as Swindoll chats about the many facets of the Christian life. Packaged as a convenient, small-sized, carry-along devotional, this is a great gift for those who want an uplifting, not-too-heavy devotional.

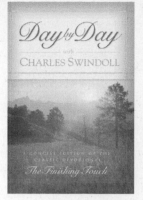

GREAT LIVES SERIES

Throughout history, people have faced the same challenges and temptations. In his "Great Lives" Series, Charles Swindoll shows us how the great heroes of the faith offer a model of courage, hope, and triumph in the face of adversity.

THE MYSTERY OF GOD'S WILL

Can we ever really know that the decisions we make are in God's will? Even popular author, pastor, and Dallas Seminary President Charles Swindoll says at times he's not been so sure. In *The Mystery of God's Will*, Swindoll examines this long-debated subject from a balanced, biblical perspective—yet honest and vulnerable—regarding his own doubts and experiences. For anyone who's ever doubted God's will, or for those who are convinced of it in every situation, this book will be a real eye-opener.

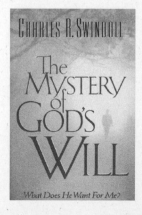